HISTORICAL AND CONSTITUTIONAL DOCUMENTS OF NORTH-EASTERN INDIA (1824-1973)

By the Same Author

- British Policy in the North-East Frontier Agency
- Development of Administration in Assam: With Special Reference to Land Revenue Justice and Police (1874-1920)
- History of Arunachal Pradesh
- Social and Cultural History of Ancient India (Revised and Enlarged Edition)
- Social History of Assam

About the Author

Prof. M.L. Bose has been teaching in the Dibrugarh University (Assam) for about thirty years and has contributed more than thirty papers in Regional and National Seminars and Journal of Repute. An Aurobindite Prof. Bose has guided many research scholars to produce Ph.D. thesis. His earliers published works are *Historical and Constitutional Documents of North-East India; British Policy in the North-East Frontier Agency; Development of Administration in Assam; Social History of Assam; Social and Cultural History of Ancient India;* and *History of Arunachal Pradesh* were well received in the academic world.

HISTORICAL AND CONSTITUTIONAL DOCUMENTS OF NORTH-EASTERN INDIA (1824-1973)

M.L. BOSE

CONCEPT PUBLISHING COMPANY PVT. LTD.
NEW DELHI-110059

ISBN-13: 978-81-8069-851-4

First Published 2017

Published and Printed by

Concept
Since 1974

Concept Publishing Company Pvt. Ltd.
A/15-16, Commercial Block, Mohan Garden
New Delhi-110059 (India)
T: 25351460, 25351794, *F*: 091-11-25357109
E: publishing@conceptpub.com, W: www.conceptpub.com
Editorial Office: H-13, Bali Nagar, New Delhi-110 015, India.

Cataloging in Publication Data--Courtesy: D.K. Agencies (P) Ltd. <docinfo@dkagencies.com>

Bose, Manilal, author.
Historical and constitutional documents of North-Eastern India (1824-1973) / M.L. Bose.
pages cm
Includes index.
ISBN 9788180698514

1. India, Northeastern--Politics and government--Sources. I. Title.

DS483.B67 2017 DDC 954.1 23

FOREWORD

Although there were political, cultural and economic links between North-Eastern India and other parts of this subcontinent in ancient and medieval times, the valleys of the Brahmaputra and the Surma came into full view only after the victories of the East India Company over the Burmese in the War of 1824-26. The great empire builder, Lord Wellesley, had his eyes on Burma, but his primary purpose was to keep the French at a distance from India's closest neighbour on the east. The destroyer of the Maratha Empire, Lord Hastings, ignored the Burmese threat to Bengal, the heart of the Company's dominions. During his successor's regime the situation became too grave to be overlooked. A war undertaken ostensibly for the defence of the eastern frontier—from Dhubri in the north to Chittagong in the south—developed into a war of conquest. Military needs dictated the development of political policy. In 1826 crippled Burma surrendered two of its own outlying provinces and renounced its claims on the principalities of the Brahmaputra and Surma valleys. It was the beginning of the modern period in the history of North-Eastern India. Quite appropriately the editor of this collection of historical and constitutional documents takes the treaty of Yandabu as the foundation of the changes which followed—inevitably if not logically—leading to the imposition of direct British rule on the entire region excluding the mountain enclave of Manipur.

Although the stories of the Ahom Kingdom and the small principalities of Cachar, Jaintia and Manipur are of primary importance, there can be no real unfolding of the history of North-Eastern India without a thorough assessment of the role played by the numerous tribes in politics, economy and culture throughout the region. This is a fact realised by workers in the academic field only in recent times. They are not to be blamed for this. Previously the tribal areas were kept isolated from the plains in the interest of British administration, and official documents needed for research were not available even for *bona fide* scholars. The curtain was raised after the dawn of Independence; the tribes were allowed to feel that they could join the mainstream of national history without losing their political and cultural identity. The Chinese invasion demonstrated the crucial importance of the tribal areas from the standpoint of the country's security. It is now necessary—and possible—to construct an integrated history of North-Eastern India. To that task the editor of this work has dedicated himself, and as a preliminary aid to his fellow students he has offered them a judicious selection of documents which would serve as a starting point for exploration of the archives.

Geography, if not anything else, brought the Ahom rulers into continuous contact with their tribal neighbours. They evolved a tribal policy which was based essentially on a recognition of mutual interests. It is interesting to compare that policy with the policy which the British rulers evolved, after their occupation of the plains, in the light of their wider political experience. They were aided by the missionaries who had no precursors in Ahom times. To what extent the tribes were drawn away from their traditional patterns of life by the joint impact of British political-cum-administrative penetration and missionary influence in its diverse forms is a really fascinating problem. It can be probed satisfactorily only when the historian and the sociologist work in co-operation. As the changes flowed directly from the working of the British imperial machinery the historian alone can draw the structural outline, it is only then that sociological explanations can follow. The editor has provided sufficient material for an introductory study along these lines.

The framers of the Indian Constitution knew that radical changes in the British system would be required if the tribes of the North-East were to be drawn into fruitful partnership with their more fortunately placed fellow citizens in other parts of the country. The democratic features of tribal life were to be reshaped for organic adjustment with the wider and sophisticated democracy of the Republic. The process of transformation was carefully regulated so as to lead—stage by stage—to the emergence of several tribal States. The principal documents reflecting this unique constitutional evolution will be found in the following pages. Autonomy, however, is not intended to serve as a barrier to co-operative pursuit of common interests. Political and administrative boundaries cannot offer the fundamental unity of North-Eastern India in respect of matters such as flood control and inter-State transport and communications, nor can they override the need of co-ordinated development projects. The creation of the North-Eastern Council is a remarkable contribution to the concept of unity in diversity and a complete negation of the British theory of government through fragmentation.

The following pages would give all serious students of the history and political evolution of North-Eastern India in modern times a good idea of the wealth of archival material available for earnest research workers. Post-Graduate students have been provided—for the first time—with an opportunity of proceeding with their work in the light of original sources. For this service to research and advanced studies the editor deserves our sincere thanks.

A.C. BANERJEE

CONTENTS

SECTION IV

Part II

SECTION V

SECTION VI

PART I

INTRODUCTION

I

The term 'North-Eastern India' in this book to means the constituents of the North-Eastern Council, except Tripura, *viz.*, the states of Assam, Meghalaya, Manipur, Nagaland and the two Union Territories of Arunachal Pradesh and Mizoram. Geographically the area may be conveniently divided into four regions, *viz.*, the valley of the Brahmaputra, the Surma valley, the hill ranges which beginning from the Pathkye Range stretch upto Goalpara and Garo Hills at the gateway of Assam, and the Sub-Himalayan ranges beginning from the trijunction of India, Bhutan and Tibet in the west to the trijunction of India, Tibet and Burma.

The valley of the Brahmaputra is a long alluvial plain about 450 miles long with an average width of 50 miles. It is shut in by mountain ranges on the north, east and south with the Brahmaputra flowing through its entire length from east to west. The uniform level of the valley is intercepted by a few low conical hills projecting like spurs. The converging hills at Goalpara appear almost to shut in the Assam valley from Bengal. The valley was inhabited by people who claimed to have descended from the Aryan stock before the Ahoms entered into it on A.D. 1226. The Ahoms, a Shan tribe of Tibeto-Burman stock of Upper Burma, crossed the Pathkye and conquered the entire valley. Gradually they were assimilated with the indigenous people and culture of the valley. From the last quarter of the eighteenth century their power began to decline. Their internal quarrels called in the intervention of the neighbouring states and in 1826 the British annexed the valley after driving out the Burmese from it.

To the south of the Assam valley lies the valley of the Barak with a chain of mountain ranges separating both. The Barak flows from a mountain to the north of Manipur. On the north of the valley lies the district of Sylhet which the British had acquired with the Dewani of Bengal in 1765. The eastern portion of the valley, which is 125 miles in length and has an average width of 60 miles, presents very diversified features. Low detached spurs, off-shoots from the main hilly tracts, bend the valley on both north and south and extend almost to the river's edge on either side with alluvial valleys between them. Two small principalities of Cachar and Jaintia existed in this valley.

The mountain ranges between the valley of the Brahmaputra and the Barak are named after the inhabitants of the hills and are known as the Naga Hills, Lushai Hills or Mizo Hills, North Cachar and Mikir Hills, Jaintia and Khasi Hills and Garo Hills. The petty tribes living there did not recognize any paramount power. Sometimes their powerful neighbours subjugated them and established some sort of overlordship over them. But this supremacy was more nominal than real. Shut in from all sides by the Naga and Lushai Hills lies the fertile valley of Manipur on the south-east border of India. An independent kingdom existed here. These hills together with Manipur felt the brunt of the First Anglo-Burmese War (1824-26) and subsequently came within the *pax Britanica.*

The Sub-Himalayan mountain upto the crest of the Himalayas, known later on as the McMahon Line, on the north from the trijunction to Bhutan, Tibet and India on the west to the trijunction where India, China and Burma meet to the north of Burma were also inhabited by numerous tribes of Tibeto-Burman stock who did not acknowledge any suzerein and lived under local chiefs. On the eve of the British occupation of Assam they had succeeded in establishing some sort of relation with the Assam valley. After the British authority was established in the valley of Brahmaputra these hills were gradually penetrated and regular administrative jurisdiction was declared over them by the Government of India.

The extension of British authority over these territories took three quarters of a century and the steps taken for the unification of the diverse people of the different regions under one Administration are both instructive and questionable. But then the authority of the British over these territories was complete and undisputed. The basis of the British authority in 'North-Eastern India' is a large body of documents of different types, such as Treaties, Engagements, Agreements, Kabulyat, Sanads, etc. In the first volume of the book in four parts such documents have been compiled. In the second volume an attempt has been made in two parts to show, first, the evolution of the Administration of the NEFA and, secondly, the break-up of 'North-Eastern India' into its present political set-up by arranging the relevant Regulations, Orders, Acts and Constitutional provisions.

II

The East India Company took very little interest in 'North-Eastern India' after it acquired the Dewani of Bengal. No strong power capable of threatening it from the flank existed in this region nor did the economy offer the prospect of lucrative trade. The region was economically self-supporting but practically no trade and commerce with the outside world existed except some exchange that took place between the Assamese people and the adjoining hill tribes. There was little money in circulation, since most of the state revenue in the Ahom kingdom was received in labour and the king's officers received remuneration in land and labour, each being allocated a number of persons to serve him for a stipulated number of days on an allotted piece of land. The state, of course, received some revenue in cash from the artisans, as also from tolls collected from export and import of goods.

The first occasion that demanded the British intervention in the north-east of Bengal was the Bhutia raid in Cooch Behar in 1772. The Bhutias had carried off the Raja of Cooch Behar; his Dewan sought British help to rescue him. The treaty that followed brought Cooch Behar under British suzerainty. It was in 1792 that the British were requested by the Ahom king, Gaurinath Singh, to help him in suppressing the Moamaria rebels in Upper Assam. The Moamarias rose in rebellion at the oppression of the Ahom king and drove out Gaurinath Singh from the seat of his government. The king sought British help; but failing to get British aid, he requested Raush, a salt farmer of Goalpara, to aid him. The privates of Raush who went to help the king were cut to a man by the rebels and in utter helplessness the Ahom prince again appealed to the British, at least to suppress the brigands who had crossed from Bengal into Assam and were ravaging his territories.

The Government of Lord Cornwallis felt an obligation to send aid, at least to suppress the irregulars, known as Barkandazes, who had marched into Assam from the Company's territory. It was also realised that a strong power in the Brahmaputra valley, friendly towards the British, would safeguard the British possessions in Bengal. Therefore a detachment of the British troops was sent to Assam under Captain Welsh. He was instructed to send an elaborate report on Assam to the Government. Captain Welsh succeeded in suppressing the rebels but found the Ahom administration oppressive, corrupt, and inefficient. He submitted to his Government the proposal of keeping in Assam a Brigade of the British army, the cost of which was to be borne by the Ahom prince. But meanwhile Cornwallis had left and his successor, Sir John Shore, who was an exponent of the non-intervention policy opposed the idea of keeping British troops on foreign soil. Therefore Captain Welsh was asked to leave Assam. Captain Welsh sent replies to a questionnaire sent to him by the Governor-General (Section I, No. 1). The same replies were later on commented upon by David Scott, the first Commissioner of Assam. The report of Captain Welsh covers a wide range of Assam history and the political system of the Ahom kingdom. It is the first-hand report of a responsible English Officer who made an on-the-spot study and prepared a full report on the conditions of Assam in 1793, its administrative system and its nature, state of economy including trade and commerce. It is more important from these points of view than the Account of Hamilton which was compiled between 1807-1814 from outside the province and was based on hearsay. The comments of David Scott made the Report of Welsh all the more important and show the condition of things in 1828 after the annexation of Assam to the British empire.

The treaty for trade and commerce between Bengal and Assam concluded by Captain Welsh with Gaurinath Singh (Section I, No. 1) envisaged the expansion of trade and commerce demolishing the monopolistic system that operated till then.

Internal strife in Assam reached its climax after the withdrawal of the British army. The non-intervention policy of the British indirectly threw Assam into the clutches of the Burmese. In 1809 an Ahom prince, Chandra Kanta Singh, was deposed from power by his ministers, and failing to obtain help from the British he went to Burma for assistance. The Burmese troops rushing into Assam to help him proved to be dangerous; Chandra Kanta whom they had set up in power was deposed and for better terms Jogeswar Singh was raised to the throne. Purandar Singh, another contendant for the throne, took refuge in British territory in Bengal.

Meanwhile, the Anglo-Burmese relations were heading towards a precipice in another part of the eastern frontier. The king of Burma had consolidated his power in his country and conquered Arakan; an independent kingdom adjoining the south-east part of Bengal. Many refugees from Arakan had taken shelter in the British territories during the combing operations by the new Burmese masters. The Burmese king demanded the surrender of these fugitives; gradually he extended his territorial claim to Chittagong, Dacca, and Murshidabad. The Burmese troops overran Manipur as also the petty principalities of Cachar and Jaintia and threatened the British district of Sylhet. Besides, a Burmese invasion of Bengal from Goalpara seemed imminent.

The East India Company had just subjugated the Marathas, the last contestant for the imperial bid; at this time the success of the Burmese in Assam and their fantastic claim upon Bengal districts had roused dangers from the flank. The capture of the Sahapuri island, off the shore of Chittagong, brought forth the war. On March 5, 1824, the Government of Lord Amherst declared war upon Burma. Bruce was sent to Assam to negotiate treaties with the tribal chiefs, and overtures of friendship were offered to the princes of Manipur, Cachar and Jaintia by David Scott. The king of Burma was compelled to sign the treaty of Yandabu on February 24, 1826. As per article 2 of the treaty, the king of Burma agreed to renounce all claims upon Assam and abstain from all future interference with the principality of Assam and its dependencies (Section I, No. 2).

Disposal of Assam proved to be a thorny problem. The Company's representative in Assam had declared that the British would withdraw from Assam as soon as peace would be restored, and called for the co-operation and assistance from the people. But the Governor-General-in-Council had declared that "by our expulsion of the Burmese from the territory of Assam the country would of right become ours by conquest". He seemed to have contemplated the idea of annexation of the territories upto Raha only, and that too, not permanently. David Scott, who had been appointed Agent to the Governor-General for Assam, submitted a detailed memorandum in which he advocated the restoration of an Ahom prince in fulfilment of the earlier declaration. The prince would be required to pay a tribute and a part of his revenue would be kept apart for the maintenance of British troops. As an alternative he suggested the annexation of the territories upto Bisvanath and the restoration of an Ahom prince in Upper Assam; the areas inhabitated by the Moamarias, Khamtis and Singphos were, however, to be kept apart for separate settlement with them.

In 1826 circumstances had changed considerably from those of 1792. Trade of Assam had increased, while the last rival of the British in imperial contest, the Marathas, had been defeated. After the expulsion of the Burmese, the British were in possession of the country. The people hailed the British as deliverers. A situation had arisen which called for a reconsideration of the north-eastern policy. The Supreme Government ordered the annexation of the country tentatively and asked the Agent to reconsider the recommendations already made by him.

Scott held fast to his view that Upper Assam was the citadel of the Ahom power, and an Ahom prince should be set up there; that would fulfil the declaration of the Government that a native prince would be set up in power after the hostilities were over. He further pointed out that Upper Assam was sparsely populated and would yield very little revenue. The people were not accustomed to pay revenue in cash; they might be asked to join the army which would serve better in case of war with Burma. An Ahom kingdom dependent on the British would thus serve better as a barrier against the Burmese. The Supreme Government realised the wisdom of the suggestion and ordered the restoration of an Ahom prince in Upper Assam. Robertson after interviewing Purandar Singh recommended him for the throne of Upper Assam; and when this was approved by the Supreme Government, he concluded a treaty with him on June 27, 1833 (Section I, No. 3).

The ghost of Burmese invasion still haunted the British for quite a long time after the Anglo-Burmese War. Scott, therefore, wanted to create a hedge of native chiefs around the Company's territory in Assam. During the later course of the war the Muttock chief, Bar Senapati, had lent cordial support and material aid to the British. So he had recommended to keep the Bar Senapati in power, conferring some distinction upon him. Therefore an engagement was entered into with him in May 1826 (Section I, No 4). The Bar Senapati acknowledged the supremacy of the British Government and undertook to furnish an armed contingent of 300 guards. In January 1835, the obligation to supply troops was commuted to a money payment of Rs. 800/- a year (Section I, No. 5). On the death of the Bar Senapati in November, 1839 his sons refused the terms offered to them by the Company's Officers. Thereupon the territories of the Bar Senapati were assumed by the Government and later annexed to the Lakhimpur district of Assam; pensions, however, were given to the members of the family of the Bar Senapati.

In course of time the British felt that the soil of Assam was fertile and the people were reconciled to the British rule. The soil of Upper Assam, that is, the territories of Purandar Singh, was best suited for the cultivation of tea. Therefore a bid was made for the resumption of this territory. Meanwhile Purandar Singh had defaulted in payment of his annual tribute and appealed for reduction of the tribute he had agreed to pay. After a tour of the territory, the Agent to the Governor-General recommended to the Supreme Government the resumption of the territory and the introduction of the direct administration of the Company. The suggestion was approved by the Supreme Government, and in October 1838 the territory of Purandar Singh was annexed by a proclamation and placed under the direct administration of the British Officers. The valley of the Brahmaputra, thus brought under the direct administration, was divided into six districts of Goalpara, Kamrup, Nowgong, Darrang, Sibsagar and Lakhimpur.

III

When the Burmese came to Assam through Manipur they advanced towards Cachar in early 1824 to reinstate Govinda Chandra, the deposed Raja. As Cachar was contiguous to the Company's territory in Sylhet the Burmese move was considered alarming. The Company's Government now took Govinda Chandra under their protection. After the war, on May 6, 18 8, the Agent to the Governor-General concluded a treaty with Govinda Chandra (Section II, No. 1). Cachar came under British control as a tributary state.

This arrangement proved to be short-lived. Govinda Chandra was murdered in 1830. He had not been allowed to choose any heir to his throne though he had no natural heir to succeed him. As the British were securely enthroned in Lower Assam and were in effective control of the Upper Valley, they did not like to forgo the revenue of Cachar which the Supreme Government had calculated to be 3 lacs of rupees. So after the murder of Govinda Chandra, on the recommendations of Crawfurd who had succeeded Scott as the Agent to the Governor-General, the plains portion of Cachar was annexed to the British territories and tracts to the east of the river Jiri was given to Gambhir Singh of Manipur.

In the hilly tracts of North Cachar and Mikir Hills Tularam Senapati had carved out a principality for himself. Govinda Chandra was induced to agree to Tularam's rule there (Section II, No. 2). In 1834 the plains portion of his principality known as central Cachar was annexed to the Company's dominions, and over the rest of hilly tracts in the east, Tularam continued to rule as per Agreements he entered into with the Company though hillmen were averse to his rule. In 1853, after the Naga atrocities were committed within this petty principality and it had been found that Tularam's descendants were not in a position to protect their people, the Company's Government took over their "jungle tracts" reluctantly, for they were uneconomic. The successors of Tularam Senapati were pensioned off.

A treaty was concluded with the ruler of Jaintia, Ram Singh, for joint action against the Burmese (Section II, No. 3). He was promised rewards for his help and co-operation with the British. After the war, he was reinstated in his state; but no territory from Assam was given to him as promised before the hostilities had begun. The Company's Agent held that Ram Singh did not exert to the extent for which any reward could be given to him in territory. The ruler of Jaintia recalcitrantly accepted the Company's protectorate but was not required to pay any tribute (Section II, No. 3).

Ram Singh died in 1832; Rajendra Singh, his nephew, succeeded him. Robertson charged him for the immolation of British subjects at the shrine of Kali; he urged him to stop such occurrence in future and hand over the culprits to him. Seizure of the British subjects had occurred during the life time of Ram Singh and his successor could not be held responsible for it. Moreover, an annual tribute of Rs. 10,000/- was asked from him for the protection of his territory by the Company; as an alternative he was asked to cede a tract of his country in lieu of the tribute. The culprits were made over to the British but Rajendra Singh declined to pay any tribute. Thereupon in 1835 Jaintiapur was annexed to the Company's possessions and Jaintia Parganas on the plains, together with the dependency of Gobha were annexed to the British dominions. Rajendra Singh, successor of Govinda Chandra, submitted a Memorial (Section II, No. 4) for his recognition as the chief of the State of Cachar to no effect.

Thus it appears that the Company's policy in dealing with these petty states was conditioned by the threat of the Burmese attack initially. The Company wanted to bring these rulers under their protection because that would preclude Burmese intrigue with them; rather these petty chiefs would help them in fighting the Burmese. But the apprehension of Burmese reprisal proved in course of time to be miscalculation; the Burmese were found to be reconciled to the loss of Assam and its dependencies. As the Company's rule was well-established in the valley of the Brahmaputra and it was found that direct administration of the territories of these chiefs would leave a surplus of revenue after defraying the expenses of administration, every excuse was availed of for annexation of their territories.

Situated between Burma and Assam, Manipur held a very important strategic position. But settlement of that kingdom in 1826 proved to be a difficult task. Initially the Manipuri princes were found unwilling to call for the Company's assistance in establishing themselves on the throne; with difficulty Gambhir Singh was reconciled to the Company's overtures. The Burmese, it was feared, would not agree to the Company's annexation of this strategically important principality which was contiguous to their territory. Therefore in the treaty of Yandabu the matter was left rather vague; it was simply stated that the Raja of Manipur, Gambhir Singh, was to be restored in power (Section I, No. 3). The Company sought a clarification from the Burmese king and found that the latter was agreeable to recognize Manipur as an independent kingdom. But the geographical situation of Manipur created complications, for in conjunction with Manipur the Burmese would have smooth movement into Assam and into Bengal the border in Sylhet; the weak ruler of Cachar would be of no helf to stop Burmese march through his territory. Moreover, Manipur with a population of 50,000 and a revenue of Rs. 10,000 had no resources to organise itself into the position of a strong power capable of resisting foreign inroads and provide for a stable government. Yet another problem arose about the boundary of Manipur with Burma, the Burmese claiming the restitution of Kubo valley which in course of the war was occupied by Gambhir Singh.

After the war Gambhir Singh became the Raja of Manipur as provided in the treaty of Yandabu. But the Company continued to pay and command the Manipur Levy. The fear of an attack of the Burmese through Manipur proved decisive in formulating the Company's policy towards it. Trade facilities through Cachar for Manipur were wrested from Govinda Chandra (Section II, No. 1). After the murder of Govinda Chandra the territories of Cachar east of Jiri river were also given to Gambhir Singh. But by an Agreement (Section II, No. 5) Gambhir Singh agreed to allow trade between Manipur and the adjoining hills and maintain the road connecting Cachar with Manipur. Further he agreed to provide a portion of his troops and hill porters to British troops in case of war with Burma. Kubo valley had to be restored to the Burmese in 1832. But the English by an Agreement agreed to pay a compensation of Rs. 500/- to Manipur for the cession of Kubo valley to the Burmese (Section II, No. 6). Manipur was relegated to the position of a vassal state and the installation of a Political Agent proved decisive in controlling its ruler.

IV

To the extreme west of the mountain range dividing the two valleys of the rivers Brahmaputra and Surma lay the Garo Hills.

The Company had begun to bring these hill tribes under its political control by recognizing the powerful local chiefs as their Jeminders. In 1811 David Scott was appointed the first Civil Commissioner of Rangpur—on the border of which stood the hills—to regularise the relations of these local chiefs with the Company. When Assam was made a Circuit of Bengal in 1826, after the peace of Yandabu, the Garo Hills were transferred to Assam together with three Dewani thanas of Bijni, Karaibari and Goalpara.

But in the Khasi Hills, where the local chiefs who were independent and powerful, the Company faced trouble. When the two valleys were brought under its possession some sort of control over the hills which separate them was felt to be necessary, and the opening of communicating route through them was imperative. Scott had mooted the idea of opening a route through the Khasi Hills as early as 1824, as the usual route through Jaintia, he felt, was inconvenient. Moreover, the unhealthy conditions prevailing in the valleys compelled him to seek a hill resort, where, by a short stay, the European Officers of the Company might recoup their health. The Company's Government initiated a policy to bring these states under their political control. A series of Engagements, or Agreements, were concluded for the purpose. The Khasi chiefs were allowed to exercise civil and criminal jurisdiction over their own people in all matters pertaining to them, but they were required to deliver up criminal refugees and obey all the mandates of the British Government.

A treaty (Section III, No. 1) with the Cherra Raja, Diwan Singh, was concluded on September 10, 1829, and on the same date the Raja ceded (Section III, No. 2) land for the station of Cherrapunji in exchange for an equivalent in the district of Sylhet. In the same year an Engagement (Section III, No. 3) was made with the Sardars of Birangpunji, by which they bound themselves to be subject to Diwan Singh. In 1876 the Birangpunji villages were resumed and brought under direct control; the inhabitants since then pay revenue (house-tax to Government) at Rupees two per house.

In 1830 Diwan Singh's nephew and successor, Subha Singh, ceded (Section III, No. 4) additional land for the station of Cherrapunji, and in 1840 Subha Singh gave a perpetual lease

(Section III, No. 5) to the British Government of the coal hills at Cherrapunji and confirmed a perpetual lease of the Birangpunji coal mines granted by the Sardars of that group (Section III, No. 6). Subha Singh was succeeded by Ram Singh, who on May 16, 1857, signed an Agreement (Section III, No. 7) confirming the Engagements of his predecessors. Ram Singh died on April 23, 1875, and a collateral member of the family, Hajan Manik, was elected to fill up the vacancy.

On the death of Singh Manik, Raja of Khyrim, his grand-nephew Rabon Singh was elected by the Chiefs and elders of the country; the election was confirmed, and an Agreement similar to that executed by the Nongkhlao Chief (Section III, No. 9) was taken from Rabon Singh. Rabon Singh died in August 1871, when his next brother, Klur Singh, was elected as his successor, and the election was confirmed on his signing the usual Agreement. Rabon Singh rendered valuable services to the British Government during the Jaintia rebellion of 1862-63 and obtained a pension of Rupees 150 per mensem; it was granted for two generations, and terminated with Klur Singh, Seim.

In the year 1878-79 the people of 25 villages in the State of Khyrim complained of long-continued oppression and undue exactions on the part of their Seim Klur Singh, and prayed that they might be allowed to become British subjects. The Seim retorted with complaints of rebellious refusal on their part to submit to his lawful authority and to his customary demands. The matter was enquired into by the Deputy Commissioner of the district and a reconciliation between the parties was effected, the disaffected villagers promising to return to their allegiance and to pay the Seim all his dues as sanctioned by the local authorities, on the following conditions:—

(1) The Government to select and appoint from among their community four Sardars to take charge of, and watch over, their interests.

(2) All petty cases in their villages to be tried and decided by the four men appointed as above.

(3) All serious and difficult cases or disputes between the 25 villages and either the Seim or outsiders to be referred to the Court of the Deputy Commissioner and to be decided by him.

The Sardars and the disaffected people subsequently applied to return unconditionally to their allegiance to the Seim, and after a local enquiry by the Deputy Commissioner, Khasi Hills, the authority of the Seim was restored.

Mut Singh, Chief of Nongstain, died in 1862, before the completion of the agreement with the British Government into which he had proposed to enter. He was succeeded by Don Singh, who had been chosen by the elders of the tribe. The title of Raja Bahadur was conferred on Don Singh on his signing an Agreement (Section III, No. 8). Don Singh was succeeded on March 15, 1878 by his brother U. Borson Singh, whose election was duly confirmed. Borson Singh died in February 1890 and was succeeded by his brother Jeesing, but before receiving the *sunnud* granted to him, he too died. He was succeeded by his nephew U. Mada, whose election was confirmed by the Chief Commissioner in December, 1890.

The most important of the following twenty-two minor States are Nongkhlao, Mylim, Langrin and Nongspung.

1 Nongkhlao.	9 Nongspung	17 Bhawal.
2 Mylim.	10 Maolong.	18 Malalsohmat.
3 Maharam.	11 Langrin.	19 Dwara Nongtyrmen.
4 Shella.	12 Maosenram	
5 Mariao.	13 Nongaohphoh	20 Maodon.
6 Rambral.	14 Maoflang.	21 Nongilwal.
7 Sohlong.	15 Jirang.	22 Pomsanngut.
8 Maolong.	16 Longlong	

A treaty (Section III, No. 9), with a view to opening up communication between Sylhet and Assam, was signed in 1826 with Raja Tirat Singh, by which the Raja, on receiving a promise of the protection of the British Government, voluntarily surrendered his independence. In 1829 Tirat Singh was prominently concerned in the massacre of two British officers, with about sixty native subjects. Hostilities ensued, and after a harassing war with the Hill Chiefs, most of whom joined Tirat Singh, the Raja surrendered. He was imprisoned for life in the Dacca Jail, and Government conferred the Chiefship on his nephew Rajan Singh, who was installed on March 29, 1834, and with whom a new Engagement (Section III, No. 10) was made.

Rajan Singh became deeply involved in debt and abdicated in favour of Jidar Singh, on condition of his debts being paid and a stipend being allowed him. Jidar Singh died in 1856, and the succession was disputed between Rajan Singh and Bor Singh, a distant collateral relation of Jidar Singh in the female line. Rajan Singh died before the dispute was settled, and as Bor Singh was considered to have no claims based on family, and was objected to by many of the Sardars, Government resumed the country. The Home Government, however, disapproved of the resumption, and directed that a Chief should be chosen by the assembled Mantris and heads of clans. The choice fell on Bor Singh, and the Chiefship was conferred on him, and his lineal heirs forever, subject to certain conditions (Section III, No. 11). In May 1866, finding himself incapable of managing his affairs, Bor Singh abdicated (Section III, No. 12) in favour of his heir Chand Rai, who was recognized in 1868 under the usual conditions as Chief of Nongkhlao. Chand Rai was succeeded on January 19, 1874, by U. Hajan Singh. This Chief was, at the request of his subjects and on proof of grave maladministration, deposed, and his cousin U. Kine Singh, was appointed in his stead on the 16th March 1876. This Chief became a convert to Christianity after his election.

Originally this State was included in that of Khyrim, but in the time of one Ron Singh, Seim of Khyrim, a dissension arose, his nephew Singh Manik disputing the succession. Ron Singh, however, fought and conquered this Singh Manik, who retired to Longkyrdem in Khyrim, where he lived in obscurity.

U. Ron Singh was succeeded by U. Lhatu Manik, and he by U. Bor Manik. In U. Bor Manik's time, a second Singh Manik, a great-grand-nephew of the Singh Manik above referred to, requested permission to reside at Nongkrem, and he and U. Bor Manik having struck up a friendship, it was agreed that U. Singh Manik should succeed U. Bor Manik on the throne. But when U. Bor Manik died U. Singh was not allowed to quietly succeed him. A nephew of U. Bor named U. Hajan Singh contested the succession. The dispute ended by the people dividing into two parties and electing U. Singh Manik Seim of the remainder of the State under the name of Myliim. After the conquest of the Mylıim country in 1829, the Chief Bor Manik, then called Chief of Khyrim, ceded to the British Government the territory on the south and east of the Umiam or Boga Pani river, called also Um-miao in the upper parts of its course (Section III, No. 13). In 1834 a proposal was made to restore this tract to the Chief, but it was never carried out.

In 1860 the chief men of Myliim presented a petition, complaining against the Chief Hajan Singh, who had succeeded U. Bor Manik. The Chief was extremely unpopular; moreover, he violated the customs of the country and gave himself up to habitual drunkenness. So he was deposed in 1861, and Milai Singh was elected by the elders and the people in his stead. A new Engagement, similar to that made with the Nongkhlao Chief, was taken from Milai Singh. In December 1863 Milai Singh signed an Agreement (Section III, No. 14) by which he ceded the lands required for the military cantonment and sanitarium of Shillong, and renounced all his sovereign and personal rights therein. By his engagements he was bound to give such lands rent-free; compensation was, however, allowed to him in the shape of a money payment of Rupees 2,000, while the rights of private proprietors were bought up for Rupees 6,325, and an annual payment of Rupees 108. Milai Singh died in January 1868, and the election of his successor, Hain Manik, was confirmed on his signing the usual Agreement.

The chief of Langrin died in December 1862, and was succeeded by his nephew U. Mit Singh, whose election was confirmed on his subscribing to an Agreement (Section III, No. 15). U. Mit Singh died on April 24, 1874, and was succeeded by U. Bor Singh on June 6, 1874, whose election was confirmed on execution of the usual agreement.

In 1872 Phanbalang, Chief of Nongspung, died and his nephew U. Step was elected as his successor. The election was confirmed under the usual conditions. On the death of U. Step, Santu Singh was duly elected on March 2, 1877 and confirmed in his appointment. Santu Singh resigned in 1885 in favour of his nephew U. Parba Singh, whose nomination was unanimously accepted by the Chiefs and elders of the State in a public darbar. U. Parba Singh was, therefore, confirmed in the Chiefship on his executing the usual agreement in December 1885.

An Agreement (Section III, No. 16) was made with U. Lar Singh, Chief of Mariao, in 1829.

U. Phan, Chief of Mariao, died in 1862, and was succeeded

by U. Ron, who signed an Agreement (Section III, No. 17) and received the title of Raja. U. Ron was, on his death, succeeded by his brother U. Jiei on October 14, 1879, who received the usual *sunnud.* U. Jiei died on April 4, 1888, and was succeeded by U. Burom Singh, his nephew, who received the usual *sunnud.*

An agreement was made with this State in 1833 but no copy of it exists. A copy, however, of the agreement with Sardar, U. Jantrai, who was appointed on May 5, 1870, is appended (Section III, No. 18).

An Agreement (Section III, No. 19) was taken from Adhor Singh, Chief of Maosenram, in 1831. The late Chief U. Mit died in 1867, and was succeeded by his nephew Adhor Singh under the usual conditions. Adhon Singh was deposed for drunkenness and inefficiency, and his nephew U. Ramon was appointed Seim in his place on January 25, 1875. He executed an Agreement (Section III, No. 20). On his death in 1889, his nephew U. Symburai, a minor, was, by an unanimous vote of the populace, elected Siem in March 1890. The election was confirmed by the Chief Commissioner on condition of his executing the usual agreement when he would come of age.

Agreements were made with the Chiefs of Maharam in 1839 and 1852 (Section III, Nos. 21-22). In October 1864 U. Sai Singh was elected Chief of Maharam in succession to U. Step Singh, and was recognized by Government on his signing an Agreement (Section III, No. 23). In 1875 U. Sai Singh was deposed for misgovernment. It had been the practice in this State to elect two Seims, a senior, called Seím-lih (Lih=white), and a junior, called Seim-iong (Iong=Black), the one being supposed to act as a check on the other; but this system which was in force in most, if not all, of the Khasi States in former times, gave rise to inconveniences, and the opportunity of U. Sai Singh's deposition was taken to abolish it, Adhor Singh, a member of the Seim-iong family, being appointed sole Chief of Maharam. On Adhor Singh's death, U. Kison Singh, his nephew, was appointed on December 15, 1877, and received the annual *sunnud.*

An Agreement (Section III, No. 24) was in December 1832 executed by U. Phaz, Chief of Bhawal Punji. In 1860, on the succession of Dhabur Singh, an Agreement, similar to that taken from Nongkhlao (Section III, No. 11), was made with him. Dhabur Singh died in 1874, and was succeeded under the usual conditions, by Lorshai Singh. U. Lorshai wass ucceeded by U. Bamon Singh, his nephew, on January 20, 1875. He executed an Agreement (Section III, No. 25). Bamon Singh died in August 1889 and was succeeded by his nephew U. Ram Singh, who received the usual *sunnud.*

U. Wan Singh, Chief of Maoiong, was killed in a tribal affray in March 1865, and his cousin U. Jan Singh was elected as his successor. The occasion of this succession was taken to introduce the general form of Agreement with him, but U. Jan Singh died before a *sunnud* could be conferred on him. U. Jit Singh was elected in his place. The first engagement with Maoiong dates from June 24, 1829, but there is no copy of that. Agreement executed by U. Jit Singh is therefore appended (Section III, No. 26).

Treaties with other Chiefs are given under Section III, Nos. 27-32. Agreements (Section III, Nos. 33-36) were made with Chiefs of Jongsohphoh, alias Nobosohphoh, Jirang and Malaisohmat.

The Chiefs of the Jaintia hills had already been brought under the direct control of the Company in 1835 when Jaintia was annexed by the Company and a Political Agent was appointed at Jowai.

The Company had no intention to bring the hill tracts to the east of these hills under its immediate control. Under pressing circumstances the territories of Tularam Senapati were gradually brought under the Company's direct responsibility; territories of Cachar east of Jiri river were made over to the Raja of Manipur. The tracts inhabitated the Naga tribes to the further east of Cachar were unattractive; the hills there were impenetrable except at certain points on the Patkai range. Prospect of revenue either from forest or land was bleak. Therefore no attempt was made to bring these tribes under the Company's administration. Chronic atrocities perpetrated by the Angami Nagas forced the Company to post an Officer at Asalu in 1854 and a line of outposts were set up along the borders of the British territory. But the results of direct control of the tribes from within the hills being satisfactory, slowly but reluctantly these hill tracts were formed into the district of Naga Hills.

Only in 1917 the present Naga Hills district took its present shape.

Similar was the case with Lushai Hills. The hills being more precipitious in character towards Burma and having no easy pass across it, and having scanty resources, did not call for any intervention by the Company till late years. On the Chittagong Hill Tracts of Bengal, the Kukis proved to be troublesome, and to administer them the Bengal Government passed an act in 1860. On the Assam side officers were appointed at Lungleh and Aijal. In 1898 the Bengal and Assam tracts were combined in one district named Lushi Hills District and placed under the Chief Commissioner of Assam.

V

East of Bhutan lay Kuriapara Duar which was held by the tribes called as Extra-Bhutan Bhutias (now known as Mompas). But they were not subject to the king of Bhutan. Their chiefs, known as Sath Rajas, were directly subordinate to the Tawang Raja, a tributory of Lhasa. This land was extremely fertile; on the charge of misdeeds, as on the Bhutan border, this land was annexed to the Darrang district of Assam. Arrangement (Section IV, No. 1) was made to pay these chiefs an amount of Rs. 5,000/- as compensation for foregoing their right of collection of dues from the Duars in 1843-44 when they appeared before Gordon, the District Officer of Darrang, in the company of the representative of the king of Tawang. They undertook not to allow the Bhutias under them to commit any crime in the plains and to subject themselves to the British courts for redress of their grievances in the plains.

Further east of Kuriapara Duar lay the extensive tracts of Char Duar or the four passes. The tribes living up the hills along the border of this tract were also known as Bhutias (Rupa and Sherdukpen, now known as Sherdukpens) but were independent of the Tawang Raja. The chiefs of these hills were also known as Sath Rajas and they also collected 'Posa' or levy from this tract. In 1826 an Agreement (Section IV, No. 2) with them was concluded by virtue of which the Darrang authority resumed the tract for a payment of Rs. 2,526-7-0 to their chiefs. The chiefs undertook not to collect revenue and oppress the ryots in the plains and to surrender the criminals from the plains to the British authorities; they also agreed to subject themselves to British courts in civil and criminal cases.

Eastward of the Bhutias, that is in the tract between Ghabru and the Bhoroli, live the Hrussos, commonly known as Akas, who realized from each house of the Khels allotted to them "One portion of a female dress, one bundle of cotton thread, and the cotton handkerchief." Similar charge of outrage was also levelled against them by the Government of the Company and David Scott forbade their entering the plains, styling them as lawless brigands. But the Akas continued to come down to the plains and gave much trouble on the score of collection of their levies. The Government of the Company gradually began to enter into Agreements with their chiefs. The first Agreement (Section IV, No. 3) was made with Tagi Raja who agreed not to commit any oppression on the ryots of the plains and became subject to the British authorities for consideration of an annual payment of Rs. 120/- for him and three other chiefs in 1892. The Hazari Khowas also entered into an Agreement (Section IV, No. 4) in which they undertook not to oppress the ryots of the plains and give asylum to criminals of the plains in their hills and to subject themselves to British courts in case of disputes, for an annual payment of Rs. 60/- and 120/- respectively.

To the east of the river Bhoroli in the hills north of Naoduar or nine passes and Chaduar or six passes, in Lakhimpur as far east as the upper course of Subansiri, live the tribes known as Daflas. The Daflas used to realize from their allotted khels on the plains from every ten houses, one double cloth, one single cloth, one handkerchief, one dao, ten heads of horned cattle and four seers of salt. For paying this import the paiks of third khels used to pay the Ahom king Rs. 3/- instead of Rs. 9/- revenue per got, the difference being remitted to enable them to meet the Dafla payment. The inconvenience of allowing them to come down to collect the 'posa' was felt by the new masters of the valley and applying force gradually the chiefs were brought to terms on condition that each clan would receive for every ten houses of their allotted khel one course askut sheet, one long cotton handkerchief, two seers of salt, one dao, and one goat. This payment in kind was substituted for cash payment of Rs. 2,54[illegible]/- and 24 maunds of salt for certain *hat* or market tolls in 1852. The Dafla chiefs were petty and numerous and they were given chits for payment. No Agreement in general was concluded with them.

The Abors were found between Dihong and Dibong rivers in the hilly tracts below. The Miris inhabitated the plains and lower hills along the north bank of the Brahmaputra from the Sissi as far as the Dihong river. To the west of Dihong Abor villages were seen here and there, but between the Dibong and Dihong no Miri village could be found. The Abors claimed absolute sovereignty over the Miris of the plains and an inalienable right to all the fish and gold dust found in the Dihong river. The Miris also acknowledged the Abors as their master. The Ahom government did not collect any revenue from the Miris who had accepted the position of go-between connecting the Assamese traders and their hill masters. The Abors collected from the villages in the island of the Brahmaputra and along the lower course of its northern villages a levy on the goldwashers and fishermen who might have descended from the hills originally.

The relations of the Abors with the new conquerers of the valley in the initial stages were friendly and all Company's servants reported the Abors to be well disposed and good mannered. But troubles began when the Company gradually tried to bring the Miris under its jurisdiction and monopolise the revenue from the goldwashers and fishermen. The Abors whose rights were encroached upon began to raid the villages which refused to pay their levy. The Company's punitive expedition into the hills met with serious reverses. At last from 1862 agreements began to be concluded between the Abors and the British Government.

The first Agreement was concluded with the Meyong Abors (Section IV, No. 5) who recognized the foot of the hills to be the boundary between them and the British. They undertook not to oppress the ryots in the plains and to subject themselves to the British court in case of grievance, in consideration of a payment of 100 iron hoes, 30 maunds of salt, 2 maunds of tobacco, 80 bottles of rum and 2 seers of opium. Similar Agreement (Section IV, No. 6) was concluded by the Dehang-Debong Abors in consideration of an annual payment of 100 iron hoes, 40 maunds of salt, 100 bottles of rum and 2 maunds of tobacco. The Kebang Abors concluded an Agreement on January 16,

1863 (Section IV, No. 7) for an annual payment of 30 maunds of salt, 40 bottles of rum, 4 maunds of tobacco, 28 iron hoes and two seers of opium. The Bor Abors also came down in 1866 and concluded similar Agreement (Section IV, No. 8) for 60 maunds of salt, 120 iron hoes, 100 bottles of rum, 3 maunds of tobacco and 2 seers of opium, 230 bottles of wine, 18 maunds and 32 seers of salt and 108 yards of red broad cloth as compensation for surrendering their claims of direct collection from the plains villages upon which they had claimed jurisdictions.

Beyond the Abors and before the Khamtis and Singphos lie the various tribes of the Mishmis in the hills which close the north-east corner of the Assam Valley. The Mishmis were the only tribes who did not realize any 'posa' from the plains villages, nor did they receive any payment from the Company. They collected tolls only from traders who went to their hills to collect forest products or catch elephant and from the Hindu pilgrims who went to Parasuramkund for pilgrimage. No boundary between their hills and the Company's territory was ever defined formally, nor any engagement was ever entered into with them.

Below the Mishmi Hills to the south of the Brahmaputra and in between the Mishmi Hills and the Singphos lived the Khamtis. The British had come into contact with them during the course of the Anglo-Burmese War of 1824-26 and received considerable help from them. Scott wished to utilize this tribe together with the Singphos as a screen between the Burmese and Assam. Accordingly in May 1826 an Agreement (Section IV, No. 9) was concluded by the Agent of the Company (Scott) with the Khamti Chief 'Chousalan Sadiya Khawa Gohain'. The latter recognized the supremacy of the British and undertook to supply in lieu of tribute a contingent of 200 men to be armed by the British. Further he was allowed to collect taxes from the Assamese emigrants who might settle within his dominions. The management of the country was left with him, but serious crimes were to be brought to the British Political Officer at Sadiya.

The relation between the Khamtis and the British was peaceful and friendly though rumours of Khamti intrigue were reported occasionally. In 1835 a fresh batch of Khamti emigrants entered Assam and were allowed to settle without payment of taxes for three years. At about this time a dispute arose between the Khamti chief of Sadiya and the Muttock chief Bar Senapati over a tract of land on the south bank of the Brahmaputra. The Political Officer at Sadiya attached the land in dispute and asked the parties to appear before him. The Khamti chief took possession of the land in defiance of the order whereupon the Political Officer in vindication of his authority ordered the suspension and then the removal of the Khamti chief from the post of Khawa Gohain. The Khawa Gohain was thereafter removed from Sadiya to a distant station down the river out of the reach of intrigue and his post was abolished. The territories were brought under the direct administration of the British Officer at Sadiya, but the tribe was left to themselves and no tax was collected from them.

Apparently the Khamtis seemed to be contented and the ex-Khawa Gohain was allowed to return to Sadiya in his private capacity. But their hatred resulted into a premeditated outbreak in January 1839 when about 500 Khamtis in arms attacked the British post at Sadiya, butchered Col. White and his men and burnt the line to the ground. The Khamtis on the southern bank of the Brahmaputra also rose in rebellion but were put down by the British troops. Successful Khamtis retreated into the Mishmi Hills and took refuge there. In 1839-40 expeditions were sent to the hills and Khamtis were dispersed from there. Finally in 1843 all the Khamtis surrendered to the British. Agreements (Section IV, No. 10) were entered into with all clan chiefs wherein on condition of good behaviour they were allowed to live within British territories. They were divided into four divisions and were despatched in four directions. One division was settled at Choonpura above Sadiya; another was settled at Saikhowa to the south bank of the Brahmaputra; a third was settled at Dhemaji and the fourth was sent to Bhodia in North Lakhimpur. Since then they ceased to be a factor in the politics of 'North-Eastern India'.

Between the Mishmis and the Khamtis on the north and the Naga tribes to the south lived the Singphos. They had come from across the Patkai range during the later part of the eighteenth century. In order to create a hedge between Burma and Assam the British entered into Agreements (Section IV,

No. 11) with sixteen Singpho chiefs in 1826. They acknowledged the supremacy of the British and gave up all connections with the Burmese. No tribute was asked of them, but they were required to supply provisions to the British army in the event of war. They were also required to report the movement of the Burmese across the border. The chiefs were to administer justice except in heinous cases which were to be brought to the Political Officer at Sadiya for trial.

By 1874, the territories of Govinda Chandra of Cachar, Ram Singh of Jaintia, Bar Senapati of Muttock, Sadiya Khowa Gohain, the Khamti Chief and the hills inhabitated by the Garos, Khasis, Jaintias, Nagas and the Lushais, were tagged to the Assam Administration. The inconvenience of administering such vast and diverse territory as an appanage of Bengal was felt in the later half of the nineteenth century. Besides the administration of Bengal had become too heavy for a single Lieutenant-Governor; the frontier affairs needed constant consultation with the Supreme Government. Some sort of reorganisation was felt to be necessary. Therefore the Commissionership of Assam was separated from Bengal and together with the district of Sylhet of the Dacca Division, constituted into the Chief Commissionership of Assam in 1874 by a proclamation of the Governor-General-in-Council. The Political Officer of Manipur was also placed in the Assam Commission. In 1898 the Lushai Hills of the Chittagong Hill Tracts were transferred to the Assam Administration and, together with the Assam tracts of the Lushai hills, constituted into the District of Lushai Hills. In 1905 Assam was combined with Eastern Bengal to make a new province, known as Eastern Bengal and Assam. In 1912 Assam was restored to its former status when the Partition of Bengal was annulled. In 1920 Assam was made a Governor's province when Reforms were introduced after the Government of India Act, 1919, was promulgated. In 1937 further changes were introduced in the system of Government when Government of India Act, 1935, was partially introduced. This position remained till August, 1947, when the British left India.

SECTION I

1. CAPTAIN WELSH'S REPORT ON ASSAM WITH DAVID SCOTT'S REMARKS THEREON

From : CAPTAIN WELSH,
To : EDWARD HAY, Esq., Secretary to Government,
Dated : 6th February, 1794.

In obedience to the orders of the Honourable the Governor-General in Council, I lose no time in replying to the questions proposed in your letter of the 6th ultimo.

The information transmitted is, I may venture to say, correct in the most material points.

1st Question

"What form of government subsisted in Assam previous to your arrival there? (In replying to this query you are to specify, as far as may be in your power, the relative degree of authority possessed by the Rajah and the different Chiefs.)"

Answer to 1st Question

At the period in question in subversion of all regular government had taken place, but the question involves the ancient form of government and the most important alterations which it may have experienced. At present the outline of the system will suffice for the information of the Board; it deserves a minute detail at a period of more leisure.

The right of conquest had vested the dominion of this Kingdom in the race of Surgee Deo and the descendants of the principal associates of Sookapah, the original conqueror. The form of government was consequently monarchical and aristocratical.

The monarchy was possessed by the descendants of Sookapah, being partly hereditary[1] and partly elective. It was hereditary in

1. In early times the succession appears to have gone generally to sons except in cases of deposal. The circumstances of the succession one to another of the four sons of Roodra Singh is said to have originated

the fraternal line. In failure of brothers in the direct line of the Monarch's sons; in failure of these in the sons of the brothers next in seniority. Beyond this line, the aristocracy exercised a latitude of election among the nearest relations of the late monarch with some attention to the claims of nearer consanguinity, but more to those of personal merit.

The Monarch was the first executive officer and presided over every department of the State. He distributed honours, titles, and offices, without the concurrence, but not without the counsel of the aristocracy. He was not lord of the soil, but would alienate lands for the legal tenure[2] of which the possessor had no written documents. All uncultivated land was entirely at his disposal. He possessed no power over the lives and property of his subjects. He could not make peace and war without the concurrence of the aristocracy. He treated with foreign powers by his own ambassadors and his own name, but with the previous concurrence of the aristocracy. In the public councils,

in the death-bed injunction of that Monarch. It was not unusual for the reigning king to appoint a successor, and it was the practice to disqualify other members of the family from reigning by causing a slight wound to be inflicted upon them which was considered as an insurmountable bar to the acquisition of the regal office.

2. With exception to Royal grants and the khats or farms of individuals, usually of small extent there is no division of the land in Assam amongst a comparatively small number of individuals such as seen in the feudal countries of Europe and in Bengal, and the cultivated soil may be considered as the property of the pykes or peasants owing service to the State to whom it is allotted. Waste land might be reclaimed by any one who had the means of bringing it into cultivation, and a property in the soil might thus be acquired, subject, however, if held without a grant from the King, to an agrarian law which rendered the whole of the transplanted rice lands (roopeet) liable to division amongst the pykes on a new census taking place, in case there should be an insufficiency of waste land for their support. Gardens, tanks, groves, etc., which are formed upon the higher description of land, were not subjected to this law, nor was ground that had been occupied for great length of time and inherited or transferred from one party to another for a valuable consideration. Land of the later description called *poyeetrick*, or ancestoral was not subject to the payment of revenue until the reign of Kumolessur when a tax in kind was imposed on it equal to from that no estate of this kind exists exceeding in extent 200 Bengal beegahs, and that no individual in the country is possessed altogether of 900 beegahs of such land of roopeet quality.

he possessed the privilege of a casting voice. In executing sentence of death on a criminal his order alone would sanction a form by which the criminal's blood might be shed. He alone coined money. His person was sacred.

The aristocracy, or *Patrah-Munttee* was composed of three Gohains and the two Prime Ministers of State. The three *Gohains* or *Patrah* were the *Burh Patrah Gohain, Bura Gohain* and *Boorah Gohain.* They were permanent and hereditary counsellors of State little inferior to the Monarch in rank. On all occasions their counsel, and on all important affairs their concurrence, were indispensable. They proclaimed the Monarch and could depose him in the instance of incapacity or great delinquency. Some doubt, however, exists of their legal power of deposition.

In the provinces allotted to each, they exercised most of the independent rights of sovereignty.[3] In the execution of sentence of death, their order could not sanction a form in which the blood of the criminal might be shed, but they could authorize his death by drowning. In the event of war or the construction of public works they furnished their proportion of militia or men. They likewise supplied some trifling articles for the King's stores, but paid no other revenue. They ruled their provinces on the principles of the general system.[4] The

3. The authority of the King was in practice probably much more despotic than is here represented, and it would not appear from the history of the country that the aristocracy had any legal means of preventing the execution of his wishes, the only remedy seeming to have consisted in the actual exercise of their power of deposing him in case of gross misconduct and neglect of their advice. It is to be regretted that the historical work to which I have had access treats with great brevity of those reigns in which no troubles occurred, and in which the Princes may be supposed to have acted in constitutional manner, but when it does afford any insight into difference of opinion between the King and his Counsellors, we usually find one or other of these parties exercising unlimited sway, the Prince in some cases dismissing and putting to death the *Gohains,* and the latter frequently treating their master in the like manner.
4. For examples of the exercise of this power vide pages 23 to 45 to the accompanying extracts of these precedents. Only three—the deposals of Sooram Pha, Sooching Pha, and Soonyut Pha—can be considered as having anything of the character of deliberate acts of the great Council of State; while from the circumstance of all of these instances

pre-eminence was possessed by the *Gohains*[5] who obtained from the Monarch the title of *Roye* and the additional services of 2,000 men.

If the son of Gohain, was incapacitated by youth, want of abilities, or other causes, he was excluded from the succession.

The Monarch, with the concurrence of the two Gohains,[6] conferred the appointment on the late *Gohain's* brother or his brother's son. In failure of incapacity or delinquency of the nearest claimants a greater latitude was allowed, but in every instance the vacancy was supplied from five families descended from the associates of *Sookapah.* In the event of delinquency *Gohain* might be removed with the concurrence of two *Gohains.*[7]

The *Burra Burwah*[8] commanded the forces, received the revenues, and administered the justice of the upper provinces of Suddea on the eastern confines to Kolliabor in Decanpah and Derung in Oaterpah with an exception in favour of the provinces under the Government of the Gohains. He could not sanction the execution of a criminal by any form of death. The ***Burra Fogon's*** office was considered of higher importance, though of later creation than the former. The jurisdiction was similar to that of *Burra Burwah,* but its distance from the seat of

---

having occurred within a period of thirty years, and two of them in the time of the same Boorah Gohain, there seems to be some ground for the doubt here expressed as to the legality of the proceedings in question.

5. The *Gohains* had altogether allotted for their own use 10,000 pykes equal, at the old assessment, to Rs. 90,000 per annum which, adverting to the relative value of money in Assam and Bengal in former times may be considered as equivalent to treble the amount in the latter country.

6. It does not appear that the *Gohains* could be selected except from three families—one furnishing a *Bur Putra Gohain,* another a *Bur Gohain,* and a third a *Boora Gohain.*

7. The members of twelve families are now eligible to these offices upon the strength of past precedents. These twelve families are distinct from the preceding three from which the two Ministers could not be chosen—a rule that was probably enacted with the view of preventing the too great accumulation of power in particular families.

8. The Bar Booroоa had the command of 14,000 pykes but they were bound to perform service to the king, and the Prime Minister's perquisite consisted in an allowance of 7 per cent, for his private use and in the fines levied from them for offences committed or on the appointment to the inferior offices of Hazarkeeya, etc.

Government rendered it necessary that he should possess the power of executing sentence of death by drowning. Appeals from his judicial decisions were scarcely practicable, and were only made on very important occasions.

Departments of Government : Civil, Military and Ecclesiastical

The civil establishment was composed of the officers who superintended the various arts, sciences, trades, sources of public revenues, employments of the King's household, and numerous other departments. About 12 *Fogons* and 20 *Burwahs*[9] were allotted for these offices, and were chosen from the nine families of hereditary nobility. They were amenable for their conduct to the Monarch only.

In the Department of Justice, the *Neeay Khodah Fogon*[10] represented the Sovereign, and received appeals from the *Burra Burwah*, and *Burra Fogon*. Every officer under Government was a Judge in his department with an appeal to his superior officer, and ultimately to the Monarch's represen'ative.[11] In the *Gohain* provinces[12] no appeal was allowed from the decision of the Chief. In the administration of Justice, witnesses were examined and written documents received in evidence, the Judge decided according to the customs of the

9. These offices were filled from the fifteen families of hereditary nobility already mentioned and such of them as did not involve military service could also be held by the higher classes of the aboriginal inhabitants of the country, but not by foreigners of their descendants for three or four generations.
10. This officer exercised jurisdiction in the absence of the king only, and in the palace or fort.
11. No record was kept in criminal trials, but in civil cases a summary of the proceedings was drawn out and delivered to the successful party called *Siddhant Puttir*. Trials were conducted before the *Bur Boorwa* or other delegate as President, and a certain number of Khattakees, Khagitstees, Ghunucks and Pundits as assessors, by whose opinion the judge was usually guided. The administration of justice is said to have been speedy, efficient, and impartial in former times, but a good deal corrupted since the commencement of the disorders occasioned by the Moamaria insurrections. No *Wakeels* were employed, the parties or one of their relations appearing personally. From the *Bur Boorwa's* Court not even the three *Gohains* were exempt.
12. After this, a force consisting of mercenaries from the western provinces was introduced, and by that means the late Boora Gohain was enabled so long to usurp the whole power of the State.

country and to the best of his judgement, as no written laws existed previous to the introduction of Brahminical religion. The Monarch would authorize any person of consequence to take cognizance of particular causes in any part of the Kingdom.

Military Establishment

The army was a militia, and organized in the following manner:

Every family furnished the Sovereign with one man in four as a permanent militia or standing army. When the public service required an additional force, two men. and in cases of great emergency either of war or public works, three men. The first was denominated *Mool,* the second *Dowal,* the third *Tewal.* The fourth who remained to cultivate the soil, and four are termed Ghote pyke Officers.[13] Twenty men were commanded by a *Burra,* one hundred by a *Khotkea,* one thousand by a *Hazaree,* three thousand by a *Fogon.* The *Burra Burwa* and *Burra Fogon* as Commanders-in-Chief, had each the particular command of a body of twelve thousand men.[14] The *Fogons, Rajekoars,* and *Hazarees* were nominated by the Monarch, but with the advice and concurrence of the Gohains. The *Khotkeas* and *Burras* were appointed by their respective *Fogons* and *Rajekoars.* The privates might demand through the regular channel the dismissal of their *Burras* and *Khotkeas,* and the appointment of an officer of their own nomination. Each officer administered justice to the men under his command with an appeal to his superior officer, and ultimately to the *Neeay Khodah Fogon.*[15]

13. The pykes are now chiefly employed as labourers; or a revenue is derived from the commutation of their services for a money payment varying from six to eight rupees per Ghote. A considerable number of the inhabitants are exempted from personal service on the score of their caste or rank or by purchase, but by far the largest portion still continue to work, in a most unprofitable manner, for the Government.
14. Since the loss of a great number of pykes in the reign of Rajeswar Sing, the number of men forming a Ghote in Upper Assam has been reduced to three. All persons below the age of 15 years and above 50 years are exempted from service.
15. This is one of the most important rights the lower orders possesses, and it extended usually to the *Hazarkeeyas,* and in case of proof of maltreatment to the higher ranks placed over them. When a dispute occurred between the retainers of two different Commanders, it was decided by the officer of highest rank.

From these services were exempted the descendants of the hereditary nobility, unless in the event of delinquency, and all who possessed offices under Government.

Military stores were under the superintendence of the Kargoriah Fogon.

Ecclesiastical

It is only necessary to observe that the Brahmanical religion has prevailed since the time of Rooder Sing, who reigned about 70 years ago.

The creation of three lesser Gohains from the same families as the former appears to have been the principal legal alteration in the Civil and Military departments. The office of Burra Fogon was of later creation also. The recent Gohains are the Suddea Koa Gohains, Governor of the eastern confines or Suddea; the Moorung Koa Gohain, Governor of the confines towards Naga and Kossaree; the Solal Gohain, Governor of Kolleabur.

In a lapse of centuries every possible deviation from regular Government might be enumerated, but it will be proper to confine the discussion to those illegal innovations, which proved the first source of the late troubles.[16]

Source of Discontent and Disaffection

The sacred regularity of succession to the Throne was violated by the power of the Burra Burwah[17] in the instance of Rajah Swar Sing who superseded his elder brother Mohun Mala Deo.[18]

The rights of the hereditary nobility were superseded by the appointment of Roop Sund, and at a later period of his son Chiste Sund, the grandfather of Joinath, to the high office of *Burra Burwah*. Joinath is the dismissed *Burra Burwah*.

16. The descendants and frequently collateral relations of nobles guilty of treason, and particularly of shedding the royal blood, were attainted and degraded so as to be incapable of holding any office.
17. This office is now held by a family of Khamptees who settled in Assam about 70 years ago.
18. This is accounted for on page 57 of the historical extracts. It appears that the elder son was disqualified for the succession in consequence of his being marked with the small-pox, any personal blemish, whether natural or artificial, being considered as an insurmountable bar to the attainment of the regal dignity in Assam.

The power of the State and the direction of the Royal Councils were now completely diverted from the lawful channel of the *Gohains.* The secret machinations of the latter co-operating with the general struggle for power under a weak and vicious administration and with the discontents of the people seem to have excited the Maran and Maimaria insurrections.

The execution of the Gooroo or High Priests of the Morarias and of his son, suspected, probably with great justice as the principal authors of the troubles, was the chief cause of the subsequent insurrections.

Mohun Meeha Deo's death by Moran poison had rendered legitimate the latter part of Luckee Sing's reign, but the sons of his elder brothers possessed a right to the succession superior to that of Gourinaut Sing; the expedient of mutilation, however, had left Gourinaut (the present Rajah of Assam) without a rival and he became lawful Sovereign at early period of life.

This debauched minority, the excrable ignorance, imbecility, caprice, cruelty, and oppression of Government, whose ministers and low favourites were the dread, detestation, and shame of the great, the scourge, and execration of the people, involved the whole Kingdom in confusion.

The *Burh Gohain* and his five sons were murdered. Adasooria, *Burra Burwah* of hereditary nobility, and numerous adherents suffered mutilation.

All the men of consequence were divided in opposite interests; but the whole seemed united in sentiments against the vile favourites of Gourinaut.

Every kind of oppression was practised on the people. The Morarias[19] succeeded probably by the connivance of the King's Generals—certainly by their supineness. The *Boora Gohain* may with great justice be suspected of having favoured the insurrection. The King fled from his capital on the approach of the

19. The Morarias still possess some power in the upper part of the country. They are united under the command of their elected chief the Bar Sinaputtee. In any arrangement that may be made for the future settlement of Assam, it will be necessary to consult the interest of this numerous body. If attached to the Government; they might become useful as a militia, but the exorbitant pretensions of their priests may render it difficult to satisfy them. Of late years it was usual with the Assam Government to keep the High Priest at Court, and after under restraint. His influence is now supposed to be on the decline.

insurgents and repaired to Gowhatty. The *Boora Gohain* and other persons of consequence, many petty Chiefs of districts and towns, and some adventurers, with a very few followers, assumed independence in various parts of the country.

The same crimes and oppressions affected the vicinity of the Monarch's residence wherever he fled. It is probable that the Diga Rajah, of Derangh, was provoked by similar oppressions to rebel, yet there is some reason to think that his principal motive was the opportunity to assert independence which the times afforded. He perished by the hands of the executioner. His son, deprived of the succession, seized Derungh and Kamroop with the assistance of the Burkandazes.

The Rajahs of the Noaduwar esteemed the times favourable to their personal independence, which was accordingly asserted, without any apparent provocation. A bold adventurer, with two or three hundred men advanced to Gowhatty, and Surgee Deo fled to Bengal.

Relative authority of the Rajah and the different Chiefs

This question has been partly answered. It remains to notice the western Rajahs of Doomriah, Derungh, Beltolah, Rannygong and Noaduwar.[20] Surgee Deo founds his title of Sovereignty over these Chiefs on the right of conquest or voluntary submission. With the concurrence of the Patrah, or Potrah Muntree, he could dismiss a Rajah,[21] and appoint his brother to fill the vacancy, or his son in failure of the fraternal line. It is doubtful whether he possessed the lawful power to put Rajah to death.

The Rajahs[22] were Judges in their own districts, but with an

20. The whole of these Chiefs are now in subjection to Assam as far as their possessions in the plains extend, but they are nearly independent in the Hills. There is every reason to believe that they are particularly well disposed towards the British Government, and the principal person amongst them, the Rajah of Burdewar, is now actively engaged in improving the road through his territory which extends nearly to Pundwa in Sylhet.
21. Of late the Bar Phookin exercised the right of dismissing and appointing the above Rajahs with exception to those of Derungh and Beltola without previous reference, but subject to an appeal to the king.
22. The powers of the Rajahs have since been much curtailed. At present they exercise judicial authority in minor cases in common with the *chowdries* by sufferance only but the facility they possess of escaping

appeal to the Burra Fogon and the Monarch. They must attend personally with their complement of men, when summoned by the Surgee Deo. All the Rajahs, except the Rance, pay an annual revenue, in addition to the number of men they might furnish on any emergency.

Confines, Suddia, Miree, Duffala, Orika, Botan, Naga, Koparee, Jointa, and the Garrows paid tributes to the Monarch of Assam.[23]

2nd Question

"How far Surgee Deo. Rajah of Assam, has been restored the exercise of his legal authority ?" You are desired to signify particularly whether any of his subjects still refuse submission to, or continue to act independently of him, and, if any should come under this description, it is wished that you should communicate their names, quality, force, and situation, with the grounds of their disaffection as far as you are acquainted therewith. It is also desired that you should take measures which are necessary to be pursued for establishing obedience to the Rajah's authority, and the period required for carrying those measures into execution."

Answer to 2nd Question

The limited degree of authority which the Surgee Deo at present enjoys, he derives from the countenance of the Company's troops.

The different Chiefs and Rajahs profess submission and obedience to the authority of the Surgee Deo, but seem all inclined to act independently of it. The grounds of their disaffection are enumerated in my reply to the first question, and their military

into the hills, when pursued by the officers of Government, has often induced them to assume still higher powers, and to mutilate and put persons to death for which a fine was usually accepted as an atonement under the Assam Government. Nothing of this kind has occurred since the full establishment of the British authority.

23. The Duplas, Bhooteeyas, and Ankas pay a nominal tributes and in return levy blackmail to very oppressive and continually increasing extent in the districts north of the river. Cachar and Jyntiah long before this period had regained their independence. Twelve of the Singpho Chiefs were also nominally subject to Assam, but did not pay tribute.

force appears to be extremely despicable. I am clearly of opinion that to establish obedience to the Rajah's authority, it is only necessary that the mediating power should more decidedly interfere, and declare its determination to support the Government of Assam in all its constituent parts.

3rd Question

"Whether you think there is any probability that the principal Rajah or Chiefs will soon be prevailed upon to accept your and the Rajah's invitation to assemble for the purpose of concerting a form of government, and in that case how long it will be before such an assembly can be formed, and admitting them to meet, whether you have any hopes from your knowledge of the characters and views of the individuals that they will be induced to agree on a plan for the settlement and tranquility of the country."

Answer to 3rd Question

By proceeding to the capital I shall have an opportunity of requiring the personal attendance of all those Chiefs who are stationed in our route and who only agreeably to prescriptive rules are necessary to establish the original form of Government convinced of the impossibility of prosecuting with success their ambitious designs, and of being protected by the mediating power against the tyranny of the Surgee Deo, they will, I doubt not, unite and agree to a plan for the settlement and tranquility of the country. The period required to effect this depends upon adventitious circumstances.[24]

4th Question

"The late Ministers having been dismissed and the Rajah's incapacity for the government of his country being asserted,

24. Although very illiterate there are nevertheless several persons amongst the Assam nobility who, with considerable talents, possess a sufficient knowledge of business to enable them to conduct the affairs of the country until it may be determined, who is to be raised to the throne. It is of course impossible to say whether or not any particular individual could be appointed with the Rajah's consent, but under the altered circumstances of the case the British Government would no doubt be justified in exercising the most decided interference in regard to the selection of the higher officers of State.

whether you know any person or persons of sufficient ability, weight, and authority in that country for supplying the places of the dismissed Ministers. If you do, you are desired to name them, and to deliver your opinion how far their appointment could be made with the Rajah's consent and would be acceptable to the principal people. It is also wished that you should specify how far the Minister lately elected by the Rajah appears to you to possess the requisite qualifications for the trust committed to him."

Answer to 4th Question

On my arrival at the capital I shall have an opportunity of consulting the three Gohains, whose concurrence is necessary in the appointment of Ministers. I cannot yet venture to recommend any one to fill the important office of Burra Burwah.

The nomination of the late appointed Burra Fogon appears to be generally acceptable to the people, and I have reasons to think that he possesses the requisite qualifications for the trust committed to him.

5th Question

"Whether Kissnarain since his admission to the Raja of Derungh has behaved with proper submission to the Surgee Deo and whether you can rely upon Kissnarain's assistance, if required, in supporting Surgee Deo."

Answer to 5th Question

Kissnarain, since his admission to the Raja of Derungh,[25] has behaved with proper submission to the Surgee Deo, or rather has acted in compliance. I do not think his regard for the interests of the Surgee Deo would induce him to contribute his assistance but I can rely upon Kissnarain's affording his services, whenever required by me.

25. The Rajahs of Derungh have been reduced to complete subjection since the date of this report, and at present they do not possess the means of disturbing the peace or assisting the Government. They are appointed and dismissed like the other officers of State, an individual of the same family being, however, always chosen. There is at present one Rajah in possession and three ex-Rajahs, all of whom entertain bitter enmity against each other.

6th Question

"What are the reasons in your opinion of the Rajah's delay in proceeding to his capital, and whether any and what obstacles occur to this measure."

Answer to 6th Question

The late Ministers, and other interested advisers, represented to their infatuated Monarch the danger of returning to his capital, and to their successful attempts to awaken his fear I partly attribute the delay. But the Rajah's extreme indolence and impotence, both of body and mind, would naturally render him averse to a measure, which must be attended with some degree of personal exertion. He is now, however, on his way thither.

7th Question

"Whether the Commercial Regulations settled between you and the Rajah are considered to be in force, whether any and what benefit has resulted from them, and whether you think they admit of any, and what, alterations, with a view to the improvement of the commercial intercourse between the two States."

Answer to 7th Question

The Commercial Regulations settled between the Rajah and myself are in full force, but the principal benefit which has arisen from them is the demolition of an iniquitous monopoly, which ultimately must be productive of great pecuniary advantage, and in the meantime removes the distresses of the people. Resulting from the collections at the Candahar chowkey the sum of Arcott Rs. 12,012-2-9 has been received during the space of nine months, after defraying incidental expenses, and from this source the Rajah is to receive annually Rs. 12,000 and the overplus is destined to defray part of the expense of the detachment.

I am of opinion that this commercial compact will admit of considerable alteration with a view to the improvement of trade between the two States. But as the efficacy of such alteration depends, in the first instance, on the restoration of order, and, in the second, on the degree of influence, the Honourable Board may be desirous of obtaining in the affairs of Assam. Before I can give a decisive answer on this subject, I beg I may be indulged with some time to be assured of the former, and to be informed of the latter.

8th Question

"Whether from your knowledge of the Rajah's character you are of opinion that, after the return of the Detachment, he will observe the stipulations he has entered into, or may further agree to."

Answer to 8th Question

From a knowledge of the Rajah's character, and the views of many individuals in power and favour, whose personal interests are affected by the stipulations entered into with him, I am decidedly of opinion[26] that none would be observed, supposing the detachment and all control on the part of the British Government is withdrawn.

9th Question

"Whether you think it probable, in the event of your detachments being recalled, that the Government of the country will be so regulated as to admit of a beneficial commercial intercourse between the two States, and to what extent and in what articles you suppose such a commerce may be carried on. In your answer to this query you will state such information as you may have obtained relating to the productions and actual commerce of Assam."

Answer to 9th Question

This query may be considered under three distinct heads, *viz.* :

1. The consequences of the recall of the detachment, with respect to commerce which will be noticed in my reply to the 13th query.

26. This opinion was completely verified by the result. On the detachment being withdrawn, the Rajah ceased to observe the commercial treaty and a virtual monopoly was again established.

2. The articles of commerce.
3. The probable extent, and actual state of commerce.

IMPORTS

Articles of Commerce

From the eastern confines or Suddea, copper, cotton, spring salt, fir trees.[27] From the northern confines Miree supplies copper, munjeet, ouka; and Duffala supply munjeet, lonj pepper, ginger goomdan, Maytoon, and animal of the kine species, Botan supplies musk, blankets, cowtails, small horses, gola borax, rock salt, Nainta, kind of cloth, Goom, Sing, an embroidered cloth, Daroka, a silk of a mixture of green, red and yellow colours.

From the southern confines, Naga supplies cotton, Luckibilla, a silk cloth, Toatbund, a silk cloth, Narakapore, an embroidered silk, red hair, and Nagazatee spears. The Garrows supply cotton, copper, iron, coarse cloth.

From the western confines or Bengal copper and other metals, red lead, woollens of Europe, chiefly of the coarser kind, cottons of Bengal, chiefly of the coarser kind, chinty particularly kinkhobs, cloves, nutmegs, mace, cinnamon, blue vitriol, assafoetida, alum, darmook, orpiment, a variety of drugs, salt.

EXPORTS

The exports to Bengal only will be noticed here, they are divided into:

(1) The produce of the other confines.

(2) The produce of Assam.

1. Cotton in considerable quantity, munjeet in doubtful quantity, fir trees probably in any quantity, ginger probably in some quantity, gold in considerable quantity, borax probably in considerable quantity, musk in considerable quantity, small horses.

2. The merchantable produce of Assam may be considered at more length under three heads of vegetable, mineral, and animal productions.

27. This statement still exhibits the principal imports. The quantity of European manufacture has of late increased, and it is probable that there may hereatter be a 'considerable outset for woollens at a sort of annual fair held on the confines of Derungh, to which merchants from Tibet and the intermediate country resort.

Vegetable Productions

Sugarcane thrives in every part of Assam.[28] The cane of the best quality affords a granulated sugar, on experiment superior to the cane of Rungpore.

The natives convert the juice into a substance (ghoor) unfit for granulation, and of little consequence as an article of export. But in respect to this article it may be confidently asserted, that proper encouragement would render it very valuable.

Paper vine is cultivated in Kamroop, Derungh, Bassadoyungh in larger quantity, Bisswenth and other provinces of the kingdom possibly, in no great abundance anywhere, although the soil in many parts would seem extremely favourable to its cultivation.

Poppy grows in luxuriance in most of the Lower Provinces. The natives, however, are as yet unacquainted with the manufacture of merchantable opium, which might be procured in considerable quantity.[29]

Indigo is cultivated in various parts of the kingdom, but in very inconsiderable quantity. Encouragement would probably render this a very valuable export.

Mustard seed. The plant is cultivated in great abundance. The seed and oil are articles of export, the latter, of universal consumption within the kingdom.

Tobacco was procured in luxuriance in the Lower Provinces and of a superior quality in the higher. It was formerly an article of export.

Sooparee was produced in great quantity everywhere; the consumption among the inhabitants was enormous, yet it was formerly an article of export.[30]

Ginger is produced everywhere in abundance.

28. The article thrives well, and the quantity would admit of being greatly increased. The price formerly used to be from ten to fifteen rupees per maund, it is now much enhanced.
29. A great quantity of opium is produced and used by the inhabitants. In point of purity it is probably equal to that of Patna or Benaras, but it is prepared in a different form, being reduced to a dry state by exposure to the air, spread on narrow slips of cloth, which are afterwards rolled up into small bales, and called Kanee or Kappa.
30. The Burmese invasion has proved very destructive to the Sooparee groves; immense numbers having been cut down and still more destroyed by wild elephants after the villages were abandoned. This article is now one of import.

Rice was, and is, produced in very great abundance. It is asserted positively that a scarcity has never been known to happen from natural causes. The nature of the season in Assam confirms the assertion. It might prove an invaluable export in times of famine in Bengal.

Mineral Production

Gold is found in considerable quantity among the sands of the Burhampooter and other streams which flow from the northern and southern mountains. It was formerly a source of considerable revenue to the monarch.[31]

Iron might be procured at Bossadyungh, as well as from the Garrows, in considerable quantities.

Saltpetre was procured everywhere in the Upper Provinces in considerable quantity, and might probably in time prove an article of export.[32]

Animal Productions

The quantity usually exported in favourable times, has not been ascertained, but we may presume, that it was not very inconsiderable from the actual produce, which we have lately observed.[33]

31. The quantity of gold would probably admit of much increase by the adoption of improved means of washing the sands containing it which is at present done by the hand and apparently in a manner involving a great deal of unnecessary labour. The gold-dust is found in conjunction with a black sandy ore of iron, probably produced from the disintegration of granite. The gold is ultimately separated in the usual manner by long washing and subsequent trituration with mercury.
32. The quantity of salt imported during the year 1824-25 was only 15,000 maunds. The consumption of this article in Assam and the adjoining parts of Rungpore is much less than might be expected, with reference to the population, chiefly in consequence of the inhabitants very generally preferring an alkaline seasoning for their food, prepared from the ashes of plants. Potash and soda are both used for this purpose, the latter being manufactured by burning certain aquatic plants, some of which are found in wild state, and others cultivated for this express purpose.
33. The quantity of lac annually exported, previously to the late troubles, amounted to about 8, or 10,000 maunds. It might be increased to a great extent, but not very speedily. The trees upon which the insect feeds requiring a long time to grow to the requisite size.

Moongah silk[34] seems to offer a most valuable and extensive article of export with proper encouragement, as the several trees on which the worm feeds, were cultivated in the utmost profusion, throughout the whole extent of the kingdom, with few exceptions. A coarser kind of silk is produced by worms which feed on the castoroil trees.

Elephant's teeth have always been an article of export, and in the present desolated condition of the country might be procured in any quantity. Increase of population will necessarily diminish the possible quantity of this export.

Rhinoceros's horn was a triflng article of export.

Buffalo's hide has not hitherto proved an article of export.

Deer's skins—The animal abounds in Assam.

Until the geography, and other particulars of this and the neighbouring countries, be more particularly known, no decided judgement can be offered relative to the probable extent of the future commerce with Assam. It is certain, that an intercourse of some kind has existed with all the neighbouring nations, particularly with Jaintia, Kossaree and even Sylhet, with the people of Mooglo, now in the possession of the King of Burma or Ava. It is possible that a communication with all the neighbouring nations might be rendered beneficial to commerce, with proper encouragement, during a considerable unless, perhaps, in the single article of Bengal salt.

Commercial intercourse is much facilitated by the number of navigable streams, which intersect Assam in every direction, especially in the season of the rains, including a period of seven or eight months. Some of these flow from the mountains on the northern and southern confines. Beyond the eastern confines, the great stream flows to a very great distance; but whether there be any navigation or commerce on that river beyond the

34. This is an article of great value and importance and which will probably prove a useful material in many of the mixed stuffs manufactured in England from its superior strength and durability to silk. The quantity as exported is small, but it may be expected to increase very rapidly. Extensive plantations of the trees required for the support of the worms being everywhere to be seen abandoned by the proprietors during the late troubles. This tree also grows wild in the upper part of the country.

Abstract of the monthly extra expense attending the detachment and deputation in Assam

European Officers etc., etc.	Average of half month, half batta to the troops, exclusive of European Commissioned Officer			Expense of the detachment in Assam support, full batta to be the average for European Commissioned and half batta for half month for the Troops			Expense of the detachments in Assam or double full batta			Extra expenses incurred by the detachments and deputation		
1	2			3			4			5		
S.	Rs.	A.	P.	Rs.	A.	P.	Rs.	A.	P.	Rs.	A.	P.
16 Battalion.												
1. Captain.	—			415	0	0	595	0	0	180	0	0
8. Lieutenants.	—			2,296	0	0	3064	0	0	768	0	0
1. Adjutant, including his staff allowance.	—			389	0	0	485	0	0	96	0	0
1. Sergeant Major.	280			5	0	0	—		—	2	0	0
1. Quarter Master.	280			5	0	0	—		—	2	8	0
The different Ranks and Departments of the Battalion.	734	12		1,469	8	0	—		—	734	12	0
Allowance for Harkarras and Guides	—			—		—	—		—	150	0	0
Probable amount for boat allowance to 9 Subalterns 16th Battalion.	—			—		—	—		—	720	0	0
Detachment, 27th Battalion.												
2. Lieutenants.	—			574	0	0	766	0	0	192	0	0
The different Ranks and Departments of this Detachment.	234	12	0	469	8	0	—		—	234	12	0
Probable amount for Boat allowance to 2 Subalterns.	—			—		—	—		—	160	0	0

1	2	3	4	5
Detachment Staff.				
1. Adjutant's staff allowance etc.	—	287 0 0	485 0 0	198 0 0
1. Quarter Master	—	287 0 0	— —	157 0 0
1. Assistant Surgeon.	—	287 0 0	383 0 0	96 0 0
1. Quarter Master Sergeant.	2 8 0	25 0 0	— —	22 0 0
Quarter Master's Establishment.	—	— —	— —	158 4 0
Tindal and 9 Lascars of Artillery.	63 0 0	74 4 0	— —	11 0 0
Boats for the transportation of the Troops on an average.	—	— —	— —	2,300 0 0
Expenses incident to the Deputation.				
Captain Welsh's Salary Sicca Rs. 1,500.	—	— —	— —	1,567 9 0
" " average of contingent bill for Durbar charges.	—	— —	— —	850 0 0
Captain Welsh's Probable boat allowance.	—	— —	— —	290 0 0
" " " for transporting public servants.	—	— —	— —	60 0 0
Assistant to the deputation, his salary Sicca—Rs. 200.	—	— —	— —	209 0 0
Assistant to the Deputation, his probable boat allowances.	—	— —	— —	145 0 0
Mr. S.P. Wade, his salary Sicca Rs. 100.	—	— —	— —	104 8 0
" " his probable boat allowances.	—	— —	— —	80 0 0
Total amount of extra expenses attending the detachment and deputation monthly.	—	— —	— —	9,489 5 0
Total " " annually.	—	— —	— —	1,13,872 0 0

Abstract of the sums to be paid annually for the purpose of defraying part of the expense of the detachment etc.

	Rs	A. P.
By the joint-Rajahs of Derungh in lieu of the levy of men	50,000	0 0
By the Beltolah Rajah ditto ditto	1,600	0 0
By Bisnarain, from Kamroop	51,000	0 0
By Collections of the Candahar Chowkey, and overplus of the sum of Rs. 12,000 to be paid to the Rajay, the amount not yet ascertained.	0	0 0
Total amount	1,02,600	0 0

limits of Assam is doubtful.[35]

Commerce could never have been very considerable in Assam, under the discouraging restraints imposed by a Government particularly jealous of strangers. The subversion of all regular Government, and the desolation of the country, reduced it to nothing.

The actual commerce is therefore very inconsiderable, though reviving, and it would be unreasonable to doubt, that it might in time, under the influence of the British Government be rendered extremely beneficial to both States.

10th Question

"How far the pecuniary commutation proposed by you to be made by the Chiefs in lieu of the supplies of men has been carried into effect, and to what extent the supplies furnished in consequence of such commutation have contributed to defray the expenses of the detachment.

Answer to 10th Question

The pecuniary commutation[36] in lieu of the levy of men proposed by the Rajahs of Derungh and Beltola in June 1793 is so far carried into effect, that since the period before mentioned the service of men has not been exacted from them; and of the stipulated annual sum of Rs. 51,600 to be paid by them and appropriated towards defraying the expenses of the detachment, I have received Rs. 10,000.

The Surgee Deo has promised that on his arrival at the capital, the arrears due on account of the detachment, etc., shall be discharged, and mode adopted for the regular payment of the expense attending it, which I have represented to him, as amounting annually to about 3 lakhs of rupees, this sum are abundant.[37] *See* table on pp. 56-57).

35. The river is not navigable much beyond Suddeya, nor is there any trade of consequence carried on in that quarter.
36. This arrangement was not adhered to. The commutation for services would be most acceptable to the peasantry and, with some restrictions rendered necessary by local circumstances, and the habits of the people, it might be adopted with much advantage.
37. The future defence of Assam will involve no expense that could otherwise be avoided, and the security of our own provinces would on

12th Question

"You are further desired to state generally what in your opinion is still necessary or proper to be done for the arrangement of the affairs of Assam, considering that arrangement as concluded by the establishment of the Rajah's authority, were authorized to make in conformity to the instructions of Marquis Cornwallis."

Answer to 12th Question

In the progress to the establishment of the Rajah's authority throughout his kingdom, I am of opinion that the original form of Government in all its parts, should be preserved as nearly as possible.[38] The little intercourse the natives of Assam were formerly permitted to have with strangers, has rendered them bigotted to the forms and customs of their own country, and innovations which would even prove beneficial to them must be introduced, with some degree to caution. They are naturally of a distrustful and jealous disposition, and it will require time to get the better of their prejudices.

All that appears to me necessary for the arrangement of affairs in Assam, is to effect the union of the Chiefs, without which energy cannot be restored to the Government, and as the Rajah is incapable of either judging or acting right, it is proper that the Government of his country should be vested in the

---

the contrary be most easily and effectually provided for by occupying the country as far as the 93 degree of East Longitude which would bring the troops on the Burhampooter into communication with those on the Soormah.

38. In the present state of society in Assam the ancient constitution would not admit of much improvement. That it is fully adequate to insure good government it would be too much to affirm, but if means were taken to raise the character and qualifications of the nobility by an improved system of education, it can scarcely be doubted that with all its imperfections this system would prove greatly superior to the simple despotism of Cooch Behar and other subordinate State where the Chief too often delegates his authority to servants who have any thing but the interest of his subject at heart and who are suffered without check or control to carry oppression and misgovernment to an extent that under other circumstances would not be compatible either with the safety of their Sovereign or the continuance of their own power.

aristocracy; and to prevent the conflict of opinions and interests among the Chiefs which would inevitably produce factions and civil discord, it appears to me advisable that the British Government should continue its mediating and controlling influence, as the only means of preserving order and tranquility.

13th Question

"What in your opinion would be the consequence of recalling the detachment from Assam without further measures or interference on the part of this Government."

Answer to 13th Question

The contest for influence, power and independence would revive among the first officers of State, the dependent Rajahs and the petty Chiefs of districts and towns. The same confusion, devastation and massacre would ensue. Assam would experience a state of desolation, greater in proportion to the temporary restraints which the British influence had imposed on the inhumanity of the monarch, the ambition and resentment of the Chiefs, and the vengeance of the people. Kissnarain would either abandon his country or recall his Burkandazes, for in defiance of any possible stipulation in his favour, he might reasonably expect and would certainly fear private assasination. The obnoxious ministers and favourites would be immediately restored to their offices. Every individual, who had been observed to cultivate the friendship of the British, would flee the country, with the well-grounded apprehension of destruction from the ministers, or their connections. Commerce would again be suppressed by the confusion prevalent in the country, and the monopoly would revive in its pristine vigour. The monarch, whose person is too sacred for assasination, would probably be compelled to abandon his kingdom again.[39]

Such would be the consequences of a cessation of the British influence, until a long course of regular administration shall have operated an entire revolution in the habits of principal Chiefs, and in the minds of the people and in predicting the evils which would result from the recall of the

39. This was not however always the case. Princes who had been disqualified by mutilation being frequently appointed to those offices.

detachment. I have been guided not by my own opinion alone, but by that of the most respectable natives, with whom I have had intercourse; the Rajah himself has repeatedly declared that with the detachments he would quit his kingdom. Sindoorah Hazaree has the charge of 1,000 Ghote Pykes, and is one of those petty Chiefs who taking advantage of the confusion of the times, asserted his own independence and became the leader of a faction. Lieutenant MacGregor invited him to attend a Kalliabar, which he evaded doing by frequent excuses, and considering his attendance necessary to effect the object of his deputation, Lieutenant Mac Gregor detached Deen Diall, Naick, with orders to bring Sindoorah Hazaree to Kalliabar.

P.S.—Omission under the head of monarchy.

To absolve the monarch from the lesser and to assist him in the greater cares of Government, two executive officers were added to the monarchy, *viz.* the Teepaum and Seringh Rajahs. Their titles are derived from districts annexed to their office; their jurisdiction in their respective districts was similar to the Gohains.

Their rank next to the monarch, their duties to communicate the deliberations or decrees of the aristocracy to the monarch, to receive, promulgate, or carry into execution, his consequent orders. On less important occasions the decrees of the aristocracy might be promulgated by these officers without application to the monarch.

The two brothers next in succession to the throne, became Teepaum and Seringh Rajahs, and in failure of brothers the senior nephew according to the usual course of succession to the throne.

2. TREATY OF YANDABO, 1826

Article 1

There shall be perpetual peace and friendship between the Honourable Company on the one part, and His Majesty the King of Ava on the other.

Article 2

His Majesty the King of Ava renounces all claims upon, and will abstain from all future interferences with, the principality of Assam and its dependencies, and also with the contiguous petty states of Cachar and Jyntea. With regard to Munnipore, it is stipulated that, should Gumbheer Singh desire to return to that country, he shall be recognized by the King of Ava as Rajah thereof.

Article 3

To prevent all dispute respecting the boundary line between the two great nations, the British Government will retain the conquered provinces of Aracan, Ramree, Cheduba, and Sandway; and His Majesty the King of Ava cedes all right thereto. The Amoupectoumieu or Aracan mountains (known in Aracan by the name of Yeoamatoung of Phokingtoun range), will henceforth form the boundary between the two great nations on that side. Any doubts regarding the said line of demarcation, will be settled by Commissioners appointed by the respective Governments for that purpose, such Commissioners from both Powers to be of suitable and corresponding rank.

Article 4

His Majesty the King of Ava cedes to the British Government the conquered provinces of Yeh, Tavoy, Mergui, and Tennasscrim, with the lands and dependencies thereunto appertaining, having the Saluen river for the line of demarcation of the frontier. Any doubts regarding their boundaries will be settled as specified in the concluding part of Article Third.

Article 5

In proof of the sincere disposition of the Burmese Government to retain the relations of peace and amity between the two nations, and as part indemnification to the British Government, for the expenses of the war, His Majesty the King of Ava agrees to pay the sum of one crore of rupees.

Article 6

No person whatever, whether native or foreign, is hereafter to be molested, by either party, on account of the part which he may have taken, or have been compelled to take, in the present war.

Article 7

In order to cultivate and improve the relations of amity and peace hereby established between the two Governments, it is agreed that accredited Ministers, retaining an escort or safe-guard, will reside at the Durbar of the other, who shall be permitted to purchase or to build a suitable place of residence of permanent materials, and a Commercial Treaty upon principles of reciprocal advantage will be entered into by the two high contracting powers.

Article 8

All public and private debts contracted by either Government or by the subjects of either Government, with the others, previous to the war to be recognized and liquidated, upon the same principles of honour and good faith, as if hostilities had not taken place between the two nations and no advantage shall be taken by either party of the period that may have elapsed since the debts were incurred, or in consequence of the war; and according to the universal laws of nation, it is further stipulated, that the property of all British subjects who may die in the dominions of His Majesty the King of Ava, shall, in the absence of legal heirs, be placed in the hands of the British Resident or Consul, in the said dominions, who will dispose of the same according to the tenure of the British law. In like manner the property of Burmese subjects dying, under the same circumstances, in any part of the British dominions, shall be made over to the Minister or other Authority delegated by his Burmese Majesty to the Supreme Government of India.

Article 9

The King of Ava will abolish all exactions upon British ships or vessels in Burman ports, that are not required from Burman ships or vessels in British ports; nor shall ships or vessels, the property of British subjects, whether European or Indian, entering the Rangoon river, or other Burman ports, be required to land their guns, or unship their rudders, or to do any other act not required of Burmese ships cr vessels in British ports.

Article 10

The good and faithful ally of the British Government, His Majesty the King of Siam, having taken a part in the present war, will to the fullest extent, as far as regards His Majesty and his subjects, be included in the above Treaty.

Article 11

This treaty to be ratified by the Burmese Authorities competent in like cases, and the ratification to be accompanied by all British, whether European or Native, American, and other prisoners, who will be delivered over to the British Commissioners; the British Commissioners, on their part, engaging that the said Treaty shall be ratified by the Right Honourable the Governor-General in Council; and the ratification shall be delivered to His Majesty the King of Ava, in four months, or sooner if possible, and all the Burmese prisoners shall, in like manner, be delivered over to their own Government, as soon as they arrive from Bengal.

Additional Article

The British Commissioners being most anxiously desirous to manifest the sincerity of their wish for peace, and to make the immediate execution of the fifth Article of this Treaty as little irksome or inconvenient as possible to His Majesty the King of Ava, consent to the following arrangement with respect to the division of the sum total, as specified in the Article above referred to, into instalments; *viz.*, upon the payment of twenty-five lacs of rupees, or one quarter of the sum total, (the other Articles of the Treaty being executed), the army will retire to Rangoon. Upon the further payment of a similar sum at that place within one hundred days from this date, with the proviso, as above, the army will evacuate the dominions of His Majesty the King of Ava with the least possible delay, leaving the remaining moiety of the sum total to be paid by equal annual instalments, in two years, from this twenty-fourth day of February, 1826 A.D., through the Consul or Resident in Ava or Pegu, on the part of the Honourable the East India Company.

3. TREATY WITH POORUNDER SINGH, RAJA OF ASSAM, 1833

Article 1

The Company give over to Rajah Poorunder Singh the portion of Assam lying on the southern bank of the Brahmapooter to the eastward of the Dhuvsiren River. and on the northern bank to the eastward of a nullah immediately east of Bishanath.

Article 2

The Rajah Poorunder Singh agrees to pay an annual tribute of 50,000 Rupees of Raja Mohree coinage to the Honourable Company.

Article 3

The Rajah Poorunder Singh binds himself, in the administration of justice in the country now made over to him, to abstain from the practices of the former Rajahs of Assam, as to cutting of ears and noses, extracting eyes or otherwise mutilating or torturing, and that he will not inflict cruel punishment for slight faults, but generally assimilate the administration of justice in his territory to that which prevails in the dominions of the H.C. He further finds himself not to permit the immolation of women by suttees.

Article 4

The Rajah Poorunder Singh binds himself to assist the passage of the troops of the Company through his territory, furnishing supplies and carriage on receiving payment for the same.

Article 5

Whether at Jorhath or elsewhere, wheresoever a spot may be required for the permanent cantonment of the troops of the British Government, the Rajah agrees that, within the limits assigned to such cantonment he shall exercise no power whatever; all matters connected with such cantonment to be decided on by the office of the British government.

Article 6

In the event of a detachment being stationed at Suddeya or elsewhere, the Rajah Poorunder Singh binds himself to render it all the assistance that it shall require in regard to provisions and carriage.

Article 7

The Rajah binds himself ever to listen with attention to the advice of the political Agent to be stationed in upper Assam, or to that of the Agent to the Governor-General with a view to the conduct of affairs in the country made over to him in conformity of the stipulations of this Agreement.

Article 8

The Rajah binds himself not to carry on any correspondence by letter or otherwise, or to enter into any contract or Agreement with the Rulers of any Foreign States. In all cases of necessity he will consult with Political Agent or Agent to the Governor-General by whom the necessary communication will be made.

Article 9

The Rajah binds himself to surrender, on demand from the Agent to the Governor-General or P.A., any fugitive from justice who may take refuge in his territory, and always to apply to those officers for the apprehension of any individuals who may fly from his territory into that of the Honourable Company, or of any other State.

Article 10

It is distinctly understood that this Treaty invests Rajah Poorunder Singh with no power over the Moamaria Country of the Bur Senapattee.

Article 11

It being notorious that the quantity of opium produced in Assam is the cause of many miseries to the inhabitants, the Rajah binds himself that, whatever measures may be determined on with a view to checking this source of mischief in the territory of the Honourable Company, corresponding measures shall be adopted in the territory made over to him.

In the event of Rajah's continuing faithful to the articles of this Treaty, the British Government engages to protect him from the aggressions of any foreign force, but if, which god forbid, he should in any way depart from a faithful adherence to the same, and be guilty of oppressing the people of the country entrusted to his charge then the right is reserved to the Government of the Honourable Company either to transfer the said country to another ruler, or take it into its own immediate occupation.

Dated the 2nd March 1833, or 20th Phagoon, 1239 B.E.

True Translation

Signed T.C. Robertson
A. 1099

4. KUBOOLYUT OF BUR SENAPUTTEE, 1826

The Bur Senaputtee, in the presence of Mr. Scott, agreed to the following Kuboolyut :—

I, Matee Bur Senaputtee of the Muttocks, write what follows : the Pykes belonging to the Phokuns Burooahs, Brahmins, and other that are under me, amount to 160 Gotes, and my own amount to 260 Gotes, of these 42 Gotes are my own Liksoos, 11 belong to the Hazaree Kuahs.

5 Sykeahs
15 Burakayees
42 are Raj Sumueyahs (provide rice)
5 to the Naoogs

120 total

300 Gotes remain, deducting these. Of these 150 are fighting men, 150 labourers; these I will furnish, according to the custom of the country, by Mal, Dewal, Tecal, and what russud the Sircar may want that I will furnish on getting the amount of its cost; over these people I will exercise jurisdiction, enquire and decide, but in case of murder, dacoity, and great wounding, and thefts above 50 rupees I will institute investigation, and send the papers and the men to the presence and whatever ordered I will obey. This Kuboolyut shall remain until another is made.

Sunnud of Bur Senaputtee.

The Agent of the Governor General, & C., to Matee Bur Senaputtee.

You are ordered, after providing yourself and the Bissyahs with Pykes for your own and their use, to keep 300 at the Sircar's disposal but of this I give you 20 for your personal use, and that of your children or others, the remaining 280 you will always have forthcoming.

13th May 1826.

Witness: Juto Zye Dewalyah Gudadhur

Signed by the Bur Senaputtee
Signed with Mr. Scott's initials

5. AGREEMENT WITH MATEE BUR BUR SENAPUTTEE, 1835

Article 1

I agree to relinquish my claim to the village of Suckhowah, which has been the cause of dispute between the Suddeya Khawah Gohain and myself; further I agree that the following shall be recognized as the territorial boundaries of my district. On the north the Brahmapooter, on the west the Boorma. Dehing River, separating my territory from that of Rajah Poorunder Singh, to the east the Dibroo River and the Dauguree Nullah, which falls into it. From the rise of the nullah a boundary line will be formed to connect it with the Boore Dehing River; for this purpose Lt. Carlton can depute one person and I will depute another.

The lands lying between the Dhul Jan and Gooroo Jan Nullahs, which falls into the Danguree Nullah, to be considered under my jurisdiction, and the persons deputed as above mentioned can connect them by definite marks, so as to form a boundary line. These are the territorial boundaries of the country under my jurisdiction and have no reference to the pecuniary questions now pending between we and the British Government.

Article 2

I cannot agree to the demand which the British government has made me to contribute towards the expenses of the state in an increasing proportion, quinquenially, or by paying a tribute of 10,000 Rupees per annum, as I engaged to do under the Assam government. But if the British government requires me no longer to furnish a military contingent of 300 men, which at the rate of 6 Rupees per head, will amount to, 1,800 Rupees per annum, I further agree to restore to the British government the arms of this force, if required. I likewise will adhere to the engagement I formed with Captain Nevfvilee, to pay 551 Rupees per annum, on account of Pykes who absconded from upper Assam, whilst that Province was under his charge in 1829; and further I agree to pay to those who have absconded from Rajah Poorunder Singh's Territories within the last two years. I will cause them to be counted, but if suspicion is entertained that a false enumeration will be given in, I agree that the British government may nominate an officer to take a new census.

Witnesses Signed Matee Bur Bur Senaputtee

Chota Gohain Khamptee, residing at Suddeya
Sadu May Jemadar, residing at Morung
Golaub Sing Jemadar, residing at Bishenath
Gopee Surma Dola Suvya Bora, residing at Jorehaut

SECTION II

1. THE TREATY WITH GOVINDA CHANDRA, RAJA OF CACHAR, 1824

Article 1

Raja Govinda Chandra, for himself and his successors, acknowledges allegiance to the Honourable Company, and places his country of Cachar, or Heruemba, under their protection.

Article 2

The internal government of the country shall be conducted by the Raja, and the jurisdiction of the British Courts of Justice shall not extend there; but the Raja agrees to attend at all times to the advice offered for the welfare of his subjects by the Governor-General in Council, and agreeably thereto to rectify any abuses that may arise in the administration of affairs.

Article 3

The Honourable Company engages to protect the territory of Cachar from external enemies and to arbitrate any differences that may arise between the Raja and other states. The Raja agrees to abide by such arbitration, to hold no correspondence or communication with foreign powers except through the channel of the British Government.

Article 4

In consideration of the aid promised by the above Article and other circumstances, the Raja agrees to pay to the Honourable Company from the beginning of the year 1232 B.S. an annual tribute of ten thousand Sicca Rupees, and the Honourable Company engages to provide for the maintenance of the Manipoorean chiefs lately accepting Cachar.

Article 5

If the Raja should fail in the performance of the above Article, the Honourable Company will be at liberty to occupy and attach in perpetuity, to their possessions, a sufficient tract of Cachar Country to provide for the future realisation of the tribute.

Article 6

The Raja agrees in concert with the British local Authorities to adopt measures that may be necessary for the maintenance in the district of Sylhet, of the arrangements in force in the Police, Opium and Salt Departments.

Executed at Buddeirpore, this 6th day of March 1824, corresponding with the 24th of Fagoon 1230 B.S.

Raja Govinda Chandra's seal (Signed) D. Scott
Agent to Governor-General

2. AGREEMENT WITH TOOLARAM SENAPATI, 1834

1. Toolaram forgoes all claims to the country between the Morihur and Dyung and the Dyeng and Keopoli Rivers, from which he was dispossessed by Govind Ram and Doorga Ram.

2. Toolaram is to hold the remainder of the country formerly in his possession, or the tract of country bounded on the west by the Dyung River, and a line to be determined hereafter, drawn from the Baree ford or the Dyung to point on the Jumoona River, between the cultivation of soil Dhurmpore and of Duboka and the Hajaee (excluding the two latter) by the Jumoona and Dyung rivers north, by the Bunsira rivers east, and to the south and southwest by the Naga Hills, and Mowter river, and he agrees to hold the above tract in dependence on the British Government, and to pay a yearly tribute, this was subsequently connected to a money tribute of Rs. 490/- a year for their protection of four pairs of elephant's teeth, each pair to weigh thirty-five seers.

3. Toolaram during his life, shall receive from the British government a stipend of fifty rupees a month, in consideration of the foregoing cessions and these agreements.

4. The British government shall have the right of placing

military parts in any part of Toolaram's country; and should there be occasion to march troops through it, Toolaram engages to furnish them with all the requisites of carriage and provisions in his power, he being paid for the same.

5. All petty offences committed within Toolaram's country he shall take cognizance of and do justice according to the custom of the country, but all heinous crimes shall be transferred to the nearest British court, and Toolaram engages to bring such to notice and endeavour to apprehend the offenders.

6. Toolaram shall not establish any custom chowkies on the rivers forming the boundaries of his country.

7. Toolaram will not commence any military operations against neighbouring chiefs without permission of the British Government and in case of being attacked he shall report the same and be protected by British troops, provided the British Authorities are satisfied that the aggression has been unprovoked on his part.

8. Ryots shall not be prevented from emigrating to and setting on either side to the bounary they may prefer.

9. In case of failing to abide by these conditions, the British Government shall be at liberty to take possession of my country.

Witnesses:	(Signed) Toolaram Senapati
Bapoor Ram Muntree	(Signed) Franso Jenkins
Burrah Phookan	Agent to Governor-General

3. THE TREATY WITH RAJAH RAM SINGH OF JYNTIA, 1824

Article 1

Rajah Ram Singh acknowledges allegiance to the Honourable Company and places his country of Jyntia under their protection; mutual friendship and amity shall always be maintained between the Honourable Company and the Rajah.

Article 2

The internal government of the country shall be conducted by the Rajah, and the jurisdiction of the British Courts of Justice shall not extend there. The Rajah will always attend to the welfare of his subjects, and observe the ancient customs of government, but should any unforeseen abuse arise in the administration of affairs, he agrees to rectify the same agreeably to the advice of the Governor-General in Council.

Article 3

The Honourable Company engages to protect the territory of Jyntia from external enemies, and to arbitrate any differences that may arise between the Rajah and other States. The Rajah agrees to abide by such arbitration, and to hold no political correspondence or communication with foreign powers, except with the consent of the British Government.

Article 4

In the event of the Honourable Company being engaged in war to the eastward of the Brahmapooter, the Rajah engages to assist with all his forces, and to afford every other facility in his power in furtherance of such military operations.

Article 5

The Rajah agrees, in concert with the British Local Authorities, to adopt all measures that may be necessary for maintenance, in the District of Sylhet, of the arrangements in force in the Judicial, Opium and Salt Department.

Executed this 10th day of March 1824, corresponding with the 28th of Fagoon 1230 B.S., at Rajahgunge.

(Signed) D. Scott
Agent to the Governor-General

Seal and signature of
Rajah Ram Singh of Jyntia

Separate Article

Rajah Ram Singh engages, that to assist in the war commenced in Assam between the Honourable Company's Troops and those of the King of Ava, he will march a force and attack the enemy to the east of Gowhatty; and the Honourable Company agrees, upon the conquest of Assam, to confer upon the Rajah a part of that Territory proportionate to the extent of his exertions in the common cause.

(Signed) D. Scott
Agent to the Governor-General

Seal and signature of
Rajah Ram Singh of Jyntia

4. MEMORIAL OF RAJUNDER SING, 1835

The memorial of Rajunder Sing, Rajah of Joyntiapore respectfully sheweth.

That your Memorialist is the descendant and successor of a race of independent Chiefs, who for a long course of ages have ruled over a territory, situated on the north eastern frontier of Bengal and known by the name of Joyntiapore.

That the first connexion between the Rajah of Joyntiapore and the British Government was in the Saka year 1695 of English year 1773/4 when Captain Oligar entered it in command of military force and took hostile possession on the part of the British Government. This occupation was however of no long duration. In the same year the British force was withdrawn and the Rajah reinstated on the same footing as before. Since that time hitherto the Raj of Joyntiapore has acknowledged the supremacy of the British Authority and has continued under its shelter and protection in the undisturbed possession of its ancient race of rulers, without claim or payment of tribute of any kind.

That on the 10th March of the Christian year 1824 the British Government being then engaged in warfare with the kingdom of Ava the Right Honourable the Lord Amherst then Governor-General of India was pleased to enter into a formal treaty with Rajah Ram Sing then the ruling prince of Joyntiapore. The terms and articles of that treaty were not only fully complied with by the Rajah but he was so fortunate as by his faithful attachment and zealous exertions in the supply of men and provisions to the military forces in Assam to obtain the esteem and approbation of the British Authorities.

That Rajah Ram Sing died on the 11th Ashwin of the Bengal year 1239 (25th September A.D. 1832) leaving no male issue, and your Memorialist, as the nearest male collateral heir in due course according to the laws and usages of the Raj became his Successor in the principality and assumed the dignities of its chief in which he was recognized by the British Government notwithstanding the open and secret intrigues and machinations of the Rajah of Poonjee and other neighbouring Chieftains who hoped to supplant him in his rights, and even entered into a league to depose him and to possess themselves of the territory and used every exertion to obtain the sanction of the British Government to such aggression. In this however they found themselves baulked by its wisdom and justice and by that sacred regard to treaties and respect for the rights of others, which has gained it the confidence of the neighbouring powers.

That being thus foiled in their unjust designs the enemies of your Memorialist tried to injure and calumniate him with the British Government by every means in their power and for that purpose availed themselves of an unfortunate occurrence which had taken place in the life time of your Memorialist's predecessor Ram Sing and which was as follows : On the 21st Assar of the Bengali year 1239 (7th July 1832) it was reported to Mr. Robertson, then Political Agent in Assam, that two subjects of the Company's territory were on their road to Assam, kidnapped by some miscreants set on by one Chutter Sing and carried off to the hills in the neighbourhood of Gobha in the Raj of Joyntiapore and there together with two others supposed to have been seized in a similar manner, decked out for sacrifice at the Shrine of Kali ; that one of them had escaped who told that tale but the other three were presumed to have been immolated.

This statement, made by a man who represented himself as the fugitive being corroborated by enquiry and information from other sources was accredited by the Agent, and laid before the Governor-General and was shortly before the death of Rajah Ram Sing the subject of remonstrance addressed to Rajah Ram Sing together with a demand for the surrender of the perpetrators, which he was in the very act of complying with, by the delivery of Chutter Sing and others, when his own sudden death set the accused at liberty.

The demand of their surrender was renewed and your Memorialist exerted himself to comply with the demand. But difficulties and confusion incident to his recent succession and a variety of other impediments made it impossible to trace or retake Chutter Sing himself or indeed any of the other offenders till a considerable time had elapsed. Your Memorialist however after repeated attempts did at length succeed in laying hold of four of them whom he delivered up to the British Authorities, as will appear by the original written acknowledgement of Captain Jenkins, the British Officer then in charge, dated the 21st

September 1834 and now in your Memorialist's hands, and of which a copy with translation is annexed marked (B). Meantime British Government wishing to vary terms of the treaty and demand tribute in lieu of the obligation to furnish a military contingent in case of war on the south eastern frontier, availed itself of the opportunity offered by the demise of Rajah Ram Sing to require a revision of the treaty : and T.C. Robertson Esqr., then Political Agent for Assam, in pursuance of instructions from the Governor-General-in-Council on the 21st May 1833 made a formal demand in writing upon your Memorialist to enter in a new engagement, in which the payment of a fixed annual tribute of Sicca Rupees 10,000 should be substituted in place of Article 4 of the former treaty ; it was natural that your Memorialist should feel surprised at this demand. It was the first time that any thing like tribute had been required by the British Government, and the compliance with such a demand was certain to alter the position and estimation of the Rajah in the eyes of the neighbouring chiefs. Surely therefore it was not unreasonable that your Memorialist should at the moment solicit a space of no more than fifteen days time for deliberation, or that, in his reply of the 23rd Joystya of the Bengal year 1240, he should have respectfully urged his objections to the variations demanded. The Political Agent, however,. without waiting for further communication was proceeding to take immediate steps for enforcing his demand and was only induced to pause by a request on the part of your Memorialist's Agent of seven days further delay. Your Memorialist immediately dispatched Gopaul-mony Duloojee and two others to the Resident, with a letter again urging his objections, and representing the fidelity with which the former treaty had been observed on the part of the Raj and the services of Rajah Ram Sing his predecessor but the Resident paid little attention to the communication and made no other reply, than by requiring your Memorialist's agents to give in a definite answer respecting the tribute demanded within twenty five days. No further communication having been made from your Memorialist the matter stood over until the 16th of Joystya 1241 (28th May 1834) when your Memorialist received a letter from Captain Jenkins, the Political Agent renewing the demand of tribute and repeating the requisition for delivery of the offenders in the affair at Gobha. The letter was complied with as above stated to the utmost of your Memorialist's ability; but your Memorialist withheld the signification of his assent to the payment of tribute trusting to the liberality of the British Government not to insist upon a demand, to which your Memorialist was unable to offer resistance otherwise than by remonstrance and representation.

That this hesitation of your Memorialist appears to have brought down upon him the heavy displeasure of his Lordship the Governor-General-in-Council for in the month of March 1835 he was both grieved and surprised by receiving a letter from His Lordship in Council intimating that the whole of your Memorialist's ancestorial possessions in the plains has been confiscated by the British Government, and that orders had been issued for taking possession of them on its behalf.

The only ground assigned for this summary act was the non-delivery of the offenders in the atro-city of Gobha and the occurrence of a similar cause of offence in the English year 1821 together with an insinuation of your Memorialist's participation either in the outrage itself or in the protection of the perpetrators. These orders were immediately carried into effect and your Memorialist has thereby been stripped of the whole of the possessions in the plains which had been the patrimony of his ancestors for many generations.

He begs leave respectfully to represent that the avowed reason for this severe and summary treatment of the heir of an old and faithful vassal was not only insufficient in itself but was wholly untrue in fact, your Memorialist having, as above stated already complied, as far as it was possible for him to do so, with the requisition to deliver up the offender in the affair of Gobha and having obtained the written acknowledgement of their surrender. Your Memorialist cannot believe that this fact could have been known to his Lordship in Council when the orders complained of were given. If it had, it must have been noticed in the time of his predecessor; still less for one that had occurred fifteen years ago upon which no measures had then been taken or insisted upon. As successor to the Raj, your Memorialist was doubtless bound to follow up the offenders whom Rajah Ram Sing had seized but was prevented by his death from surrendering; and so he did. Nor it is to be wondered at that delay should have occurred in a matter of so much embarrassment and amongst tribes so wild and impatient of all rule. Your Memorialist on receiving the acknowledgement from the British Officer, without comment or further demand naturally concluded that his compliance with the requisition had been accepted. Had any thing more been called for it would surely have been intimated to him in the interval between September 1834 and March 1835 and had any such intimation been made, it would appear on the records of the proceedings of the British Authorities. But none such has ever been made or pretended.

Your Memorialist scarcely knows how to advert to the charge against himself of participation in the atrocity of Gobha or at least of harbouring the perpetrators; for the charge is rather insinuated than brought forward in the letter from His Lordship in Council and it was new to the ears of your Memorialist who can impute it to nothing else but the secret malevolence of his enemies and calumniators. Had there been any foundation for such a charge it would have been an effectua bar to the recognition by the British Government of your Memorialist as successor to Rajah Ram Sing. The best reputation is the bare fact of your Memorialist having in the interim braced out and delivered up four of the offenders, before the charge was even insinuated.—His Lordship's knowledge of that fact alone would have effectually silenced the calumniator by whom the suggestion must have been made.

It will however naturally occur to your Lordship that the outrage at Gobha was merely the ostensible ground of charge, and that the real offence of your Memorialist, which has been thus heavily visited was the silence of your Memorialist as to the demand of tribute. Indeed the total omission of this topic in the communication of the ground of offence can be no otherwise accounted for than by the consciousness that it was untenable. In time of war or other emergency, the demand of a subsidy or money payment by the paramount state from its vassal is usual and just. But the demand of a permanent tribute in time of profound peace in lieu of an existing obligation to furnish temporary aid in men and supplies upon the contingency of war on the neighbouring frontier which might not occur for a century, seems neither usual nor equitable, and could appear to the vassal in no better light than an alarming innovation. But even the direct refusal of such a demand could scarcely be a just ground of forfeiture. Your Memorialist however never did refuse compliance. He was sensible of his position and of the impossibility of refusal. Had that course been taken towards Memorialist, however reluctant to part with the shadow of independence his exemption from tribute appeared to leave to him, or grieved at the necessity of discharging those retainers of his family which the exaction of a tribute equivalent to nearly half of the rent of the territory taken from him must render him unable longer to entertain, he must needs have yielded to the demand. If the interests of the British Government require that the tribute in question should be insisted upon as the condition of renewed treaty with the Rajah of Joyntiapore, your Memorialist was and is ready to subscribe to those terms. But he respectfully submits that his reluctance to part with the privileges of his forefathers was not unnatural and ought not to be construed as a mark either of contumacy or of disaffection.

In conclusion your petitioner confidently hopes, that, on full consideration of the case, it will be found by your Lordship that the forfeiture and degradation he has been subjected to have been inflicted upon him under misapprehension of the facts—and without regard to the actual circumstances of the Raj of Joyntiapore and of your Memorialist himself. And he earnestly solicits that he may be restored to the possession of the small territory of which he has been deprived and that the treaty of the British Government with the Rajah of Joyntiapore may be renewed on such terms either of tribute or otherwise, as your wisdom and justice shall dictate.

Calcutta, 18th July 1836 Signed (in Bengali)

5. CONDITIONS IMPOSED UPON GUMBHEER SING RAJAH OF MUNNIPORE, 1835

The Governor-General and Supreme Council of Hindoostan declare as follows: With regard to the two ranges of Hills, the one called the Kalanaga Range, and the other called the Noon-jai Range, which are situated between the eastern bend of the Barak and the western bend of the Barak, we will give up all claim on the part of the Honourable Company thereunto, and we will make these Hills over in possession to the Rajah, and give him the line of the Jeeree and the western bend of the Barak as a boundary, provided that the Rajah agrees to the whole of what is written in this paper, which is as follows :

1. The Rajah will, agreeably to instructions received, without delay, remove his Thanna from Chundrapore, and establish it on the eastern bank of the Jeeree.

2. The Rajah will in no way obstruct the trade carried on between the two countries by Bengali or Munnipooree merchants. He will not exact heavy duties, and he will make a monopoly of no articles of merchandise whatsoever.

3. The Rajah will in no way prevent the Nagas inhabiting the Kalanaga and Noon-jai Ranges of Hills, from selling or bartering ginger, cotton, pepper, and every other article, the produce of their country, in the Plains of Cachar, at the Banskandee and Oodharbun bazaars, as has been their custom.

4. With regard to the road commencing from the eastern bank of the Jeeree and continued via Kalanaga and Kowpoom, as far as the Valley of Munnipore—after this road has been finished, the Rajah will keep it in repairs, so as to enable laden bullocks to pass during the cold and dry seasons. Further, at the making of the road, if British officers be sent to examine or superintend the same, the Rajah will agree to everything these officers may suggest.

5. With reference to the intercourse already existing between the territories of the British Government and those of the Rajah, if the intercourse be further extended, it will be well in every respect, and it will be highly advantageous to both the Rajah and his country. In order, therefore, that this may speedily take place, the Rajah, at the requisition of the British Government, will furnish a quota of Nagas to assist at the construction of the road.

6. In the event of war with the Burmese, if troops be sent to Munnipore, either to protect that country, or to advance beyond the Ningthee, the Rajah at the requisition of the British Government, will provide Hill porters to assist in transporting the ammunition and baggage of such troops.

7. In the event of anything happening on the Eastern Frontier of the British territories, the Rajah will, when required, assist the British Government with a portion of his troops.

8. *The Rajah will be answerable for all the ammunition he receives from the British Government, and will, for the information of the British Government, give in every month a statement of expenditure to the British Officer attached to the levy.

Seal

I, Shree Joot Gumbheer Sing of Munnipore, agreeto all that is written above in this paper sent by the Supreme Council.

Dated 18th April 1833

(A true translation)

(Signed) Geo. Gordon, Lieut.,
Adjutant, Gumbheer Sing's Levy

Signed and sealed in my presence,
(Signed) F. J. Grant,
Commissioner

(Signed) Shree Joot Rajah
Gumbheer Sing

6. AGREEMENT REGARDING COMPENSATION FOR THE KUBO VALLEY, 1834

Major Grant and Captain Pemberton, under instructions from the Right Honourable the Governor-General-in-Council, having made over the Kubo Valley to the Burmese Commissioners deputed from Ava, are authorized to state :

1. That it is the intention of the Supreme Government to grant a monthly stipend of five hundred Sicca Rupees to the Rajah of Munnipore, to commence from the ninth day of January One Thousand Eight Hundred and Thirty-four, the date at which the transfer of Kubo took place, as shown in the Agreement mutually signed by the British and Burmese Commissioner.

2. It is to be distinctly understood that should any circumstances hereafter arise by which the portion of territory lately made over to Ava again reverts to Munnipore, the allowance now granted by the British Government will cease from the date of such reversion.

(Signed) F.J. Grant, Major, ⎤
,, R. Boileau Pemberton, Capt. ⎦ Commissioners.

Langhthabal Munnipore,
January 25, 1834

*As the connection of the British Government with the Munnipore Levy and the supply of ammunition to the Levy have ceased, this clause is inapplicable to present circumstances.

SECTION III

1. AGREEMENT WITH DEWAN SING, 1829

The Rajah having lost his eye-sight, Soobha Singh, Rajah, has put his mark hereto on the part of Dewan Sing, Rajah

(True copy from the original)
(Sd.) Rajkissur Mozimdar

To
The Honourable Company

The written Agreement of Dewan Sing, Rajah, and the Ministerial Officers and other *Cossiahs* residing at Cherra Poonjee, executed in the present English year 1829, to the following purport :

We acknowledge our subjection to the Honourable Company with the object of having our country protected, and enter into this Deed of Agreement to the effect that we hereby place our territory under the protection of the Honourable Company.

1. We are to conduct the affairs of our country in concert with the Ministerial Officers according to the former usages and customs, keeping the people pleased and contented, and to have no concern in such matters with any of the Honourable Company's Courts; but should any person, who has committed any wrongful act in the Government territories, come to our country, we will, on demand, immediately apprehend him and deliver him up.

2. If we should have any disputes with the Rajahs of other countries which it may be deemed proper to investigate we will abide by and submit to any judgment that may be given on the part of the Government, and we will not enter into any quarrels with the Rajahs of other countries without the permission of the Honourable Company.

3. If there should be any hostilities in the Hills with the Honourable Company, we will immediately proceed there with our forces, and render assistance to the Government.

Mr. David Scott, Agent to the Governor-General, hereby promises that your territory will we properly protected on the part of the Government if you act according to the aforesaid conditions; and if any quarrels should arise between you and the Rajahs of other countries, they will be disposed of and settled, and you will receive a fitting reward for the services referred to. To which purport this Agreement is executed by both parties.

Dated the 10th September, corresponding with the 26th Bhadra 1236 B.S.

(Sd.) W. Cracroft,
A.A.G.G.

2. AGREEMENT WITH DEWAN SING, 1829

The Rajah having lost his eye-sight, Soobha Sing, Rajah, has put his mark hereto on the part of Dewan Sing, Rajah.

(True copy from the original)

(Sd.) Rajkissur Mozimdar

To
Mr. David Scott,
Agent to the Governor-General.

The written Agreement of Dewan Sing, Rajah of Cherra Poonjee, executed in the present English year 1829, to the under-mentioned effect :

Some land having been required of me for erecting Government edifices and for gentlemen to build houses on, I voluntarily cede this land, and enter into the following Agreement :

1. For the erection of these buildings, etc., I have given up some land in a place to the east of Cherra Poonjee, bounded on one side by the dell or below the rest of the valley, and on the other by the Seit Oodoi river, where bamboos have been put up on the part of Government; and if more land is required, it will be furnished to the east of that spot; but in exchange for as much land as I may give up altogether in my territory, I am to receive an equal quantity of land in the vicinity of Punduah and Companygunge, within the boundary of Zillah Sylhet.

2. I am to establish a haunt in Mouzah Burryaile, on a spot of ground that I have purchased, pertaining to the aforesaid zillah, and I am always to manage the haunt, and to make investigations there according to the customs of my country; and in such matters I am to have nothing to do with the Honourable Company's courts. This place is moreover to be transferred from the aforesaid zillah, and made over, as a rent-free grant, to my Cossiah territory; and if any person who has committed a wrongful act in the Government territories should come and stay on this land belonging to me, I will apprehend him and deliver him up on demand.

3. Wherever limestone may be found on the Cherra Poonjee Hills in my territory, I will allow the Government to take it gratis when required for their own use.

4. If any quarrels and disturbances should take place between Bengalees themselves, it will be necessary for you to investigate them, and I am to investigate disputes occurring between Cossiahs. Besides which, if any dispute should occur between a Bengalee and a Cossiah, it is to be tried in concert by me and a gentleman on the part of the Honourable Company. To which purport I have executed this Agreement.

Dated the 10th September, corresponding with the 26th of Bhadro 1236 B.S.

(Sd.) W. Cracroft,
A.A.G.G.

3. AGREEMENT WITH CHIEF OF BYRUNG POONJEE, 1829

(Sd.) Oojoy Cossiah
,, Mon Sing
,, Jeerkha Cossiah
,, Ram Sing
,, Konrai
,, Ramrai

To
The Honourable Company,

The written Agreement of Oojoy and Mon Sing, residents of Byrung Poonjee, Jeerkha and Ram Sing residents of Oomtheelay Poonjee, and Kollaprai and Ramrai, residents of Eamdah Poonjee, executed in the English year 1829 to the following purport :

We have no faith in the Cossiah Mountaineers, who have taken up arms against the Government, and having therefore joined the Honourable Company, enter into this Agreement to this effect :

1. That we have not made war with the Government, nor will we ever enter into hostilities with the people on the part of the Honourable Company; and we will apprehend and deliver up any Cossiahs who have absconded, and regarding whom proclamations have been issued, if they should come into our territory.

2. That if we should find any proclaimed persons who have absconded, and fail to apprehend and deliver them up, or conceal them, and this should be proved, we will make no objection to our villages being burnt.

Dated in the English year 1829, 2nd N. (November seemingly, judging from the year mentioned).

We further state that we will obey the orders of Dewan Sing, Rajah of Cherra Poonjee, and will never do anything without his sanotion.

(Sd.) W. Cracroft,
A.A.G.G.

4. AGREEMENT WITH RAJAH SOOBHA SING, 1830

(Sd.) Soobha Sing, Rajah,
And others of the 12 tribes
Sirdar Cossiahs of Cherra Poonjee

To

The Honourable Company

The written Agreement of Soobha Sing, Rajah, and the Officers, Sirdars and other Cossiahs, residing at Cherra Poonjee, executed in the current year 1237 B.S. to the following purport :

Whereas the locality ceded by Dewan Sing, Rajah, during his lifetime, to the Honourable Company, under an Agreement he furnished for the purpose of erecting buildings on for gentlemen and convalescent persons, is now insufficient for that object in consequence of a great number of Government subjects having resorted to the place; we therefore, in compliance with the request of Mr. David Scott, Agent to the Governor-General, cede to the Government, agreeably to the terms of the previous Agreement furnished by the late Rajah, the land lying to the south-east of that place, extending up to the valley and river as specified in the said Agreement and give this Agreement to the effect that we will abide by, and act in accordance to, the conditions specified in the late Rajah's Agreement. To which purport we have executed this Agreement.

Dated the 19th October 1830, corresponding with Cartick 1237 B.S

(Sd.) T.C. Robertson,
Agent to the Governor-General

5. LEASE OF COAL HILL AT CHERRA POONJEE, 1840

To

The Political Agent at Cherra Poonjee

A perpetual lease, executed to the following purport, by Soobha Sing, Rajah of Cherra Poonjee :

I hereby give a perpetual lease, for all future time, of the Hills called Oosider, Ooksan, and Nowkrem, within my territory, pertaining to Cherra Poonjee, where Coal is being worked by the Government, agreeably to the terms mentioned below, which are to be acted up to :

1. I am to receive taxes from the Government at the rate of one Rupee per hundred maunds for as much Coal as may be broken up in the places mentioned. I will never demand more than this rate, and my Cossiah subjects are not to be prohibited by the Government from working Coal in these localities; they are to work it free of charge, and will settle with me for the taxes on it; but no other person is at liberty to quarry Coal in these places without the sanction of the Government, nor have I the right of granting such permission to any other person.

2. The Government can quarry Coal hereafter, whenever they wish to do so, according to the conditions of this pottah, and no new objections will be raised, and if made, they are to be rejected.

3. Besides the above stated localities, the Government have the right to the Coal in such places in my territory as it may be discovered in, according to conditions of this pottah, to which effect I have executed this perpetual lease, the 20th April 1840, corresponding with the 9th of Bysack 1247 B.S.

Seal of the Rajah (Sd.) Soobha Sing, Rajah

Witnesses :

Soomur Sing, Cossiah, resident of Cherra Poonjee

Jattrah Sing, -do- -do- -do-

Chund Rai, Dubashia -do- -do-

Bungsee Sing, Burkundaz of the Office

6. LEASE OF COAL-FIELDS OF BYRUNG POONJEE, 1840

I, Soobha Sing, Rajah, resident of Cherra Poonjee, having made myself acquainted with the purport of this document, hereby confirm the conditions specified in this pottah, given by the Sirdars of Byrung Poonjee, dated the 20th April 1840, corresponding with the 9th of Bysack 1247 B.S.

Seal of the Rajah (Sd.) Soobha Sing Rajah

To

The Political Agent at Cherra Poonjee

A perpetual lease, executed to the following purport, by Beerah Sing and Ramrai, Cossiah Sirdars of Byrung Poonjee, belonging to the territory of Cherra Poonjee.

We hereby give a perpetual lease to the Government, for all future time, of the places pertaining to this Poonjee, where Coal has been found, and those localities where it may hereafter be discovered, agreeably to the terms mentioned below, which are to be acted up to :

1. We are to receive taxes from the Government at the rate of one Rupee per hundred maunds, for as much Coal as may be broken up in all places belonging to our Poonjee. We will never demand more than this rate, and the Cossiahs of the Poonjee we reside in are not to be prohibited by the Government from working Coal in these localities. They are to work it free of charge, and will settle with us for the taxes on it; but no other person is at liberty to quarry Coal in these places without the sanction of the Government, nor have we the right of granting such permission to any other person.

2. The Government can quarry Coal hereafter, whenever they wish to do so, agreeably to the conditions of this pottah,

and no new objections will be raised, and if made they are to be rejected.

3. Besides the above stated localities, the Government have the right, according to the conditions of this pottah, to those places where Coal may at any time be discovered. To which effect we have executed this perpetual lease, dated the 29th April 1840, corresponding with the 9th of Bysack 1247 B.S.

(Sd.) Beerah Sing and Ramrai,
Cossiah Sirdars

Witnesses:

Soomur Sing, Cossiah, resident of Cherra Poonjee
Jattrah Sing, -do- -do- -do-
Chund Rai, Dubashia, -do- -do-
Bungsee Sing, Burkundaz of the Office

7. AGREEMENT OF RAM SING OF CHERRA POONJEE, 1857

Rajah's Seal

(Sd.) Ram Sing, Rajah

To
The Honourable Company

The written Agreement of Ram Sing, Rajah and his Ministerial Officers and Sirdars, and other Cossiahs residing at Cherra Poonjee executed in the year 1857 to the following purport:

Having, on the demise of my uncle, the late Soobha Sing, Rajah of this territory, taken his place as his successor, and come into possession of the Raj, I have been required by the Principal Assistant Commissioner of Cherra Poonjee, to furnish a new Agreement, based on those given by my predecessors; and as all the conditions of the engagements entered into by my predecessors, the late Dewan Sing, Rajah, on the 10th of September 1829, and the late Soobha Sing, Rajah, on the 19th of October 1830, are acceptable to me, I will act according to them hereafter.

Dated the 16th of May 1857, corresponding with the 8th of Joisto, 1264 B.S.

Written by Bhoyrobnath Dahn.

Presented this day by Radha Krishno Dutt, Mooktiar, and Bhoyrobnath Dahn, on the part of Ram Sing, Rajah, with his letter of this date, the 16th of May 1857, corresponding with the 4th of Joisto 1264 B.S.

(Sd.) C.K. Hudson,
Principal Assistant Commissioner,
In charge of Cossiah and Jynteah Hills

8. AGREEMENT OF DUN SING OF NUSTENG, 1862

I, Dun Sing, Rajah, son of Oola Beang Koonwur, of Nusteng, in the Cossiah Hills, having been appointed ruler of Nusteng, do hereby agree and promise to conduct myself agreeably to the following rules :

Article 1

I consider myself under the general control and authority of the Political Officer at Cherra Poonjee. All disputes between myself and Chieftains of other Cossiah States shall be referred for trial and decision to the British Court.

Article 2

I shall always reside in the Nusteng ilaka, and decide without partiality, on open Durbar, with the assistance of my Muntrees, Sirdars and elders, according to the ancient and established customs of the country, all civil suits and criminal cases occurring there that are beyond the cognizance of the Police in which only the people of that ilaka may be concerned. All cases in which Europeans and inhabitants of the plains, or of other Cossiah States, are parties to be tried by the Political Officer at Cherra Poonjee.

Article 3

I shall obey all orders issued to me by the Political Officer at Cherra Poonjee, and make over, on demand, to the local authorities, all refugees and civil and political offenders coming to, or residing in, my ilaka.

Article 4

I shall furnish full information regarding my State and its inhabitants whenever I may be required to do so by Government Officers. I shall always endeavour to promote the welfare and happiness of my subjects, give every help and protection in my power to Government Officers and travellers passing through my country, or to settlers residing there; and use my best endeavours to facilitate free intercourse, and trade between the people of my country and British subjects and the people of other Cossiah States.

Article 5

The British Government reserves to itself the right of establishing military and civil sanitaria, cantonments and posts, in any part of my ilaka where that may be required, full compensation being given for the lands thus occupied for those or other Government purposes, and of opening roads in any direction through the country, in which matter I must render my utmost assistance when requisite.

Dated 22nd July 1862, corresponding with 7th Srawun 1269 B.S.

Sunnud conferring the title of Rajah Bahadoor upon Dun Sing, the elected ruler of Nusteng, dated the 26th January 1863.

Whereas you have been elected to be Ruler of Nusteng, I do hereby confer upon you the title of Rajah Bahadoor on condition of your faithfully and fully observing the conditions specified in the Agreement made with you on 22nd July 1862, corresponding with 7th Srawun 1269 B.S.

(Sd.) Elgin and Kincardine

9. AGREEMENT OF TEERUT SING OF NUNGKLOW, 1826

Article 1

Rajah Teerut Sing, the Ruler of Nungklow and its dependencies, with the advice and consent of his relations, dependent Lushkurs and Sirdars in Council assembled, voluntarily agrees to become subject to the Honourable Company, and places his country under their protection.

Article 2

The said Rajah agrees to give a free passage for troops through his country to go and to come between Assam and Sylhet.

Article 3

The Rajah agrees to furnish materials for the construction of a road through his territories, receiving payment for the same and after its completion to adopt such measures as may be necessary to keep it in repair.

Article 4

The Agent to the Governor-General agrees, on the part of the Honourable Company, to protect the Rajah's country from foreign enemies, and if any other Chief injures him, to enquire into the facts, and if it appears that he has been unjustly attacked, to afford him due support. The Rajah on his part agrees to abide by such decision, and not to hold any intercourse or correspondence on political matters with any foreign Chief without the consent of the British Government.

Article 5

The Rajah agrees that, in the event of the Honourable Company carrying on hostilities with any other power, he will serve with all his followers as far to the eastward as Kulliabar in Assam, his men being entitled to receive subsistence money from the British Government when employed on the Plains.

Article 6

The Rajah promises to rule his subjects according to laws of his country, keeping them pleased and contented, and carrying on the public business according to ancient custom, without the interference of the British Government; but if any person should commit violence in the Honourable Company's Territory, and take refuge in the Rajah's country, he agrees to seize and deliver them up.

Dated at Gowhatty this 30th November 1826, corresponding with the 16th Aghun 1233.

(A true translation)

(Sd.) D. Scott,
Agent to the Governor-General

Similar Agreement entered into by the Chief of Khyrim.

10. AGREEMENT OF RUJJUM SING OF NUNGKLOW, 1834

To
Captain Francis Jenkins,
Agent to the Governor-General, North-East Frontier,
On the part of the Honourable Company

The written Agreement of Rujjum Sing, resident of Nungklow, executed to the following purport :

The Government having appointed me to the Raj of the late Teerut Sing Rajah, I hereby execute the Articles of Agreement detailed below, and promise never to act in violation of them, and that my Muntrees will also abide by the terms thereof.

1. That I have no objection to land being taken up by the Honourable Company for the purpose of making a road in any direction chosen between Zillah Sylhet and the Plains of low lands of Assam.

2. That I have no objection to bridges, bungalows of sorts, store-rooms, fortifications, and stockades for sepoys being built for the Honourable Company wherever it may be deemed expedient to select sites for them.

3. That I and my Muntrees will furnish labourers and workmen for building and repairing the above-mentioned roads, buildings, etc. without objection, whenever they may be required.

4. That whenever it may be considered expedient to erect any buildings within the country consigned to me by the Government, I and my Muntrees will immediately furnish the undermentioned materials for them, and we shall not be able to raise any objection about doing so :

List of Materials : Timbers, stones, slates, lime, fire-wood, and any other articles procurable in the country, will be readily furnished.

5. That I and my Muntrees will provide shelter and pasturage for any cows, oxen, etc., that the Honourable Company may send into the country, and I will be responsible for any losses of these animals.

6. That if any criminals or convicts should escape from the Honourable Company's territory and come into my country, I will immediately render assistance in apprehending them.

7. That I will act as stated in the above-mentioned Articles and if I should do anything in contravention of them, I and my Muntrees will submit to such fines as the Governor-General's Agent may think proper to impose on us.

8. That I promise to fulfil the aforesaid stipulations, and am to continue to receive my present monthly stipend of 30 Rupees for one year, as this stipend to me from the Government will enable the people of the country to settle down again in it comfortably without being pressed for any demand. This stipend to me is to cease after the completion of one year, and I am then to make arrangements for myself as formerly.

Dated the 29th of March 1834, corresponding with the 19th of Choitra of the Bengal year 1240.

We, Rai Mon and Oojoor, residents of Nungbree, Ooram of Myrung, Ootep of Mouther, Ooboo Boshan of Singshang, Oosep Lungdeo of Kenchee, Oophan of Monai, and Omeet of Nongsay, having been nominated as Muntrees to the Rajah, approve of the Agreement executed by him, and will be responsible for the fulfilment and violation of it.

(Copy)

(Seal) (Sd.) H. Inglis,
Assistant Political Agent,
Cossiah Hills

11. CONDITIONS IMPOSED UPON THE RAJAH OF NUNGKLOW

1. The Rajah is to consider himself under the general control and authority of the Political Officer at Cherra Poonjee, to whom he must refer all disputes between himself and the

Chieftains of other Cossiah States; and he is clearly to understand that he holds his appointment under authority from the British Government, which reserves to itself the right of removing him from office, and of appointing another Chieftain in his stead, if he should fail to give satisfaction to the British Government, and to the people of the district.

2. The Rajah must reside in the Nungklow district, and he is to be permitted to decide in open Durbar, with the assistance of his Muntrees, Sirdars, and Elders, according to the ancient and established customs of the country, all civil suits and criminal cases occurring there that are beyond the cognizance of the Police and in which only the people of the Nungklow district may be concerned. All cases in which Europeans and inhabitants of the Plains or of other Cossiah States are parties are to be tried by the Political Officer at Cherra Poonjee.

3 The Rajah is to obey all orders issued to him by the Political Officer at Cherra Poonjee, and to make over on demand to the local authorities all refugees and civil and political offenders coming to, or residing in, the Nungklow district.

4. The Rajah is to furnish full information regarding the Nungklow district and its inhabitants, whenever he may be required to do so by Government Officers; to render every assistance in developing the resources of the country; to give every help and protection in his power to Government officials and travellers passing through the country or to settlers residing there; and to use his best endeavours to facilitate free intercourse and trade between the people of the country and British subjects and the people of other Cossiah States.

5. The British Government reserves to itself the right of establishing military and civil sanitaria, cantonments and posts, in any part of the Nungklow district where they may be required, of occupying rent-free any lands that may be required for these or other government purposes, and of opening roads in any direction through the country, in which matter the Rajah must render his utmost assistance when requisite.

6. The Rajah must make grants of the waste lands in Nungklow upon the same terms as those that may be adopted

at the time being by the British Government in granting out its own waste lands.

Similar Agreements entered into by the Chiefs of Moleem and Bhawul Poonjee.

12. AGREEMENT WITH THE CHIEF OF NUNGKLOW, 1866

I, Bor Sing, Seim of the State of Nungklow in the Cossiah Hills admitting my incapacity to the conduct of affairs in my territory, do hereby record my written assent and agreement to the appointment of my relative and heir Chand Rai to be Regent of Nungklow, and that the general management of affairs in Nungklow, together with the carrying out of all orders of the British Government, shall lie with him, and that all communications and precepts shall be addressed to, and received by him.

Signed and sealed by me this day, the 18th May 1866.

(Sd.) Bor Sing,
His+mark, U Seim Jong ka Nungklow

This document was executed by Bor Sing, Seim of Nungklow, in my presence, this 21st day of May 1866.

(Sd.) W.S. Clarke,
Officiating Deputy Commissioner
Cossiah and Jynteah Hills, Assam

Sunnud recognizing the Succession of Chand Rai

Whereas you have been elected to be Ruler of Nungklow, I hereby recognize you as Chief of that place, on condition of your faithfully and fully observing the conditions entered in the separate agreement to be made by you with His Honour the Lieutenant-Governor of Bengal.

Dated 19th August 1868 (Sd.) John Lawrence

13. AGREEMENT WITH BUR MANICK OF KHYRIM, 1830

(Sd.) Bur Manick,
Rajah of Khyrim

To
David Scott, Esquire,
Agent to the Governor-General

My country having been taken possession of by the Honourable Company in consequence of my having made war with them, and thereby caused considerable losses, I now come forward, and placing myself under the protection of the Honourable Company, and acknowledging my submission to them, agree to the following terms as sanctioned by the Presidency authorities :

1. I cede to the Honourable Company the lands I formerly held on the south and east of the Oomeeam river, and I promise not to interfere with the people residing on those lands without the orders of the Agent to the Governor-General.

2. I consent to hold the remaining portion of the territory agreeably to the sunnud of the Honourable Company as their dependents and to conduct its affairs according to ancient customs; but I am not at liberty to pass orders in any murder case without the permission of the Governor-General's Agent, and will report to him any case of this kind that may occur.

3. When any of the Honourable Company's troops pass through my territory, I will furnish them with such provisions as the country produces, so that they may not be put to any inconvenience, receiving payment for these supplies from Government; and I will construct bridges etc., when ordered to do so, and am to be paid for the expenses incurred thereon.

4. In case of any Hill Chieftains making war with the Honourable Company, I will join the Government troops with the fighting men of my country, but they are to receive subsistence from the Government.

5. I relinquish my former claim regarding the boundary of Desh Doomorooah, and agree to the Afdee Nuddee being the future boundary. I am, however, to be assigned some land near the Sonapore Market for the purpose of trading there.

6. I agree to pay a fine of 5,000 Rupees to the Honourable Company on account of the expenses now and previously incurred by them in the subjugation of my country.

7. If Teerut Sing, Rajah, who is inimical to the Honourable Company, or any other of his guilty followers, should enter my territory, I will immediately apprehend them and deliver them up, and I promise to produce all criminals who may come and

take refuge in my country from any place in the Honourable Company's dominions.

To which effect I have executed this Agreement on this 15th day of January 1830, corresponding with the 4th of Maugh 1236 B.S.

14. AGREEMENT WITH THE CHIEF OF MOLEEM, 1863

Whereas it was stipulated in the Agreement entered into by me, Melay Sing, Rajah of Moleem, under date 19th March 1861, with the British Government, that the right of establishing civil and military sanitaria, posts and cantonments, within my country should remain with the British Government; whereas Lieutenant-Colonel J.C. Haughton, Agent to the Governor-General, North-East Frontier, under the instructions of the said Government, has selected, for the purpose of civil and military sanitaria, etc., the land hereinafter described, I hereby renounce with the advice and consent of my Muntrees and the heads of my people, all sovereign and personal rights therein to Her Majesty the Queen of England and the British Government. It is, however, stipulated, should the proprietors, of any of the land within the limits hereinafter described be unwilling to sell or part with their land to the British Government, the said persons shall continue fully to enjoy the same without impost or taxation as heretofore, but that in all other respects the jurisdiction and sovereignty of Her Majesty the Queen of England, and of the British Government, and the officers of Government duly appointed, shall extend over the said land and over all persons residing thereon, and to all offences committed therewithin.

Boundary: The boundary of the lands of Oo Don Sena to the south and east of the Oom Ding Poon stream which have been purchased; the boundary of the lands of Ka Stang Rapsang, south of the stream south of the Oom Ding Poon adjoining the village of Sadoo which have been purchased; the boundary of the lands of Oo Bat Khaobakee touching the Oom Ding Poon stream which have been purchased; the boundary of the lands of Ka Doke adjoining the last named which have been purchased; the boundary of the land of Sooaka adjoining the last named which have been purchased; the boundary of the Shillong lands which have been purchased, from which point the boundary will follow the north and west sides of the present Government roads till the boundary of the lands of Borjon Muntree which have been purchased is met. It will then follow the boundary of the said Borjon's land till the boundary of the said land again meets the Government road now existing, which it will follow till the boundary of the Raj lands purchased are met. It will follow the boundary of the Raj lands till that dividing the Longdo lands of Nongseh from the Raj land and the land purchased from Oo Reang-Karpang of Nongseh, and will go between the two last on the east side of a hill by a path till the boundary stone of the Longdo of Nongseh at the head of a watercourse is met. It will then follow that watercourse to the junction of it with the Oom Soorpee, leaving the hill with the Lungdo jungle of the fir trees on it to the left or north and west side. The boundary will then cross the Oom Soorpee river and ascend by a ravine opposite inclining somewhat to the right hand to monumental stones (Mowshin Ram), near one of which a peg and pile of stones is placed. The boundary will then descend the hill backwards towards the point of Youdoe Hill, that is, the hill on which the Youdoe Bazar is held, to a pile of stones and a peg not far from the Government road which it crosses and not far from the Oom Soorpee river. The boundary thence turns north-east by ascending the hollow to the ridge which divides the waterflow on which is a mark, to the hollow to the north-east, which it follows by the water to the Oom Kra river leaving the Youdoe Bazar hill and the village of Mao Kra on the left hand. The boundary thence turns eastward, following the base of the hills and excluding all cultivation in the plains, including within it the hill lands given to the Government by Oo Beh till the lands of Oo Dor given to Government are met, whence the boundary, in the same way, follows the base of the hills excluding the cultivation in the plains till the river Pomding Nayam is met. Opposite a cave at the mouth of this stream, when it enters the plain, a peg and pile of stone is met. The boundary thence follows the same stream to its head in the rice lands of Oo Beh aforesaid; thence it follows the foot of the hills, leaving the village of Limera to the left or east side, and excluding the rice cultivation of Oo Beh, but including the hill land given by him to Government till it reaches the head of the said rice cultivation, where it turns sharply to the left or east between two hills till it reaches the banks of the stream Oom Ponteng Kom, the downward course of which it follows till the junction of the same water, now called Oom Soorpee, with the Oom Jussaci is reached. This river is the boundary till its source is reached from a pile of stones, near which, marking the boundary of land purchased from Oo Don Sena, the boundary crosses over south-westerly to the point where the Oom Shillong makes a bend; at that point stones have been placed opposite ten fir and five oak trees on the spur of a hill. The boundary then follows the Oom Shillong till the boundary of Oo Don Sena's land is met, which it follows the point from whence it started is reached. I agree that the Government, or the possessor of the land within named, as well as the Shillong lands, shall have the joint right of turning off all water adjoining the said land for use, subject to such rules as the Government may prescribe. I promise also, as far as in me lies, to preserve the sacred groves whereon the water supply is dependent, and to punish any of my subjects found cutting the trees of the said groves and to deliver up for punishment any British subject found so offending.

SHILLONG : (Sd.) Melay Sing Rajah+His mark
The 10th December 1863 (Sd.) Lormiet Montang+His mark
Witness :
(Sd.) U. Joymonee,
Interpreter

Before me, this 18th December, 1863, explained in Cossiah and signed.

(Sd.) J.C. Haughton

Witnesses present not called on to sign, being unable to write :

Oo Ram, Muntree
Oo Sona, ,,
Oo Jee, ,,
Oo Don Sena, ,,
Rajah Singh, Koonwur
Kunrace, of Khyrim

Oo Don, Koonwur
Oo Jon, Sirdar
Purbut, Interpreter
Tama, Koonwur
Alop, Koonwur

I, Melay Sing, having, on behalf of myself and my Muntrees, and all others concerned, ceded the Raj rights and title in the land at Shillong, known as the Shillong lands; the Raj lands south of the Oom Soorpee, known as the Kurkontong Nongseh land; the land near Youdoe, known as the Shillong Labang land; hereby renounce all right and title thereto, resigning the same to Her Majesty the Queen of England, with the trees, water, and all things thereon or therein, and hereby acknowledge to have received, in full satisfaction therefor, the sum of Rupees 2,000 (two thousand) from Lieutenant-Colonel Haughton, Governor-General's Agent, North-East Frontier.

YOUDOE : (Sd.) Melay Sing+His mark
The 8th December, 1863 (Sd.) Raja Rabon Sing+His mark

Rajah Rabon hereby acknowledges to have ceded all rights on part of himself and his people.

(Sd.) J.C. Haughton,
Offg. Governor-General's Agent,
North-East Frontier

Witness :
(Sd.) U. Joymonee

Sree Arradhun Doss,
Mohurir

Present :

(Sd.)	Oo Ram,	Muntree	
,,	Oo Jee,	,,	Moleem Poonjee
	Oo Soobah,	,,	
	Oo Sonah,	,,	
	Oo Raimon,	,,	
	Oo Bamon,	,,	
	Oo Mooik Longskor		Khyrim Poonjee
	Oo Sonkha Longdo		

(Sd.) J.C. Haughton,
Offg. Governor-General's Agent,
North-East Frontier

15. ENGAGEMENT EXECUTED BY THE CHIEF OF LUNGREE, 1864

I, Oomit Sing, having succeeded to the Raj of Lungree on

the death of Soonder Sing, my uncle, late Rajah according to the custom of the country and with the approval of the Chiefs and Elders, and also with the sanction of the Viceroy and Governor-General of India promise to be faithful in allegiance to Her Majesty the Queen of England, her heirs and successors, and I bind myself to the following Articles :

Article 1

That I shall consider myself under the general control and authority of the Deputy Commissioner in the Cossiah and Jynteah Hills, or such other Officer as may be from time to time appointed by Government, to whom I shall refer all disputes between myself and the Chieftains of other Cossiah States, and that I clearly understand I hold my appointment under authority from the British Government, which reserves to itself the right of removing me from office and appointing another Chieftain in my stead if I should fail to give satisfaction to the British Government and the people of the district.

Article 2

That I shall reside in the Lungree District, and decide in open Durbar, with the assistance of the Muntrees, Sirdars, and the Elders, according to ancient and established custom of the country, all civil and criminal cases, not of a heinous nature, in which the inhabitants of the said district only are concerned. I agree to refer to the Deputy Commissioner in the Cossiah and Jynteah Hills, or other Officer appointed for the purpose by Government, all cases civil or criminal, in which Europeans or other foreigners, including the inhabitants of the plains, are concerned, also all cases in which inhabitants of other Cossiah States are concerned, and all heinous criminal cases.

Article 3

That I shall obey all orders issued to me by the Deputy or other Officer appointed to the charge of the Hill districts, and make over, on demand to the local authorities, all refugees and civil and political offenders coming to, or residing in, the Lungree District.

Article 4

That I shall furnish full information regarding the Lungree District and its inhabitants whenever I may be required to do so by Government Officers, will render every assistance in developing the resources of the country, will give every help and protection in my power to Government officials and travellers passing through the country, or to settlers residing there, and will use my best endeavours to facilitate free intercourse and trade between the people of the country and the British subjects and the people of other Cossiah States.

Article 5

The British Government shall have the right of establishing military and civil sanitaria, cantonments, and posts, in any part of the Lungree District where they may be required. I agree to give all lands required for such purposes, the possessors, where the land does not belong to the Raj being duly compensated therefor.

Article 6

Lastly, I, my heirs and successors, will abide by the terms of the Agreement entered into with the Government by the late Rajah on the 22nd September 1859, by which he ceded, in consideration of receiving half the profits, all his mineral rights, except those connected with the limestone tracts leased to the late Mr. Henry Inglis upto 1283 B.S., and all the waste lands not paying revenue, which are not being brought into cultivation by the people of Lungree, and by which being brought into cultivation they will not be sufferers.

Dated Cherra Poonjee, 25th January 1864.

Seal and mark of :
Oomit Sing,
Rajah of Lungree

Witnessed by :
J.B. Shadwell,
Assistant Commissioner in charge

⊙ Mark of Scidee, Muntree of Lauring
⦸ Mark of Oowan, Muntree of Lauring
± Mark of Oosam, Muntree of Lauring
/m Mark of Oo Ramsing, Muntree of Lauring

Sealed and signed in my presence on the 25th day of January 1854, when it was explained to the Rajah that a Sunnud and Khillut would be forwarded by the Viceroy and Governor-General.

(Sd.) J.B. Shadwell,
Assistant Commissioner in charge

Sunnud conferring the title of "Rajah" upon Oomit Sing, the Chief of Lungree

Whereas you have been elected to be Ruler of Lungree, I do hereby confer upon you the title of Rajah on condition of your faithfully and fully observing the conditions specified in the Agreement made with you on the 25th January 1864.

Dated 7th June 1864 (Sd.) John Lawrence

16. RECOGNIZANCE OF OOLAR SING OF MURRIOW, 1829

(Sd.) Oolar Sing,
Rajah of Murriow

To
David Scott, Esquire,
Agent to the Governor-General

Whereas I, Oolar Sing, Rajah of Murriow, formerly conspired against the Honourable Company's people and made war with them. I now come forward for my own good and give this recognizance, to the effect that I will not again enter into such a conspiracy or quarrel, or make war with the people on the part of the Government, and that if I do so, I shall be liable to such punishment as is usually inflicted on riotous persons.

1. My country now remains under the control of the Government, and I will keep the people contented, and conduct the Cossiah affairs in the usual way.

2. I will investigate such cases as take place in my country according to its established customs; but if any heinous crimes, such as murders, etc. should occur, I will give you information of them, and I will obey and act in other matters according as you may order me to do. To which purpose I hereby give

this recognizance on this 12th day of October 1829, corresponding with the 27th of Assin 1236 B.S.
Witnessed by :

Ram Singh Dubashia, Resident of Cherra Poonjee
Dewan Singh Dubashia, Resident of Cherra Poonjee

17. AGREEMENT WITH THE CHIEF OF MURRIOW, 1865

I, Ooron, resident of Murriow, Cossiah Hills, according to the custom of country, and with the approval of the Chiefs and Elders of Murriow, being the lawful heir and successor to the late Oo-Phan, Rajah of Murriow, in anticipation of being duly created under the orders of the Viceroy and Governor-General of India Rajah of Murriow, do hereby promise to be faithful in allegiance to Her Majesty the Queen of "Great Britain" and its dependencies, to her heirs and successors, and I bind myself to the following Articles:—

1. I consider myself under the general control and authority of the Deputy Commissioner in the Cossiah and Jynteah Hills, or such other Officer as may, from time to time, be appointed by Government, and I will refer all disputes between myself and the Chieftains of other Cossiah States to the Deputy Commissioner aforesaid; and I clearly understand that I hold appointment under the authority from the British Government, which reserves to itself the right of removing me from office and appointing another Chieftain in my stead, if I shall fail to give satisfaction to the British Government or to the people of Murriow.

2. I agree to reside in Murriow District, and promise to decide in open Durbar, with the assistance of the Muntrees, Sirdars, and Elders, according to ancient and established custom of the country, all civil and criminal cases not of a heinous nature, in which the inhabitants of the said country only are concerned. I agree to refer to the Deputy Commissioner in the Cossiah and Jynteah Hills, or to any other Officer appointed by Government for the purpose, all cases, civil or criminal, in which Europeans or other foreigners, including the inhabitants of the plains, are concerned, as also all cases in which subjects of other Cossiah States are concerned, and all heinous criminal cases.

3. I bind myself to obey all orders issued by the Deputy Commissioner, or other Officer appointed to the charge of the hill district, and to make over on demand to the duly constituted authorities all refugees and civil and political offenders coming to, or residing in, the Murriow District.

4. I also agree to supply full information regarding the Murriow District and its inhabitants whenever I may be required so to do by the officers of Government. I will also render assistance in developing the resources of the country, and will give aid and protection to Government officials and travellers passing through Murriow, as also to settlers residing therein; and I will use my best endeavours to facilitate free intercourse and trade between the people of the country under me and British subjects and people of other Cossiah States.

5. The British Government shall have the right to construct roads in any direction through the Murriow District, and I bind myself not to levy transit taxes or other dues on such roads unless permitted to do so.

6. The British Government will have the right of establishing military and civil sanitaria, cantonments, and posts in any parts of the Murriow District under my control, and I agree to give all land or lands which do not belong to the Raj on condiion that the proprietors shall receive compensation.

7. Lastly, I bind myself, my heirs and successors, to the terms of the Agreement entered into with the Government of British India by the late Rajah Oo-Phan, by which he ceded, in consideration of receiving half the profits, all his mineral rights and all the waste lands not paying revenue, which are not being brought under cultivation by the people of Murriow, and by which they will not be sufferers.

Ooron Rajah, his mark and seal

Witnessed by:

Ooshirob Longdoh, his mark
Ooksun Longdoh, ,, ,,
Oo-Phan Songdoh, ,, ,,
Oollan Mateebar, ,, ,,

Oodhoo Mateebar, his mark
Oohir Mateebar, ,, ,,

Explained before me and in my presence, clause by clause, to the Rajah, to the Elders, and to the people assembled, and acknowledged by the Rajah to be his voluntary act and deed, this twentieth day of February, Anno Domini 1865, at Murriow, Cossiah Hills.

(Sd.) H.S. Bivar, Major,
Deputy Commissioner, Cossiah and Jynteah Hills

Sunnud conferring the tittle of Rajah upon Ooron, elected Ruler of Murriow

Whereas you have been elected to be Ruler of Murriow, I do hereby confer upon you the tittle of Rajah on condition of your faithfully and fully observing the conditions specified in the Agreement made with you on the 20th February 1865.

The 19th October 1865 (Sd.) John Lawrence

18. AGREEMENT WITH THE CHIEF OF DWARA NONGTURMEN, 1870

I, Jantrai, Sirdar, resident of Dwara, Ellaka Dwara Nongturmen, having been appointed to the Sirdarship of the said Ellaka Dwara Nongturmen, hereby agree and promise that I will conduct myself agreeably to the following rules:—

1. I consider myself under the orders and control of the Deputy Commissioner of the Khasi and Jaintia Hills, and in the event of any disputes arising between myself and the Chief of any other State, they shall be decided by the Deputy Commissioner of the Khasi and Jaintia Hills, or any other duly authorised Officer appointed by the Lieutenant-Governor of Bengal.

2. I will adjudicate and decide all civil and all criminal cases not of a heinous kind which may happen within the limits of my State, and in which the people of my territory alone are concerned; but in regard to heinous offences, I will report their occurrence immediately to the Deputy Commissioner of the Khasi and Jaintia Hills, and will take upon myself the arrest of persons concerned, whom I will deliver up to be dealt with by the Deputy Commissioner or other Officer appointed by him for that purpose.

3. In all disputes which may arise with other Khasi Chiefs, and in all cases in which persons of other States, Europeans or Natives of the plains may be concerned within the limits of my territory, I promise to refer the matter for adjudication by the Deputy Commissioner of the Khasi and Jaintia Hills, or other duly constituted British authority. The authority of the British Government in connection with my Sirdarship extends so far that in case of my using any illegality, or in the event of my people being dissatisfied with me, Government will be at liberty to remove me from my said rank, and appoint another Sirdar in my stead.

4. I bind myself to submit to all orders issued by the Deputy Commissioner of the Khasi and Jaintia Hills, or other duly authorised Officer, and to make over, on demand, all refugees and civil and political offenders coming to, or residing within, my territory.

5. I also agree to supply any information relative to my territory and its inhabitants whenever I may be required to do so by the officer of the British Government. I will always use my best endeavours to maintain the well-being of my people residing in my territory, and I will give aid and protection with all my might to Government officers and travellers passing through, also to people of other ellakas residing in, my territory. I will also endeavour to facilitate free intercourse and trade between the people of the territory under me and the people of other districts and States.

6. I acknowledge the right of the British Government to establish civil and military sanitaria, cantonments, and posts in any part of my State, and to occupy the lands necessary for the purpose rent-free. I will give Government every assistance which may be required in opening roads within my State.

7. I will implicitly obey all orders issued to me by the Deputy Commissioner of the Khasi and Jaintia Hills, otherwise I agree to suffer fine or such other penalty for my misconduct as the Government may think fit to inflict.

8. I hereby add my agreement to the cession by my predecessors of all the lime, coal, and minerals within my State, as also to the cession, after the expiry of the present leases, of the Boot Sermai and Chellai Gang lime quarries on condition of receiving half the profits arising from their sale, lease or

other disposal, and on the same terms to the cession also of all such waste lands, being lands at the time unoccupied by villages, cultivation, plantation, orchards, etc. as may be required to be sold as waste lands.

Fully understanding the terms of this Engagement, I hereby affix my hand and seal this 5th day of May 1870.

His mark + (Sd.) U. Jantrai,
Sirdar

Before me:
(Sd.) R. Stewart,
Deputy Commissioner

19. AGREEMENT WITH AHDOR SING OF MOWSUNRAM POONJEE, 1831

(Sd.) Ahdor Sing, Rajah

To
The Agent to the Governor-General,
North-East Frontier

The written Agreement to Ahdor Sing, Rajah, resident of Mowsunram Poonjee, given to the following effect:

My village having been burnt down on the part of the British Government, and being now a waste, I hereby acknowledge my submission to the Government, and furnish this Agreement, with the object of again settling on the spot, to the effect that I and my people will re-build and re-occupy the village as subjects of the Government, and will obey such orders as you may, from time to time, issue to us.

That I will take measures for apprehending the enemies of the Government if I should hear of their being in my village or its vicinity, and I will also convey immediate information of the same to Captain Townshend, and if I have no particular news to communicate, I will merely wait on him every month.

That if I violate these Engagements, I will, without any demur, abide by whatever orders you may think proper to pass.

Dated this 17th of December 1831, corresponding with the 3rd of Pous 1238 B.S.

Witnessed by:

Dewan Sing Dubashia, resident of Cherra Poonjee
Oomer Cossiah, -do- -do-

Sunnud* recognizing Ahdor Sing, as Chief of Mowsunram in the Cossiah Hills

Whereas you have been elected to be Ruler of Mowsunram, I hereby recognize you as Chief of that place, on condition of your faithfully and fully observing the conditions entered in the separate Agreement to be made by you with His Honour the Lieutenant-Governor of Bengal.

Fort William, (Sd.) John Lawrence
The 17th April, 1867

20. AGREEMENT WITH THE CHIEF OF MAOSENRAM 1875

I, U. Rammon, of Maosenram, having been appointed by the Chief Commissioner of Assam, under orders conveyed in his Secretary's letter No. 506, dated the 18th February 1875, to be Chief of the State of Maosenram, in the district of Khasi and Jaintia Hills, in the room of U. Ahdor Singh, Seim, deposed, do hereby agree and promise that I will, in the administration of the said State, conduct myself agreeably to the following rules:

1. I consider myself to be under the orders and control of the Deputy Commissioner of the district of Khasi and Jaintia Hills. In the event of any dispute arising between myself and the Chief of any other Khasi State, such dispute shall be decided by the Deputy Commissioner of the Khasi and Jaintia Hills, or by any other Officer duly authorised in that behalf by the Chief Commissioner of Assam or by the Government of India.

2. I will adjudicate and decide all civil and criminal cases not of a heinous kind which may arise within the limits of the State in which my subjects alone are concerned. I will report the occurrence of heinous offences within the limits of the State immediately to the Deputy Commissioner of the Khasi and Jaintia Hills, and will arrest the persons concerned in them,

*This Sunnud was, by an oversight, issued by the Government of India, instead of by the Agent to the Governor-General, North-East Frontier.

whom I will deliver up to be dealt with by the Deputy Commissioner or by any Officer appointed by him for that purpose. I promise to refer all civil and criminal cases arising within the limits of the State, in which the subjects of other Khasi States or Europeans, or natives of the plains may be concerned, for adjudication by the Deputy Commissioner of the Khasi and Jaintia Hills, or by other Officer appointed by him for that purpose.

3. In case of my using any oppression, or of my acting in a manner opposed to established custom, or in the event of my people having just cause for dissatisfaction with me, the Chief Commissioner of Assam may remove me from my Chiefship and appoint another Chief in my stead.

4. I will surrender to the Deputy Commissioner of the Khasi and Jaintia Hills, on demand, all civil and political offenders coming to, or residing within my jurisdiction.

5. I will supply any information relative to the country under my control and its inhabitants whenever I may be required to do so by the Deputy Commissioner of the Khasi and Jaintia Hills. I will always use my best endeavours to maintain the well-being of the people subject to my rule, and I will give aid and protection with all my might to officers of the British Government and travellers passing through, also to people of other jurisdictions residing in, my jurisdiction. I will also endeavour to facilitate free intercourse and trade between the people of the State under me and people of other districts and States.

6. I acknowledge the right of the British Government to establish civil and military sanitaria, cantonments, and posts in any part of the country under my control, and to occupy the lands necessary for that purpose rent-free. I will give to the British Government every assistance which may be required in opening roads within the State of Maosenram.

7. I will implicitly obey all orders, issued to me by the Deputy Commissioner of the Khasi and Jaintia Hills, or other officer duly authorized in that behalf by the Chief Commissioner of Assam or by the Government of India. In case of my violating this rule, I shall suffer fine or such other penalty for my misconduct as such officer may think fit to inflict.

8. I hereby add my Agreement to the cession by my predecessor of the natural products of the soil of the State, *viz.* lime, coal and other minerals, and of the right to hunt and capture elephants within the State on condition that I shall receive half the profits arising from the sale, lease, or other disposal of such natural products or of such right; on the same condition, I agree to the cession of all waste lands, being lands at the time unoccupied by villages, cultivation, plantations, orchards, etc., which the British Government may wish to sell or lease as waste lands.

9. I will not alienate to any person any property of the State, movable or immovable, which I possess, or of which I may become possessed as Chief of the State without the sanction of Government.

10. I will have defined areas set aside for the growth of trees to supply building timber and firewood to the inhabitants of the State, and I will take efficient measures to secure these areas against destruction by fire and by jhuming.

Fully understanding the terms of this Engagement, I hereby affix my hand this 15th day of June 1875.

His mark X (Sd.) U. Rammon,
Seim, Maosenram

Executed before me, the 15th day of June 1875.

Shillong (Sd.) H.S. Bivar,
15th June 1875 Deputy Commissioner

21. AGREEMENT OF SONGAPH OF MAHRAM, 1839

To
Major Lister,
Political Agent to the Governor-General, at his Court House

1. I, Songaph, Rajah, resident of the Mahram country, having wantonly made war against the Honourable Company, and caused great loss of life to their people, and put them to considerable expense, have myself been driven through fear a fugitive to the jungles, and acknowledge having committed great faults; but I now crave an amnesty for the past offences of myself and my Cossiah people and enter into this Agreement, in the hope of being permitted to remain in my country in the capacity of a Sirdar (Chief) on the following terms :

2. That I acknowledge my dependency on the Government, and agree to stay in my country, as a Sirdar (Chief), or as if I have been appointed a Sirdar by the Government. I am, however, to adjudicate, amongst my own people, according to custom, but will not put any other to death.

3. That if any of the Government troops should pass through my country, I will attend and furnish them with such provisions as they may require, receiving payment for the same at the customary rates.

4. That should any disturbances arise in the hills, I will, if so ordered, attend with all the Cossiahs of my country, and remain in attendance as long as I may be required to do so, receiving merely subsistence for my people from the Government.

5. That if any murderers or dacoits should take refuge in my country, I will apprehend them and deliver them up when called on to do so.

6. That, in atonement for my faults, I promise to pay the Government a total fine of 2,000 Rupees; but I am to lodge this amount within a month from the present date.

7. That I give Chand Manick Rajah, and Bur Manick, Rajah of Moleem Poonjee, as my securities for the fulfilment of the terms of this Agreement, and I also place at Moleem Poonjee my nephew, Soolong Rajah, who will carry out all orders that may be given at any time regarding my country.

To which end I have executed this Agreement.

Dated this 13th February 1839, corresponding with the 3rd Falgoon 1254 B.S.

22. PERWANNAH ISSUED TO OOSEP SING, OF MAHRAM IN 1852

Seal of Office (Sd.) F. G. Lister,
Political Agent

To

Oosep Sing, Dhollah Rajah,
Resident of Rongthong Poonjee, in the Mahram Territory.

Know Hereby :

It appears that Oober Sing, Dhollah Rajah of the Mahram territory, having deceased, you requested to be appointed Rajah there, on the ground of the country having been under the control of your uncle, the late Songaph, Dhollah Rajah, your application being supported by a petition from Oomen Muntree, Oolar Sing Rajah, and other persons consenting to it; but final orders were deferred on it, in consequence of Ramsye, Kallah Rajah of Nongland Poonjee, in that territory, having set up a claim founded on the right of his uncle, the late Ram Sing, Kallah Rajah, to which Oojeet Lungdeo, Ooksan Sirdar, and certain other persons signified their assent in a petition they presented. As you and Ramsye Rajah have, however, this day come to an amicable arrangement, and filed a deed of compromise to the effect, that of the two Kallah and Dhollah Rajahs of Mahram, the Kallah Rajah is to be subordinate to the Dhollah Rajah, and the investigations connected with the duties of the Raj are to be conducted by them together in consultation, and the profits derived therefrom are to be enjoyed by them both, and as you have therein stated that you are to be Rajah in the place of the aforesaid Dhollah Rajah, retaining the said Ramsye Rajah as your subordinate, and investigating and deciding cases occurring in the country in concert and consultation with him, which are otherwise to be considered null and void, and the aforementioned Ramsye Kallah Rajah has expressed his willingness to remain as your subordinate, and according to former custom to investigate and decide cases taking place in the country in company and consultation with you, the decisions being invalid, unless so conducted, etc., besides which, you two presons are, agreeably to previous practice, to enjoy the profits derived from the country, and to share the losses incurred therein, and as you have assented to the above stated terms, and requested that a Perwannah may be given to you, appointing you as Rajah in accordance therewith, you are, therefore, informed that you are hereby appointed Rajah in the room of the Dhollah Rajah of the territory of Mahram, and it will be your duty to conduct investigations and give decisions there as stipulated in the deed of compromise, and according to your own sense of proper justice, retaining Ramsye Kallah Rajah as your subordinate, and both of you acting together and in consultation to do what is incumbent on you. You will, moreover, obey all orders that may be issued to you, from time to time, on the part of the Honourable Company, without delay, observing the terms agreed on in the deed of compromise referred to.

Dated the 28th of September 1852, corresponding with the 14th of Assin 1259 B.S.

23. ENGAGEMENT WITH RAJAH OF MAHRAM, 1864

I, Oo Sai Sing, resident of Mahram, according to the custom of country and with the approval of the Chiefs and Elders of Mahram, being the lawful heir and successor to the late Oosep Sing, Dhollah Rajah of Mahram, in anticipation of being duly created, under the orders of the Viceroy and Governor-General of India, Dhollah Rajah of Mahram, do hereby promise to be faithful in allegiance to Her Majesty the Queen of Great Britain and its dependencies, her heirs and successors, and I bind myself to the following Articles :

Article 1

I consider myself under the general control and authority of the Deputy Commissioner in the Cossiah and Jynteah Hills, or such other Officer as may be from time to time appointed by Government, and I will refer all disputes between myself and the Chieftains of other Cossiah States to the Deputy Commissioner aforesaid, and I clearly understand that I hold my appointment under authority from the British Government, which reserves to itself the right of removing me from office and appointing another Chieftain in my stead, if I should fail to give satisfaction to the British Government or to the people of Mahram.

Article 2

I agree to reside in the Mahram District, and promise to decide in open Durbar, with the assistance of the Muntrees, Sirdars, and the Elders, according to ancient and established custom of the country, all civil and criminal cases, not of a heinous nature, in which the inhabitants of the said country only are concerned. I agree to refer to the Deputy Commissioner in the Cossiah and Jynteah Hills, or to any other Officer appointed by Government for the purpose, all cases, civil and criminal, in which Europeans or other foreigners, including the inhabitants of the plains, are concerned, as also all cases in which subjects of other Cossiah States are concerned, and all heinous criminal cases.

Article 3

I bind myself to obey all orders issued by the Deputy Commissioner or other officer appointed to the charge of the Hill districts, and to make over, on demand, to the duly constituted authorities all refugees and civil and political offenders coming to, or residing in, the Mahram District.

Article 4

I also agree to supply full information regarding the Mahram District and its inhabitants whenever I may be required so to do by the officers of Government. I will also render assistance in developing the resources of the country, and I will give aid and protection to Government officials and travellers passing through Mahram, as also to settlers residing therein, and will use my best endeavours to facilitate free intercourse and trade between the people of the country under me and British subjects and people of other Cossiah States.

Article 5

The British Government will have the right of establishing military and civil sanitaria, cantonments, and posts, in any part of the Mahram District under my control, and I agree to give all lands required for such purposes on the understanding, when the land or lands do not belong to the Raj, that the proprietors shall receive compensation.

Article 6

Lastly, I bind myself, my heirs and successors, to the terms of the Agreement entered into with the Government of British India by the late Rajah Oosep Sing on the 22nd September 1859, by which he ceded, in consideration of receiving half the profits, all his mineral rights (except those connected with the Mahram tracts leased to late Mr Henry Inglis up to 1283 B.S.), and all the waste lands not paying revenue which are not being brought under cultivation by the people of Mahram, and by which they will not be sufferers.

His seal and mark,
Oo Sai Sing, Rajah

Dated Yondae (fifth) 5th October 1864

Witnessed by:

Grish Chunder Bose

Mark of Ram Sing, Muntree	Mark of Tor Sai, Muntree
Mark of Oo Sugi, ,,	Mark of W. Sona, ,,
Mark of W. Tar, ,,	Mark of W. Saih, ,,
Mark of W. Sar Sing, Gooshtee	Mark of U. Ram, Gooshtee
Mark of Suntoo, ,,	Mark of Khalet Vasued

Signed and sealed in my presence the 5th day of October 1864 when it was explained to the Rajah that a Sunnud and Khillut would be furnished on receipt of the orders of Government.

(Sd.) H. S. Bivar,

Deputy Commissioner, Cossiah and Jynteah Hills.

Sunnud confirming the election of Oo Sai Sing as Rajah of Mahram

Whereas you have been elected by the chief men and people of Mahram to succeed the late Rajah Oosep Sing in the Chieftaincy, I hereby recognize and confirm your election to be Rajah of Mahram.

Be assured that so long as you remain faithful in your allegiance to the British Crown, and fully and faithfully fulfil your engagements with the British Government, the State of Mahram will remain to you in undisturbed possession.

(Sd.) John Lawrence

Dated 5th December 1864

24. RECOGNIZANCE OF OOPHAR OF BHAWUL POONJEE, 1832

Seal of Oophar Rajah

To

The Agent to the Governor-General

I, Oophar Rajah, Resident of Bhawul Poonjee, have this day, of my own free-will and accord, and without any compulsion, executed this Recognizance before Captain Townshend, at Cherra Poonjee, as detailed in the following paragraphs, and I will be responsible for the violation of any of the terms thereof, and will obey the orders of the Gentlemen.

1. That if the Cossiahs should kill, or in any way harm or injure any of the Honourable Company's people within the

boundaries of the Ooahn Churrah of Hatee Khodda on the west, and the Dhoolai Nuddee on the west bank of the Dongdongiah on the east, I will immediately produce the guilty persons and make reparation for the losses sustained.

2. That I will not give any shelter, assistance, or provisions to the enemies of the Honourable Company, and whenever I may receive any news regarding them, I will send information thereof to the Government people through the Dooahradars.

3. That I will not allow any of the Honourable Company's enemies to come to my Ahrung of Seemai when it is re-opened.

4. That whenever I may be called for by the Gentlemen, I will attend immediately on receipt of the written order to do so, and if I act contrary to stipulations made in the above paragraphs, I will submit to any orders the Gentlemen may choose to pass. To which end I have executed this Recognizance.

Dated the 11th December 1832, corresponding with the 27th Ahgran 1239 B.S.

Witnessed by:

Goopeeram, resident at present at Chattarkonah
Askur Mahmed, resident of Pergunnah Mahram,
Mouzah Nolegong
Rohoomot Dooahradar, resident of Ghasegong
Ramjan Dooahradar, resident of Pergunnah Mahram,
Mouzah Kandeegong
Robaie Dooahradar, resident of Chorgong

25. AGREEMENT WITH THE CHIEF OF BHAWAL, 1877

I, U. Bamon Singh, resident of Bhawal, having been appointed to be Chief of the State of Bhawal alias Warbah, in the district of Khasi and Jaintia Hills, do hereby agree and promise that I will, in the administration of the said State, conduct myself agreeably to the following rules:

1. I consider myself to be under the orders and control of the Deputy Commissioner of the district of the Khasi and Jaintia Hills. In the event of any dispute arising between myself and the Chief of any other Khasi State, such dispute shall be decided by the Deputy Commissioner of the Khasi and Jaintia Hills, or by any other officer duly authorized in that behalf

by the Chief Commissioner of Assam or by the Government of India.

2. I will adjudicate and decide all civil cases and all criminal cases, not of a heinous kind, which may arise within the limits of the State, in which my subjects alone are concerned. I will report the occurrence of heinous offences within the limits of the State immediately to the Deputy Commissioner of the Khasi and Jaintia Hills, and will arrest the persons concerned in them, whom I will deliver up, to be dealt with by the Deputy Commissioner, or by any other officer appointed by him for that purpose. I promise to refer all civil and criminal cases arising within the limits of the State, in which the subjects of other Khasi States, or Europeans, or Natives of the plains may be concerned, for adjudication by the Deputy Commissioner of the Khasi and Jaintia Hills, or by any other officer appointed by him for that purpose.

3. In case of my using any oppression, or of my acting in a manner opposed to established custom, or in the event of my people having just cause for dissatisfaction with me, the Chief Commissioner of Assam may remove me from my Chiefship and appoint another Chief in my stead.

4. I will surrender to the Deputy Commissioner of the Khasi and Jaintia Hills, on demand, all civil or political offenders coming to, or residing within, my jurisdiction.

5. I will supply any information relative to the country under my control and its inhabitants whenever I may be required to do so by the Deputy Commissioner of the Khasi and Jaintia Hills. I will always use my best endeavours to maintain the well-being of the people subject to my rule, and I will give aid and protection with all my might to officers of the British Government and travellers passing through, also to people of other jurisdictions residing in, my jurisdiction. I will also endeavour to facilitate free intercourse and trade between the people of the State under me and the people of other districts and States.

6. I acknowledge the right of the British Government to establish civil and military sanitaria, cantonments, and posts in any part of the country under my control, and to occupy the lands necessary for that purpose rent-free. I will give to the British Government every assistance which may be required in

opening roads within the State of Bhawal or Warbah.

7. I will implicitly obey all orders issued to me by the Deputy Commissioner of the Khasi and Jaintia Hills, or other officer duly authorized in that behalf by the Chief Commissioner of Assam or by the Government of India. In case of my violating this rule, I shall suffer fine or such other penalty for my misconduct as such officer may think fit to inflict.

8. I hereby add my agreement to the cession by my predecessors of the natural products of the soil of the State, *viz.* lime, coal, and other minerals, and of the right to hunt and capture elephants within the State, on condition that I shall receive half the profits arising from the sale, lease, or other disposal of such natural products or of such right. On the same condition, I agree to the cession of all waste lands, being lands at the time unoccupied by villages, cultivation, plantations, orchards, etc., which the British Government may wish to sell or lease as waste lands.

9. I will not alienate to any person any property of the State, movable or immovable, which I possess, or of which I may become possessed, as Chief of the State.

10. I will cause such areas as may be defined by the British Government for that purpose to be set aside for the growth of trees to supply building timber and firewood to the inhabitants of the State of Bhawal. I will take efficient measures to secure these areas against destruction by fire and jhuming.

Fully understanding the terms of this agreement, I hereby affix my hand this twenty-third day of July 1877.

His mark X (Sd.) U. Bamon Singh, Seim

Executed before me this 23rd day of July, 1877.

(Sd.) W.S. Clarke,
Deputy Commissioner,
Khasi and Jaintia Hills

Shillong:
The 23rd July 1877

26. AGREEMENT WITH THE CHIEF OF MAOIANG, 1869

I, Jit Singh, Seim, resident of Umkrem, Ellaka Maoiang, having been appointed to the Chiefship of the said Ellaka Maoiang, hereby agree and promise that I will conduct myself agreeably to the following rules:

1. I consider myself under the orders and control of the

Deputy Commissioner of the Khasi and Jaintia Hills, and in the event of any disputes arising between myself and the Chief of any other State, they shall be decided by the Deputy Commissioner of the Khasi and Jaintia Hills, or any other duly authorized officer appointed by the Lieutenant-Governor of Bengal.

2. I will adjudicate and decide all civil and all criminal cases, not of a heinous kind, which may happen within the limits of my State and in which the people of my territory alone are concerned; but in regard to heinous offences I will report their occurrence immediately to the Deputy Commissioner of the Khasi and Jaintia Hills, and will take upon myself the arrest of persons concerned, whom I will deliver up to be dealt with by the Deputy Commissioner or other officer appointed by him for that purpose.

3. In all disputes which may arise with other Khasi Chiefs, and in all cases in which persons of other States, Europeans or Natives of the plains, may be concerned within the limits of my territory, I promise to refer the matter for adjudication by the Deputy Commissioner of the Khasi and Jaintia Hills or other duly constituted British authority. The authority of the British Government in connection with my Chiefship extends so far that, in case of my using any illegality, or in the event of my people being dissatisfied with me, Government will be at liberty to remove me from my said rank and appoint another Chief in my stead.

4. I bind myself to submit to all orders issued by the Deputy Commissioner of the Khasi and Jaintia Hills or other duly authorized officer, and to make over, on demand, all refugees and civil and political offenders coming to, or residing within, my territory.

5. I also agree to supply any information relative to my territory and its inhabitants whenever I may be required to do so by the officers of the British Government. I will always use my best endeavours to maintain the well-being of the people residing in my territory, and I will give aid and protection with all my might to Government officers and travellers passing through, also to people of other ellakas residing in, my territory. I will also endeavour to facilitate free intercourse and

trade between the people of the territory under me and the people of other districts and States.

6. I acknowledge the right of the British Government to establish civil and military sanitaria, cantonments, and posts in any part of my State, and to occupy the lands necessary for the purpose rent-free. I will give Government every assistance which may be required in opening roads within my State.

7. I will implicitly obey all orders issued to me by the Deputy Commissioner of the Khasi and Jaintia Hills, otherwise I agree to suffer fine or such other penalty for my misconduct as the Government may think fit to inflict.

8. I hereby add my agreement to the cession by my predecessors of the lime, coal, and minerals within my State, on condition of receiving half the profits arising from their sale, lease, or other disposal, and on the same terms to the cession also of such waste lands being lands at the time unoccupied by villages, cultivation, plantations, orchards, etc., as may be required to be sold as waste lands.

Fully understanding the terms of this agreement, I hereby affix my hand and seal this sixth day of May 1869.

His mark X (Sd.) U. Jit Singh,
Seim of Maoiang

Executed before me this sixth day of May 1869.

(Sd.) R. Stewart, Major
Officiating Deputy Commissioner,
Khasi and Jaintia Hills

27. AGREEMENT WITH ZUBBER SINGH OF RAMRYE, 1829

(Sd.) Zubber Singh,
Rajah of the country of Pantan

The written Agreement of Zubber Singh, Rajah of the territory of Ramrye, executed in the English year 1829, to the following purport:

I and my subordinate officers and all my people, acknowledging our dependence and subjection to the Honourable Company, promise to obey and act agreeably to such orders as may, from time to time, be passed regarding our country.

1. Our country having been invaded and taken possession of by the Government troops, in consequence of our people having quarrelled with those of the Government, I promise to realize from my Hill subjects all the expenses that have been incurred thereon.

2. I will investigate and decide all petty cases occurring in my country agreeably to custom with Punchayats; but I will report all cases of murder that may take place; and when the culprits shall have been apprehended and given up, they will be tried by the laws that are current in the hills.

3. I will not oppress or wrong my people, and will keep them satisfied and contented.

4. I and my subordinates will never fight or quarrel with the Honourable Company, and, if we do so, we shall be punished according to the regulations like other refractory persons.

5. I will appoint and remove the Lungdeos of my country with your approval and consent, and act in all matters after consulting with the people.

6. Whenever any hostilities may occur between the Hill people and the Government, I will assist the Government with my troops. To which effect I have executed this Agreement, dated this 27th of October of the present year.

I have filed a separate list of the expenses that I will pay.

(Sd.) W. Cracroft,
A. A. G. G.

28. AGREEMENT WITH THE SIRDARS OF RAMRYE, 1835

(Sd.) Oohn Sirdar
,, Ookiang Lungdeo
,, Oohn Sirdar
,, Oomoi Sirdar
Of the Territory of Ramrye

To
The Agent to the Governor-General

The written Agreement of Oohn Sirdar, resident of Soojor Poonjee, Ookiang Lungdeo, resident of Nongkland, Poonjee, Oohn Sirdar, resident of Khenderiag, and Oomoi Sirdar, resident of Oomshem, pertaining to Ramrye, executed to the following purport :—

Having this day attended before the Commanding Officer, Captain Lister, we hereby, of our own free-will and accord, furnish the Agreement detailed in the under-mentioned paragraphs. Dated this 21st of January 1835, corresponding with the 9th of Maugh 1241 B.S.

1. That we are under the protection of the Government, and acknowledge our submission to them.

2. That if any murders or serious cases occur in our country they will be investigated by the Government, to which we are willing and agreeable and the punishments awarded, on investigation of such cases, are to be by the Government.

3. That if there should be a likelihood of hostilities occurring between us and the people of another State, we will act as the Government may direct and in the event of our having any quarrel with such foreign people, we will submit to the decision given by the Government.

4. That our debt to the Government of Rupees 8,485-13 (Eight thousand four hundred and eightyfive and thirteen annas) is this day remitted, and we agree to pay a sum of Rupees 200 annually in the month of Kartic at any place where we may be directed to do so, and on lodgement of the money we will take receipts for it from Government authorities.

5. That if we act in contravention of the stipulations in the above paragraphs, the Government may do whatever they consider just and proper, and we will make no objection to it. To which effect we have executed this Agreement of our own accord.

Witnessed by :
Ram Sing, Jemadar
Borjooram Dubashia

29. AGREEMENT WITH THE WAHADADARS OF CHEYLA POONJEE, 1829

(Sd.) Mishnee Wahadadar
„ Bursing Wahadadar
„ Soomen and Ooksan Wahadadars
Residents of Cheyla Poonjee

To
The Honourable Company

The written Agreement of Mishnee, Bursing, Soomen, and

Ooksan, Wahadadars of Cheyla Poonjee, and other villages, twelve in number, whereas a disturbance or battle took place in the Hills, and we did not join with the Government or make our appearance, in consequence of which troops were sent to our villages ; we now come forward and give this Agreement to abide by the following stipulations :

1. That having committed these faults, we agree to pay by instalments to the Government, amongst our twelve villages, a fine of Rupees 4,000 for the payment of which sum we four persons are responsible.

2. That from the limestone situated on the banks of the Bogah River in our territory, we agree to allow the Government always to remove gratis, as much as they require, in any locality selected by their officers, but it is not to be taken from any other place.

3. That should any persons concerned in any acts in Zillah Sylhet or other places come and take shelter with us, we will immediately deliver them up on their being called for by the Zillah Courts.

4. That we promise not to dispute or make war with the Honourable Company, or with any of the Rajahs who are in confederacy with the Government.

5. That if any quarrels should arise between us and the Rajahs alluded to, the Government is to investigate and settle them, and to this effect we have executed this Agreement.

Dated the 3rd September, 1829 corresponding with the 19th of Bhadro 1236 B.S.

Petition of the Wahadadars of Cheyla Poonjee to the Political Agent of the Cossiah Hills in 1851, soliciting his assistance in causing the attendance, at their Durbars, of persons resisting their authority and offering to abide by his decisions in appeals preferred to him against their orders, or in complaints made to him against their acts.

(Sd.) Mishnee Wahadadar
,, Bursing ,,
,, Larsing and Sonarai Wahadadar
,, Ookhang and Beehai ,,
Residents of Cheyla Poonjee

Respectfully Sheweth,

That previous to the occupation of these Hills by the Honourable Company, we were appointed to the offices of the four Wahadadars of our village of Cheyla Poonjee, and protected the people by conducting enquiries and investigations in our country. That when these Hills afterwards came into the possession of the Honourable Company, we were confirmed in our appointments, agreeably to former custom, with the approval of the late Mr. David Scott, and most efficiently protected the inhabitants by investigating cases in the country by our own authority ; but during the last two or three years, certain Cossiahs of our village, who are unruly, powerful, and evil-advising persons have formed themselves into a party to carry out their own purposes, and are oppressing and harassing some of the poor Cossiahs, and if they complain, and we send for these persons through our officers, they openly resist our authority and assault them, besides making various remarks about us. When we also summon defendants in cases under trial before us, these violent individuals screen them, and in resistance of orders beat our men and snatch away the defendants from them; thus causing great annoyance to the poor people under our control, which we have frequently complained of to you by petitions ; and the individuals of this party who harass the poor people in this manner are, moreover, not unknown to you. It is besides probable that unless this faction is put down, serious affrays and murders may hereafter occur, attended with ruination to our country, which it will be difficult for us to account for to you, and we shall be punished by Providence if the poor are violently oppressed by such persons of our village as have numerous friends and relatives, and we, as rulers of the country, do not redress their grievances. But as the calamities of our poor people cannot be removed, or the country rendered tranquil without your assistance, we therefore throw ourselves on your protection, and voluntarily present this petition, soliciting that the persons under our control, who resist our officers, may be tried by you, and that you will, on our solicitation, grant us your help to bring to our Durbars all such persons as pertinaciously refuse to attend there when we send for them ; and if any persons who are dissatisfied with our orders should appeal to you against them, or if we oppress or injure any persons, and they complain to you about it, we will agree to any investigations and orders that you may pass, and will never act in contravention of them, but will obey them without urging any objections. There is no prospect of relief to our country, unless you so favour us, and in this your power is absolute.

Dated the 30th of Bysack 1258 B.S. (Received 14th May 1851)

Present : Colonel Lister, Political Agent

The request of the Wahadadars is granted, and it is hereby ordered that a perwannah be written to them, to the effect that if any person hereafter oppress or injures another, and the person so oppressed complains to the Wahadadars and the oppressor, when called for by them obstinately and in disobedience of the Wahadadars' orders refuses to attend at their Durbars, they must send him to Cherra Poonjee with the witnesses to the fact of the opposition made to their authority, and the prosecutor and his witnesses, when proper orders will be passed.

Dated the 16th May 1851, corresponding with the 3rd of Jyet 1258 B.S.

(Sd.) F.G. Lister,
Political Agent

30 AGREEMENT WITH CHOTA SAHDOO SING OF JEERUNG, 1841

The written Agreement of Chota Sahdoo Sing, Rajah of the territory of Bur Jeerung Poonjee, executed in the present year 1248 B.S., to the following purport :

Having solicited permission to be continued in charge of the three villages of Bur Jeerung, Choto Jeerung, and Pathor Khallee, now held by me on condition of my repairing the road and bridges in the hills agreeably to orders, I have been called on by a Perwannah, No. 494 dated the 7th of Choitro of the past year for an Agreement, and in compliance with that order I now furnish this Agreement stating that I promise, as customary, to make the annual repairs of the bridges, road, ghats, and stockades, etc., in the hills and other places without payment the above-mentioned three villages remaining in my charge for the performance of these services ; and if I negligently delay to execute these works, and the road, bridges etc., should not be kept in repair, I will submit to whatever orders you may think proper to pass. To which effect I have given this Agreement dated the 8th of June of the English year 1841, corresponding with the 27th Joisto 1248 B.S.

Whereas Sahdoo Sing, Rajah, has personally presented this Agreement it is hereby ordered to be accepted and filed with the record.

Dated the 8th of June of the English year 1841, corresponding with the 27th Joisto 1248 B.S.

31. PERWANNAH ISSUED TO THE SIRDARS OF MOWLONG POONJEE, 1857

Seal of Office

(Sd.) C.K. Hudson,
Principal Assistant Commissioner,
In charge of Cossiah and Jaintia Hills

To
Oojee Lusker and Chonglah Lusker,
Residents of Mowlong Poonjee
Know Hereby,

That whereas you represented yourselves, on the demise of Zuffer Lusker, Sirdar of the Mowlong District, as being the sons and heirs of the deceased, and solicited that you two brothers might be permitted to conduct the duties of that office by turns for one year each, you are now therefore appointed to the office of the Late Zuffer Lusker, pending the preferment of any substantial claim that may be worthy of notice being made to that district, and are hereby informed that agreeably to the terms of the Deed of Compromise you previously filed, you will conduct the duties of the office of that Sirdar, as is incumbent on you, by turns, for one year each. Herein fail not.

Dated the 25th of March 1857, corresponding with the 13th of Chaitro 1263 B.S.

32. AGREEMENT WITH THE SIRDARS OF SOOPAR POONJEE AND ALLIED VILLAGES, 1829

(Sd.) Oomit Khye, of Soopar Poonjee
,, Oohn Khye, of Nongrong
,, Oodoor Cossiah, of Noskin

To
Mr. David Scott,
Agent to the Governor-General

Agreement of the Sirdars, Elders, and Inhabitants of Soopar Poonjee, Nongrong Poonjee, and Noskin Poonjee, executed in the year 1829, to the following purport :

1. The people of our villages having entered into hostilities with and killed the subjects of the Honourable Company, our villages have been taken possession of by the Government. We, therefore, having now attended at Moosmai Poonjee, enter into this Agreement, for ourselves and all the people of the aforesaid villages, to the effect that we acknowledge our submission to the Honourable Company as being their people, and we agree to obey all orders that may at any time be given regarding us.

2. The inhabitants of our above-mentioned three villages having wantonly made war with and killed the subjects of the Government, we, instead of paying a fine in money, hereby divide with the Government one-half of all the limestone, good, bad, and indifferent, in our aforementioned three villages. We are to have half, and we give half to the Government, and to this effect we have executed this Agreement on the 29th day of October 1829, corresponding with the—Kartick 1236 B.S.

Witnessed by :

Soomer Giri, resident of Cherra Poonjee
Ram Doloie, -do- -do-
Lall Sing Giri -do- -do-

(Sd.) W. Cracroft,
A. A. G. G.

33. RECOGNIZANCE OF THE RAJAHS OF MULLAI POONJEE, 1832

(Sd.) Ooksan Rajah
,, Ooahnloka Rajah

To
The Agent to the Governor-General

We, Ooksan Rajah and Ooahnloka Rajah, residents of Mullai Poonjee, having this day appeared before Mr. Harry Inglis, on the bank of the Jadookata River, do, of our own accord and free-will execute this Recognizance as detailed in the following paragraphs, and we will be responsible for the violation of any of the terms thereof, and will obey the orders of the Gentlemen.

1. That if any Cossiahs kill, or otherwise harm or injure, any of the Honourable Company's people within the Dholai River on the west, and the Khagoorah Churrah on the east, we will immediately produce the guilty persons and make reparation for the losses sustained.

2. That we promise not to give shelter, assistance, or provisions to the enemies of the Honourable Company, and if we should obtain any information regarding them, we will send notice of the same to the Government Officers through the Dooahradars.

3. That we will not allow the enemies of the Government to come to our bazar of Nokhoreeah Burtikrah when it is re-opened.

4. That whenever we are summoned by the Gentlemen, we will present ourselves as soon as we receive the written order to attend, and if we infringe these terms we will abide by any orders that may be passed by the Gentlemen. To which end we have hereby executed this Recognizance on this 21st of November 1832 corresponding with the 7th Aghran 1239 B.S.

Witnessed by:

Mohomed Ansor, resident of Mouzah Noigong, Pergunnah Mahram.

Bobaraie, resident of Mouzah Mookeergong, Pergunnah Barakheeah.

Bottai Dubashia, resident of Pergunnah Chorgong.

34. AGREEMENT WITH THE CHIEF OF NONGSOHPHOH, 1870

I, U. Ksan, Seim of Nongsohphoh, resident of Nongsohphoh, Ellaka Nongsohphoh, having been appointed to the Chiefship of the said Ellaka Nongsohphoh, hereby agree and promise that I will conduct myself agreeably to the following rules :

1. I consider myself under the orders and control of the Deputy Commissioner of the Khasi and Jaintia Hills, and in the event of any disputes arising between myself and the Chief of any other State, they shall be decided by the Deputy Commissioner of the Kashi and Jaintia Hills, or any other duly authorized officer appointed by the Lieutenant-Governor of Bengal.

2. I will adjudicate and decide all civil and all criminal cases not of a heinous kind, which may happen within the limits of my State and in which the people of my territory alone are concerned; but in regard to heinous offences, I will report their occurrence immediately to the Deputy Commissioner of the Khasi and Jaintia Hills, and will take upon myself the arrest of persons concerned, whom I will deliver up to be dealt with by the Deputy Commissioner or other officer appointed by him for the purpose.

3. In all disputes which may arise with the other Khasi Chiefs, and in all cases in which persons of other States, Europeans or Natives of the plains, may be concerned within the limits of my territory, I promise to refer the matter for adjudication by the Deputy Commissioner of the Khasi and Jaintia Hills, or other duly constituted British authority. The authority of the British Government in connection with my Chiefship extends so far that in case of my using any illegality, or in the event of my people being dissatisfied with me, Government will be at liberty to remove me from said rank and appoint another Chief in my stead.

4. I bind myself to submit to all orders issued by the Deputy Commissioner of the Khasi and Jaintia Hills or other duly authorized officer and to make over, on demand, all refugees and civil and political offenders coming to, or residing within, my territory.

5. I also agree to supply any information relative to my territory and its inhabitants whenever I may be required to do

so by the officers of the British Government. I will always use my best endeavours to maintain the well-being of the people residing in my territory, and I will give aid and protection with all my might to Government officers and travellers passing through, also to people of other ellakas residing in, my territory. I will also endeavour to facilitate free intercourse and trade between the people of the territory under me and the people of other districts and States.

6. I acknowledge the right of the British Government to establish civil and military sanitaria, cantonments, and posts in any part of my State, and to occupy the lands necessary for the purpose rent-free. I will give Government every assistance which may be required in opening roads within my State.

7. I will implicitly obey all orders issued to me by the Deputy Commissioner of the Khasi and Jaintia Hills, otherwise I agree to suffer fine or such other penalty for my misconduct as the Government may think fit to inflict.

8. I hereby add my agreement to the cession by my predecessors of the lime, coal and minerals within my State, on condition of receiving half the profits arising from their sale, lease, or other disposal, and on the same terms to the cession also of such waste lands, being lands at the time unoccupied by villages, cultivation, plantation, orchards, etc., as may be required to be sold as waste lands.

Fully understanding the terms of this engagement, I hereby affix my hand and seal this 31st day of August 1870.

SHILLONG
The 31st August 1870

His mark X (Sd.) U. Ksan
Seim of Nongsohphoh
Before me,
(Sd.) R. Stewart

35. AGREEMENT WITH THE CHIEF OF JIRANG, 1883

I, U. Bang of Jirang, having been appointed by the Deputy Commissioner of the Khasi and Jaintia Hills to be Sirdar of the State of Jirang, in the district of Khasi and Jaintia Hills, do hereby agree and promise that I will in the administration of the said State, conduct myself agreeably to the following rules :

1. I consider myself to be under the orders and control of the Deputy Commissioner of the district of the Khasi and Jaintia

Hills. In the event of any dispute arising between myself and the Chief of any other Khasi State, such dispute shall be decided by the Deputy Commissioner of the Khasi and Jaintia Hills, or by any other officer duly authorized in that behalf by the Chief Commissioner of Assam or by the Government of India.

2. I will adjudicate and decide all civil cases and all criminal cases not of a heinous kind, which may arise within the limits of the State in which my subjects alone are concerned. I will report the occurrence of heinous offences within the limits of the State immediately to the Deputy Commissioner of the Khasi and Jaintia Hills, and will arrest the persons concerned in them, whom I will deliver up to be dealt with by the Deputy Commissioner or by any other officer appointed by him for that purpose. I promise to refer all civil and criminal cases arising within the limits of the State, in which the subjects of other Khasi States, or Europeans, or Native of the plains may be concerned, for adjudication by the Deputy Commissioner of the Khasi and Jaintia Hills, or by any other officer appointed by him for that purpose.

3. In case of my using any oppression or of my acting in a manner opposed to established custom, or in the event of my people having just cause for dissatisfaction with me, the Deputy Commissioner may remove me from my Sirdarship and appoint another Sirdar in my stead.

4. I will surrender to the Deputy Commissioner of the Khasi and Jaintia Hills, on demand, all civil and political offenders coming to, or residing within, my jurisdiction.

5. I will supply any information relative to the country under my control and its inhabitants whenever I may be required to do so by the Deputy Commissioner of the Khasi and Jaintia Hills. I will always use my best endeavours to maintain the well-being of the people subject to my rule, and I will give aid and protection with all my might to officers of the British Government and travellers passing through, also to people of other jurisdictions residing in, my jurisdiction. I will also endeavour to facilitate free intercourse and trade between the people of the State under me and the people of other districts and States.

6. I acknowledge the right of the British Government to establish civil and military sanitaria, cantonments, and posts in

any part of the country under my control, and to occupy the lands necessary for that purpose rent-free. I will give to the British Government every assistance which may be required in opening roads within the State of Jirang.

7. I will implicitly obey all orders issued to me by the Deputy Commissioner of the Khasi and Jaintia Hills or other officer duly authorized in that behalf by the Deputy Commissioner. In case of my violating this rule, I shall suffer fine or such other penalty for my misconduct as such officer may think fit to inflict.

8. I hereby add my agreement to the cession by my predecessors of the natural products of the soil of the State, *viz.*, lime, coal, and other minerals, and of the right to hunt and capture elephants within the State, on condition that I shall receive half the profits arising from the sale, lease, or other disposal of such natural products or of such right. On the same condition I agree to the cession of all waste lands, being lands at the time unoccupied by villages, cultivation, plantation, orchards, etc., which the British Government may wish to sell or lease as waste lands.

9. I will not alienate to any person any property of the State, movable or immovable, which I possess or of which I may become possessed, as Chief of the State.

10. I will cause such areas as may be defined by the British Government for that purpose, to be set aside for the growth of trees, to supply building timber and firewood to the inhabitants of the State of Jirang. I will take efficient measures to secure these areas against destruction by fire and jhuming.

Fully understanding the terms of this agreement, I hereby affix my hand and seal this 14th day of May 1883.

His mark X (Sd.) U. Bang
Sirdar, Jirang

Executed before me this day at Shillong by U. Bang,
Sirdar of Jirang

(Sd.) W.S. Clarke,
Deputy Commissioner

The 14th May 1883

36. AGREEMENT WITH THE CHIEF OF MALAI SOHMAT, 1869

I, U. Shongnam Singh, Chief resident of Malai Sohmat, Ellaka Malai Sohmat, having been appointed to the Chiefship of the said Ellaka Malai Sohmat, hereby agree and promise that I will conduct myself agreeably to the following rules :

1. I consider myself under the orders and control of the Deputy Commissioner of the Khasi and Jaintia Hills, and in the event of any disputes arising between myself and the Chief of any other State, they shall be decided by the Deputy Commissioner of the Khasi and Jaintia Hills, or any other duly authorized officer appointed by the Lieutenant-Governor of Bengal.

2. I will adjudicate and decide all civil and all criminal cases not of a heinous kind, which may happen within the limits of my State, and in which the people of my territory alone are concerned; but in the regard to heinous offences I will report the occurrence immediately to the Deputy Commissioner of the Khasi and Jaintia Hills, and will take upon myself the arrest of persons concerned, whom I will deliver up to be dealt with by the Deputy Commissioner or other officer appointed by him for that purpose.

3. In all disputes which may arise with other Khasi Chiefs, and in all cases in which persons of other States, Europeans, or Natives of the plains may be concerned within the limits of my territory, I promise to refer the matter for adjudication by the Deputy Commissioner of the Khasi and Jaintia Hills, or other duly constituted British authority. The authority of the British Government in connection with my Chiefship extends so far that in case of my using any illegality or in the event of my people being dissatisfied with me, Government will be at liberty to remove me from my said rank, and appoint another Chief in my stead.

4. I bind myself to submit to all orders issued by the Deputy Commissioner of the Khasi and Jaintia Hills, or other duly authorized officer, and to make over, on demand, all refugees and civil and political offenders coming to, or residing within, my territory.

5. I also agree to supply any information relative to my

territory and its inhabitants whenever I may be required to do so by the officer of the British Government. I will always use my best endeavours to maintain the well-being of the people residing in my territory. I will give aid and protection with all my right to Government officers and travellers passing through, also to people of other ellakas residing in, my territory. I will also endeavour to facilitate free intercourse and trade between the people of the territory under me and the people of other districts and States.

6. I acknowledge the right of the British Government to establish civil and military sanitaria, cantonments, and posts in any part of my State, and to occupy the lands necessary for the purpose rent-free. I will give Government every assistance which may be required in opening roads within my State.

7. I will implicitly obey all orders issued to me by the Deputy Commissioner of the Khasi and Jaintia Hills, otherwise I agree to suffer fine or such other penalty for my misconduct as the Government may think fit to inflict.

8. I hereby add my agreement to the cession by my predecessors of all the lime, coal, and minerals within my State, as also to the cession, after the expiry of the present lease, of the Sinjara, Cherra and Solai Cherra, lime, quarries, on condition of receiving half the profits arising from their sale, lease, or other disposal; and on the same terms to the cession also of all such waste lands, being lands at the time unoccupied by villages, cultivation, plantation, orchards, etc., as may be required to be sold as waste lands.

Fully understanding the terms of this engagement, I hereby affix my hand and seal this Ist November, 1869.

(Seal)
Seim of Malai Sohmat

Executed before me this 1st November 1869.

(Sd.) R. Stewart,
Deputy Commissioner

SECTION IV

1. AGREEMENT WITH THE SATRAJAHS OF NAREGOON AND TAKHAL TOOROOM

It having been ordered by His Lordship the Governor-General-in-Council that we should be allowed annually one-third of the whole of the proceeds of Koreeahpara Dwar *viz.* 5000 Rupees, we voluntarily pledge ourselves to adhere to the following terms most strictly:

1. We pledge ourselves to be satisfied, now and for ever, with the above mentioned sum of 5000 rupees, and relinquish all right over any proceeds that may accrue from the Dwar.
2. In our traffic we pledge levies to confine our dealings to the established market places at Oodalgooree and Mungledye and never interfere with the ryots, neither will we allow any of our Booteahs to commit any acts of aggression.
3. We have relinquished all power in the Dwar and can no longer levy any rent from the ryots.
4. We agree to apply to the British courts at Mungledye for redress in all our grievances in their territories.
5. Should we ever infringe any of the foregoing terms, we shall forfeit our right to the above pension.

(True translation)

Frans Jenkins
Agent, Governor-General

2. AGREEMENT WITH THE RAJAHS OF BOOTAN

Under the supposition that we are concerned with Niboojoo Rajah Kawree Bhoot, and Bogah Bhoot, in the murder of Muddoo Sykeah, of Osang, in Chardoar and therefore require to give up the above mentioned supposed murderers, which we were unable to do in consequence of which the Dwars were attached and we forbidden to frequent them; and it being now ordered that we be allowed a pension in lieu of Black Mail and may again visit the plains for the purposes of traffic under a Sworn Agreement to ensure the ryots from any oppressions from us: We hereby pledge ourselves to act up to the following terms, swearing according to our customs by placing salt on a daw or Bootan sword and biting it, and cutting the skins of tiger and bear.

1. We pledge ourselves to report our arrival in the plains to the Patgaree, and never to commit any fraud or theft against any ryot or Patgaree in traficking with them or any act of oppression. Neither will we allow any of our people to do so, or we shall forfeit our privilege of visiting the plains.

2. We pledge ourselves never to join any person or persons that may be at enmity with the British Government, and furthermore to oppose any effort made against the Government the instant it shall be brought to our knowledge and report faithfully any intelligence we may get of any conspiracy being carried on. We also pledge ourselves to act up to any orders we may get from the British Authorities. Should it ever be proved that we have joined in any conspiracy, we shall not be allowed to visit the plains.

3. We will never come into the plains armed, and in our traffic, confine ourselves exclusively to the established market places at Lahabarree, Balle, Barah Oobung, and Toopur, and not deal with the ryots in their private houses, neither will we permit any of our people doing so.

4. We consider ourselves in all civil aggrievances bound to abide by the decisions of the British Courts.

5. I Durjee Rajah, am content to receive a monthly pension of 25 rupees and for the rest of any people 20 rupees each, altogether 145 rupees in lieu of our Black Mail, and we relinquish every other right in Chardoar.

6. The moment we hear that any of our people have been guilty of any crime in the plains we engage to give up the offender.

7. We pledge ourselves to act up to the foregoing terms, or forfeit our pension.

(True translation)

Frans Jenkins,
Agent, Governor-General

Increased to Rs. 2,526-7-0 in 1852

3. AGREEMENT WITH THE TAGI RAJAH OF THE AKA PURBAT

Although I entered into an Agreement on the 28th January 1842 A.D., that I should in no way injure the ryots in my dealings with them, and have received from the British Government, since 1842, a Pension of 20 Rupees, and traded in all the villages in Chardoar. It being now considered that my trading in this way is oppressive to the ryots, and therefore required to be discontinued, I bind myself to confine my trade to the established market places at Lahabarree and Baleepara, and to adhere to the following terms:

1. Myself, with my tribe, will confine ourselves in our trade exclusively to the markets in Lahabarree, Baleepara, and Tezpor. We will not, as heretofore, deal with the ryots in their private houses.

2. I will be careful that none of my Tribe commit any act of oppression in the British territories.

3. We will apply to the British Courts for redress in our grievances, and never take the law in our own hands.

4. From the date of this Agreement I bind myself to abide by the foregoing terms, on condition that the following pensions are regularly paid:

To Seemkolee Aka Rajah	....	32 Rupees
To Soomo Rajah	....	32 ,,
To Nesoo Rajah	....	26 ,,
		120 Rupees

5. In the event of my infringing any of the foregoing terms, I subject myself to the loss of my Pension of 20 Rupees, and shall also forfeit the privilege of visiting the Plains.

(True translation)

Frans Jenkins,
Agent, Governor-General

4. AGREEMENT WITH THE HAZAREE KHOWAH AKA CHIEFS

We hereby swear, according to our customs, by taking in our hands the skin of a tiger, that of a bear, and elephant's dung, and by killing a fowl, that we will never be guilty of any violence or oppression towards any of the ryots of the British Government, and that we will faithfully abide by the following terms :

1. Whenever any of us come down into Chardoar, we will report our arrival to the Patgarree, and fairly barter our goods, being guilty of no theft or fraud in any way with any of the ryots.

It shall also be our particular care that none of our people shall be guilty of any crimes in the territories of the Honourable Company.

2. We also engage never to join any parties that are or may hereafter be enemies to the British Government, but pledge ourselves to oppose them in every way in our power. We will also report any intelligence we may get of any conspiracy against the British Government, and act up to any order we may receive from their authorities. Should it ever be proved that we have participated in any conspiracy, we shall have forfeited our privilege of coming into the British territories.

3. In coming into the Plains we will always appear unarmed, and confine ourselves exclusively to the hauts or market-places established at Lahabarree, Baleepara, Oorung or Tezpor, and not, as heretofore, traffic with the ryots at their private dwellings; neither will we allow our people to do so.

4. All civil debts with the ryots shall be recovered through the Courts, as we acknowledge ourselves subservient to the British laws in their country.

5. I, Kapasorah Aka Rajah, agree to take in lieu of the Black-Mail of Chardoar a yearly Pension of 60 Rupees; and I, Hazaree Khowah Aka Rajah, a Pension, in like manner, of 120 Rupees. This will be considered to deprive us of any connection with Chardoar, and of exacting anything from the ryots. We pledge ourselves to abide strictly by the above terms, or forfeit our Pension.

(True translation)

Frans Jenkins,
Agent, Governor-General

5. AGREEMENT WITH THE MEYONG ABORS, 1862

Whereas it is expedient to adopt measures for maintaining the integrity of the British territory in the District of Luckhimpoor, Upper Assam, on the Meyong Abor Frontier, and for preserving peace and tranquility, and whereas by virtue of letter No. 11 of 11th October 1862, from the Officiating Commissioner of Assam, transmitting orders from the Government of Bengal conveyed in a letter No. 265T., dated 8th August 1862, from the Officiating Junior Secretary to the Government of Bengal, the Deputy Commissioner of Luckhimpoor has been authorised to proceed in this matter, an Engagement to the following effect has been entered into with the Meyong Abors this 5th day of November A.D. 1862 at Camp Lallee Mookh :

Article 1

Offences committed by the Meyong Abors in a time of hostility towards the British Government, and for which the assembled heads of villages have sued for pardon, are overlooked and peace is re-established.

Article 2

The limit of the British territory which extends to the foot of the hills is recognized by the Meyong Abors, who hereby engage to respect it.

Article 3

The British Government will take up positions on the frontier in the plains, will establish stations, post guards, or construct forts, or open roads, as may be deemed expedient, and the Meyong Abors will not take umbrage at such arrangements, or have any voice in such matters.

Article 4

The Meyong Abors recognize all persons residing in the plains in the vicinity of the Meyor Hills as British Subjects.

Article 5

The Meyong Abors engage not to molest or to cross the frontier for the purpose of molesting residents in the British territory.

Article 6

The communication across the frontier will be free both for the Meyong Abors and British subjects, going to the Meyong villages for the purpose of trading or other friendly dealings.

Article 7

The Meyong Abors shall have access to markets and places of trade which they may think fit to resort to; and on such occasions they engage not to come armed with their spears and bows and arrows, but merely to carry their daos.

Article 8

Any Meyong Abors desiring to settle in or occupy lands in the British territory engage to pay such revenue to Government as may be fixed upon by the Deputy Commissioner; the demand, in the first instance, to be light.

Article 9

The Meyong Abors engage not to cultivate opium in the British territory or to import it.

Article 10

In event of any grievance arising, or any dispute taking place between the Meyong Abors and the British territory, the Abors will refrain from taking the law into their own hands, but they will appeal to the Deputy Commissioner for redress and abide by his decision.

Article 11

To enable the Meyong Abors of the eight khels or communities, who submit to this engagement, to keep up a Police for preventing any marauders from resorting to the plains for sinister purposes, and to enable them to take measures for arresting any offenders, the Deputy Commissioner, on behalf of the British Government, agrees that the communities referred to shall receive yearly the following articles :

100 Iron hoes (one hundred)
80 Bottles of rum (eighty)
30 Maunds of salt (thirty)
2 seers of Abkaree opium (two)
2 maunds of tobacco (two).

Article 12

The articles referred to above, which will be delivered for the first year on the signing of this engagement, will hereafter be delivered from year to year to the representatives of the eight khels or communities of the Meyong Abors as aforesaid on their meeting the Deputy Commissioner at Lalee Mookh or at any other convenient place on the Meyong Doar side.

Article 13

On the occasion of meeting the Deputy Commissioner, the Meyong Abors in earnest of their continued friendly feeling, engage to make a tribute offering of a mithun, pigs, and fowls, in exchange for which they will obtain usual suitable acknowledgments.

Article 14

In the event of Meyong Abors infringing or failing to act up to any of the provisions of this engagement, it will be considered null and void, and will no longer have effect.

Article 15

The original of the above engagement, which is drawn up in English, will remain with the Deputy Commissioner of Luckhimpoor, Upper Assam, and a counterpart or copy will be furnished to the subscribing Meyong Abors.

Article 16

In ratification of the above engagement contained in fifteen paragraphs, the Deputy Commissioner of Luckhimpoor, Assam, on behalf of the British Government, puts his hand and seal, and recognized headmen or Chiefs of the eight khels or communities of the Meyong Abors affix their signatures or marks, this 5th day of November A.D. 1862.

(Sd.) H.S. Bivar, Major

Seal Deputy Commissioner, Ist Class, Luckhimpoor, and Agent, Governor-General, North-East Frontier

On behalf of the community of Munkoo	Lomiur Gham, his mark	X
	Tankoor ,, ,,	X
	Yabang ,, ,,	X
	Chapeur ,, ,,	X
	Taying ,, ,,	X
On behalf of the community of Ramkong	Pooruding Gham, his mark	X
	Azragi ,, ,,	X
	Kakoh ,, ,,	X
	Koling ,, ,,	X
	Goling ,, ,,	X
	Daling ,, ,,	X
On behalf of the community of Bokoong	Moozung Gham, his mark	X
	Sootam ,, ,,	X
	Gandal ,, ,,	X
	Bidoo ,, ,,	X
	Takoor ,, ,,	X
	Yaleng ,, ,,	X
On behalf of the community of Padamneh	Kerie Gham, his mark	X
	Taddang ,, ,,	X
	Tutto ,, ,,	X
On behalf of the community of Kemi	Tassee Gham, his mark	X
	Somning ,, ,,	X
	Takokh ,, ,,	X
	Taneeh ,, ,,	X
	Takoom ,, ,,	X
	Takor ,, ,,	X
	Loling ,, ,,	X
	Lomeh ,, ,,	X
On behalf of the village of Lekang	Basing Gham, his mark	X
On behalf of the village of Galong	Taming Gham, his mark	X
	Takir ,, ,,	X
	Tussif ,, ,,	X
	Dookang ,, ,,	X
On behalf of the village of Ledom	Looking ,, ,,	X
	Taying ,, ,,	X

6. ENGAGEMENT WITH THE KEBANG ABORS, 1863

Whereas it is expedient to adopt measures for maintaining the integrity of the British Territory in the District of Luckhimpur, Upper Assam, on the Kebang Abor Frontier, and for preserving peace and tranquility; and whereas by virtue of a letter, No. 11 of the 11th October 1862, from the officiating Commissioner of Assam, transmitting orders from the government of Bengal, conveyed in a letter No. 265T, dated the 8th August 1862, from the officiating Junior Secretary to the government of Bengal the Deputy Commissioner of Luckhimpur has been authorised to proceed in this matter, an engagement to the following effect has been entered into with the Kebang Abors, the 26th of January, A.D. 1863, Camp: Lallee Mookh.

1. Offences committed by the Kebang Abors in a time of hostility towards the British government and for which the assembled Heads of villages have sued for pardon are overlooked and peace is re-established.

2. The limit of the British territory, which extends to the fort of the Hills, is recognized by the Kebang Abors, who hereby engage to respect it.

3. The British government will take up positions on the Frontier in the plains, will establish Stations, post Guards, construct Forts or open Roads as may be deemed expedient and the Kebang Abors will not take umbrage at such arrangements, or have any voice in the matter.

4. The Kebang Abors will recognize the persons residing in the plain in the vicinity of Kebang Hills as British subjects.

5. The Kebang Abors, engage not to molest or to cross the Frontier for the purpose of molesting residents in the British territory.

6. The communication across the Frontier will be free both for the Kebang Abors and for any persons, British subjects, going to the Kebang villages for the purpose of trading or other friendly dealings.

7. The Kebang Abors shall have access to markets and places of trade which they may think fit to resort to, and on such occasions they engage not to come armed with their spears and bows and arrows, but merely to carry their daos.

8. Any Kebang Abors desiring to settle in or occupy lands in the British Territory engage to pay such revenue to government as may be fixed upon by the Deputy Commissioner, the demand in the first instance, to be light.

9. The Kebang Abors engage not to cultivate opium in the British Territory or to import it.

10. In the event of any grievances arising, or any dispute taking place between the Kebang Abors and British subjects, the Abors will refrain from taking the law in their own hands, but they will appeal to the Deputy Commissioner for redress and abide by his decision.

11. To enable the Kebang Abors of one Khel or community who submit to this engagement to keep up a police for preventing any marauders from resorting to the plains for sinister purposes, and to enable them to take measures for arresting any offenders, the Deputy Commissioner, on behalf of the British Government, agrees that the communities referred to shall receive yearly the following articles :

Thirty maunds of salt.
Forty bottles of rum.
Four maunds of tobacco. Rs. 28 for tobacco
Twentyeight iron-hoes.
Two seers of opium.

12. The articles referred to above, which will be delivered for the first year on the signing of this engagement, will hereafter be delivered from year to year to ten representatives of the one Khel or community of the Kebang Abors as aforesaid on their meeting the Deputy Commissioner at Lallee Mookh or at any other convenient place on the Kebang Doar side.

13. On this occasion of meeting the Deputy Commissioner the Kebang Abors, in earnest of their continued friendly feeling, engage to make a tribute of a mithun, pigs, and fowls, in exchange for which they will obtain usual suitable acknowledgments.

14. In the event of Kebang Abors infringing or failing to act upto any of the provisions of this engagement it will be considered null and void and will no longer have effect.

15. The original of this engagement, which is drawn up in English, will remain with the Deputy Commissioner of

Luckhimpur, Assam and a counterpart or copy will be furnished to the subscribing Kebang Abors.

16. In ratification of the above engagement contained in fffteen paragraphs, the Deputy Commissioner of Luckhimpur, Upper Assam, on behalf of the British Government, puts up his hand and seal and the recognized Headmen or Chiefs of the one Khel or community of the Kebang Abors affix their signature or marks the 16th day of January in A.D 1863.

On behalf of the Community of Kebang Taking Gam
Taing ,,
Kebatain Gam
Kesa
Takeer
Feture

Sd/-A.K. Comber
Deputy Commissioner of Luckhimpur

7. AGREEMENT WITH THE DEHANG DEBANG ABORS DOARS, 1862

Whereas, with a view to maintain the integrity of the British territory and to preserve peace and tranquility in the district of Luckhimpoor, Upper Assam, in the frontier bordering on the "Padoo", the "Meyboh", the "Silookh", the "Bompon", and the "Bor Abor" Hills, it is expedient to adopt certain measures, and whereas that the policy enjoined under a letter from the Officiating Commissioner of Assam, No. 11, of the 11th October, conveying the orders of the Government of Bengal in a letter No. 265T., dated 8th August 1862, might with advantage be adopted towards the Abor clans aforesaid, pursuant thereto, at a meeting between the representatives of the Abor communities named, and the Deputy Commissioner of Luckhimpoor, Upper Assam, at Camp Dihang, Dibang Mookh, on the 8th day of November A.D. 1862, the following engagement was entered into :

Article 1

The British territory which extends to the foot of the hills will be respected by the Abors of the communities named in the preamble.

Article 2

The Abors hereby recognize all persons residing in the plains to be British subjects.

Article 3

The Abors engage to take measures for preventing any parties from amongst their clansmen from molesting residents in the British territory.

Article 4

The British Government may take up positions in the frontier, in the plains, may establish stations, post guards, or construct forts, or open roads, as may be deemed expedient, and the Abors will not take umbrage at such arrangements or have any voice in such matters.

Article 5

The communication across the frontier will be free for the Abors and for residents in the British territory going to the Abor villages for the purpose of trade or other friendly objects.

Article 6

The Abors shall have access, as heretofore, to markets and places of trade in the British territory they may think fit to resort to; but when trading, they, the Abors, engage not to come armed with their spears, bows, and arrows, but merely to carry their daos.

Article 7

Any Abors settling or occupying lands in the British territory engage to pay such revenue to Government as may be fixed upon the demand, in the first instance to be light.

Article 8

The Abors engage not to cultivate opium in the British territory or to import it.

Article 9

In event of the Abors having any grievance, or in case of any dispute arising between them and the British subjects, the

Abors will refrain from taking the law into their own hands; but they will in all cases appeal to the Deputy Commissioner and abide by his decision.

Article 10

To enable the Abors of the clans or communities mentioned in the preamble to keep a Police for preventing any marauders from resorting to the plains for sinister purposes, and to enable them to take measures for arresting any offenders, the Deputy Commissioner, on behalf of the British Government, undertakes that the Abor communities referred to shall receive yearly the following articles :—

One hundred iron hoes,
Forty maunds of salt,
One hundred bottles of rum,
Two maunds of tobacco.

Article 11

The articles referred to above, which will be delivered for the first year on the signing of this Engagement, will hereafter be delivered from year to year to the representatives of the communities or clans named in the preamble.

Article 12

On the occasion of the yearly meeting of the Deputy Commissioner and the Abors, the usual exchange of offerings and presents will take place.

Article 13

In event of the Abors failing to act up to the provisions of this Engagement it will be null and void.

Article 14

The original of this Engagement, which is drawn up in English, will remain with the Deputy Commissioner of Luckhimpoor, Upper Assam, and a counterpart or copy will be furnished to the representatives of the Abor communities aforesaid.

Article 15

In ratification of the above Engagement contained in fourteen paragraphs, the Deputy Commissioner of Luckhimpoor,

Upper Assam, puts his hand and seal, and the representatives of the Abor communities affix their marks or signatures, this eighth day of November 1862.

(Sd.) H.S. Bivar,
Deputy Commissioner

On behalf of Meyvoh	... Popang Gham, his mark +
On behalf of Padoo	... Toomkur ,, ,, +
On behalf of Silookh	... Moskokh ,, ,, +
On behalf of Bomjeon	... Joloong ,, ,, +
On behalf of the Bor Abors	... Junbang ,, ,, +
On behalf of the Bor Silookh Abors	Karmood, son of Onoo Gham, his mark +
On behalf of Toomkoo Padoo Abors	Meyong Gham, his mark +

8. AGREEMENT WITH THE BOR ABORS, 1866

1. We, the representatives of the 12 Bor Abor tribes, who have not as yet entered into any Agreement with the British Government, do hereby express our desire to enter into the same compact as that agreed upon between the other Abor tribes and the Deputy Commissioner of Luckhimpoor.

2. We agree to abide by the provisions of the Abor Treaties of 1862-63, on condition that we receive from Government yearly to defray our expenses, by preserving the tranquility of our frontier, the following articles: Salt, (60) sixty maunds; iron hoes (120) one hundred and twenty; rum (100) one hundred bottles; tobacco (3) three maunds; opium (2) two seers.

3. Should we at any time transgress the provisions of the above Treaties, the same to be null and void.

4. In ratification of this Agreement we hereto affix our signatures or marks.

For Lalam Gam	+	his mark
Soosoo Gam	+	-do-
Ikirug Gam	+	-do-
Moohing Gam	+	-do-
Liloot Gam	+	-do-

Linkong Gam	+	his mark
Loothing Gam	+	-do-
Maling Gam	+	-do-
Likoh Gam	+	-do-
Tinteh Gam	+	-do-
Tinkoh Gam	+	-do-
Linkoh Gam	+	-do-
Boomoot Gam	+	-do-
Koonang Gam	+	-do-

Before me, this fifth day of April, one thousand eight hundred and sixty-six.

(Sd.) W.W. Hume, Lieut.,
District Superintendent of Police
Luckhimpoor

9. KUBOOLYUT OF SUDDEYA KHOWAH GOHAIN, 1826

Salan Suddeya Khowah Gohain makes the following Agreement : I am made Khowah Huddah of Suddeya for the purpose that I perform all the duties of the Company, and which I agree by this writing to do. The 12 Sirings under me have 43 Gotes of 3 Pykes, and of Khamptees there are 40 and 1 Poa, and of Dooms there are 12 Gotes, 1 Poa—total 95 Gotes, 2 Poa. Of these the Siring Burrooah has 1 Gote 1 Poa and 8 Gotes of Siksoos, and my own are 10 Gotes with 1 Poa for Runnut Mura. Also the Bura of Khamptees and Dooms has 4 Gotes—remaining 72 Gotes. Of these 40 are fighting men, and 20 working men, and 12 fishermen : these shall be forthcoming according to the customs of the country by Mal, Dewal, Teeal; and I will do justice to the people under me, but in cases on murder, the papers, witnesses, and offenders shall be sent to the Huzoor, and I will be always ready to obey the orders of the Huzoor, and what russud shall be given on payment. This paper is written before every one.

(Sd.) Salan Suddeya Khowah

Witnesses:
Kagessur, Duftry
Sundee Sing, Chupprassee

Signed with Mr. Scott's initials

*15*th May *1826*

10. AGREEMENT WITH THE KHAMPTI CHIEFS, 1843

We, late inhabitants of Derack and Suddeya, were engaged in the attack upon the latter place, and fled to the Mishmee country; we have offered our submission to return back, if our former offences were overlooked, and now we have returned agreeably to the orders of the Political Agent, with our followers, *viz*., Chowdung, Chawding, Long Fong, Poychoy, Chalan, Sham, Poom, Metong, and Chowlah, but the whole of the Khamptees are unable to return for the present, owing to their crops being uncut. However, they hereby promise to come in with all their families after their crops have been gathered, or within a month and half from this date.

1. We shall be allowed a sufficient quantity of lands for our support, either at Choonpoora or at Noa Dehing, for a term of five years rent-free, and after the expiration of that period we agree to pay a moderate rent for the lands we may cultivate, or pay a house-tax, as Government may choose to authorize. Any orders that may be issued respecting the Abkarry shall be duly attended to.

2. We engage also to endeavour to prevent or intercept any inroads of the Singhphoos or Mishmees on the Suddeya ryot, and shall obey all orders of the Civil or Political authorities on the frontier.

3. We further engage that we shall desist from trafficking in slaves according to the regulations of Government generally.

4. All petty crimes and offences occurring amongst ourselves shall be settled by the Chiefs of the villages, but in all heinous offences, such as robbery, murder, dacoity, wounding, and counterfeiting the coin, we promise to make over the offenders to the Political Agent, with their respective witnesses for trial; and disputes between the heads of the different villages or clans shall also be referred to the same authority.

5. At the expiration of ten years the whole of our engagements will be subject to a revision and alteration, as it may seem best to His Lordship to determine on.

6. Should we or any of the Khamptees in any way depart from the faithful adherence of the above Agreement, and commit any acts of violence, we shall be subject to be driven

out of the province, and be without further excuse.

(True translation)

Frans Jenkins,
Agent, Governor-General

11. AGREEMENT WITH THE SINGPHOE CHIEFS, 1826

Whereas we, the Singphoe Chiefs, named Bum, Koomjoy, Meejong, Jow, Chowkhen, Jowrah, Jowdoo, Chow, Chumin, Neengun, Tangrung, Chowbah, Chamuta, Chowrah, Chowdoo, Choukam, Koomring, etc., are under the subjection of the British Government, we execute this Agreement to Mr. David Scott, the Agent to the Governor-General, and hereby engage to adhere to the following terms, *viz.* :

1. Assam being now under the sway of the British Government, we and our dependent Singphoes, who were subjects of the Assam State, acknowledge subjection to that Government. We agree not to side with the Burmese or any other King to commit any aggression whatever, but we will obey the orders of the British Government.

2. Whenever a British Force may march to Assam to protect it from foreign aggression, we will supply that Force with grain, etc., make the repair roads for them, and execute every order that may be issued to us. We should on our doing so be protected by that Force.

3. If we abide by the terms of this Agreement, no tribute shall be paid by us; but if any Assam Paeeks of their own accord reside in our villages, the tax on such Paeeks will be paid to the British Government.

4. We will set at large or cause to be liberated any Assam people whom we may seize, and they shall have the option to reside wherever they please.

5. If any of the Singphoes rob any of the Assam people residing in our country, we will apprehend the former and surrender him to the British Government; but if we fail to do so, we will make good the loss thus sustained by the latter.

6. We will govern and protect the Singphoes under us as heretofore and adjust their differences; and if any boundary dispute occur among us, we will not take up arms without the knowledge of the British Government.

7. We will adhere to the terms of this Agreement and never depart from them. This Agreement shall be binding upon our brothers, sons, nephews, and relatives, in such way as the Agent to the Governor-General may deem proper. We have executed this Agreement in the presence of many.

Written at Saddeya on Friday, the 5th May 1826, or Sukabda 1748, or 24th Bysakh 1233 B.S.

Names of Singphoe Chiefs who have signed the Agreement:

Chowtow	Cowkhen
Topomka	Chowrah
Towallah	Sowdoo
Hokap	Chow
Chowcha	Chanlong
Insala	Ningon
Donphoomla	Tunrong
Ahringla	Chowun
Katanchawpha	Samtang
Tangsung Zung	Chowra
Dothemjowphea	Chowdoo
Latham Thoyrung	Chowkam
Chekangla	Sowrno
Singnien	Seerola San
Moonlankoo	Panjow
Beesa Bum	Latxejabong
Koomjoy	Pooingnong
Meejong	Oraon

PART II

INTRODUCTION

I

The North-East Frontier as distinct from Assam began to emerge when in 1875-76 the Inner Line of Lakhimpur and Darrang districts was specified applying Regulation II of 1873 (Section V, No. 1). The Inner Line separated some tracts inhabited by tribal people from the districts of Assam Administration and journey beyond the Inner Line was restricted. It was found inconvenient to administer these tracts inhabited by unsophisticated tribes by applying Regulations and Acts prevailing in the Assam plains. The Scheduled Districts Act passed in 1876 (Section V, No.2) authorised the Government to administer these tracts inhabited by tribal people in a rude and rough manner by issuing Regulations. Therefore in 1880 under the authority of the Scheduled District Act of 1874, the Assam Frontier Tract Regulation was passed (Section V, No.3). This Regulation authorised the Chief Commissioner of Assam, with the prior consent of the Governor-General, to prohibit or permit the operation of any law or part thereof passed by the Government of India and to propose Rules for the administration of the Frontier Tracts which, when approved by the Governor-General-in-Council would have the force of law. In 1886 under the authority of the Scheduled District Act, 1874, the Chief Commissioner of Assam passed Rules for the administration of justice in the Lakhimpur Frontier Tract (Section V, No. 4).

The Rules for the administration of justice laid the foundation of administration of the Frontier Tracts of Assam. These were promulgated in 1914 in all three sections in which the Assam Frontier Tracts were then divided. In the Deputy Commissioner or his Assistant was vested the power to create local authorities and to entrust to them the functions of plain and petty criminal and civil justice. The Deputy Commissioners and their Assistants were both magistrates and judges in the Frontier Tracts to whom lay appeal from the local authorities. The Chief Commissioner of Assam was the highest court of justice in the

Frontier Tracts and the High Court of Calcutta did not have jurisdiction over them. No professional lawyers were allowed to counsel the contesting parties in the Frontier Tracts. In 1914, when Political Officers were appointed, the Deputy Commissioners did not have any jurisdiction in the Frontier Tracts except the Deputy Commissioner of Lakhimpur to whom the Lakhimpur Frontier Tract was committed for administration.

In 1920, when the Government of India Act, 1915, as amended in 1919 (Section V, No. 5) was promulgated, the North-East Frontier was put under the charge of the Governor of Assam, as distinct from the Government of Assam, as deputy of the Governor-General of India. The Government of India Act, 1935 (Section V, No. 6) kept the position almost the same. An Order in Council by His Majesty the King of England (Section V, No. 7) vested the administration of the Frontier in the Governor of Assam.

Indian provisional constitutional order vested the administration of Frontiers in the Government of Assam (Section V. No. 8).

The Constitution of India (Section V, No. 9) put the administration of the Frontier in charge of the President of India who delegated to the Governor of Assam his responsibility in this respest. Representation of NEFA was provided by an Act in 1950 (Section V, No. 10). The administration continued to be carried on by the Political Officers and their Assistants. In 1954 (Section V, No. 11) the Frontier Tracts were named Divisions, and administration of Frontiers was named North East Frontier Agency (NEFA). But in 1965 these Divisions were termed Districts and Political Officers were designated as Deputy Commissioner as in the province of Assam (Section V, No. 12).

In 1969 Panchayat Raj Regulation of 1967 (Section V. No. 13) was promulgated to introduce the same pattern of Local Self-Government as existed in other parts of India. First there is an Anchal Samiti consisting of the members of the Gram Panchayats, representatives of the co-operative societies and nominated members in each bloc which is coterminous with the Community Development Bloc. Next there is the Zilla Parishad over every district consisting of the representatives of the Anchal Samitis, and members nominated by the Deputy Commissioner of the district. At the top over the entire territory of the present Arunachal Pradesh there is the Pradesh Council consisting of the representatives of the Zilla Parishads and such other members of the Pradesh as may be nominated by the Chief Commissioner. While the first two have administrative and supervisory powers the last has only supervisory and advisory powers.

The crude Frontier Tracts which emerged in 1875-76 as a result of the application of Regulation 3 of 1873 gradually developed over a century into an Administration and in 1973 it became a Union Territory of the Republic of India.

II

Till August 1947, when India became independent, Assam consisted of six Brahmaputra valley districts, of Goalpara, Kamrup, Nowgong, Darrang, Sibsagar and Lakhimpur, the two Surma valley districts of Sylhet and Cachar, the four hill districts of Garo Hills, Khasi and Jaintia Hills, Naga Hills and Lushai Hills, and the North-East Frontier Tracts. But then the administration of the Hill Districts and the North-East Frontier was a responsibility of the Governor of Assam and the Indian Ministers had no jurisdiction except over some subjects in the Hill Districts. The Indian Constitution Order of 1947, after Independence, placed all these areas under the direct charge of the Government of Assam, instead of the Governor of Assam, who had held special responsibility till Independence. But the Constituent Assembly, as recommended by the Bordoloi Committee, again made special provision in the Indian Constitution for the administration of the Frontier Tracts and the Hill Districts of Assam. Therefore in 1950, when the Indian Constitution came into force, the Hill Districts and the Frontier Tracts were again placed under the Governor of Assam, as the deputy of the President of India ; the Government of Assam was given no jurisdiction over the Frontier Tracts and over the Hill Districts. The Government had power only over those subjects, which had been given to it by the Sixth Schedule of Constitution (Section VI, No. 1).

The Sixth Schedule of the Constitution provided autonomy for the tribes in tribal matters and in matters of purely local interest. The Bordoloi Committee envisaged gradual development of the Hill Areas and integration of these areas into Assam by stages.

But with the development of education in the Hill Areas the tribes became conscious of their ethnic and linguistic separateness from the people of Assam. Fear of being exploited, together with the apprehension of losing their language, made these tribes restive. In the Naga Hills the tribes were already fighting for complete independence from India in fear of being dominated by the neighbouring people. They set up a parallel underground Government and demanded loyalty and revenue from the Nagas. Regular guerilla warfare was carried on by them against the Indian Government and only a separate State within the Indian Union reconciled the moderate among them in 1963. By an Act of the Indian Parliament (Section VI, No. 2) in 1963 Naga Hills were constituted into a separate State named Nagaland to which had already been transferred the Tuensang Division of the North-East Frontier Agency.

The movement of the Hill Tribes in the Hill Districts continued unabated. The language disturbances of 1960 in Assam and the creation of Nagaland spurred the leaders of the Hill State movement. In the Khasi-Jaintia and Garo Hills they launched a peaceful movement for a separate state. The Government of India appointed a Commission to investigate and report on the issue. The Hill leaders accepted as a compromise the recommendation of the Pataskar Commission. An Autonomous Hill State, as a temporary expedient, was created in 1969 (Section VI, No. 3). In 1970 again the movement for a full-fledged and separate state began to gain momentum and the Government of India took the decisive step of reorganising the North-Eastern region (Section VI, No. 4). By an Act Meghalaya, Tripura and Manipur were made full-fledged states of the Indian Union (Section VI, No.5).

But meanwhile there developed another major disturbance in the Lushai Hills. In 1971 the Mizo National Front, a nationalist organisation of the Lushais, tried to constitute the Mizo Hills into a separate state like the rebel Nagas. The rising was quickly suppressed by the Indian Government ; but it realised the necessity of quick and planned development of the border hills and stable and efficient administration in the region. Therefore in December 1971 Parliament passed amendments to the Constitution and also an Act by which Mizo Hills and the North-East Frontier Agency were constituted into two

Union Territories (Section VI, No.6), to be known as Mizoram and Arunachal Pradesh respectively.

In the Hill Districts of Assam and Manipur the people possess democratic traditions and experience ; in the Hill Districts the tribes successfully conducted the business of the District Councils ; in Manipur the people had run the administration creditably. It is expected that the attainment of statehood by Manipur has fulfilled the aspirations of the people of Manipur and in the state of Meghalaya the tribes would prove capable of running democratic institutions. In the newly created state of Manipur and in Mizoram there are some minor tribes who require special consideration and safeguards to speed up their development. Autonomous Regions and District Councils have been provided for them (Section VI, No. 8). By an Act of Parliament the hill areas of Manipur have been divided into six districts for each of which a District Council would be constituted. In Mizoram likewise Autonomous Regions for each tribe would be constituted.

The break-up of the former political set-up in this region would naturally generate some difficulties ; the entire region was politically, economically and culturally interwoven into a single structure. The smooth development of the region, which is geographically a unit with similar characteristics, requires joint planning and united efforts on part of the present constituents. To provide a framework for the purpose an organisation known as the North-Eastern Council (Section VI, No. 7) has been provided by Parliament. The Council has been authorised to draw up proposals for joint development in matters of common interest to the members of the Council and to seek the financial assistance of the Union Government. The Council would make arrangements for the sharing of the benefits of the joint ventures and may recommend to members the measures necessary for the security and public order in the region.

Thus the North-Eastern Region which was practically under the Government of Assam till 1947 gradually disintegrated and formed a unique mosaic. The North-Eastern Council perhaps holds out the prospect of reunification of the region when the present constituents of the Council, fully developed, would come forward for coalition on the basis of equal status and identity of interests.

SECTION V

1. INNER LINE REGULATION, 1873

Whereas the Secretary of the State for India in Council has by resolution in Council declared the Provisions of Act XXXIII Vic. Cap. 3 Section, to be applicable to the districts of Kamrup, Darrang, Nowgong, Sibsagar, Lakhimpur, Garo Hills, Khasi & Jaintia Hills, Naga Hills, Cachar and Cheettagong Hills.

And whereas the Lt. Governor of Bengal has proposed to the Governor-General in Council a draft of the following Regulation, together with the reasons for proposing the same, for the peace and good government of the said districts.

And whereas the Governor-General-in-Council has taken such draft and reasons into consideration and has approved of such draft and the same has received the Governor General's assent.

The following Regulation is now published in the Gazetteer of India and will be published in the Calcutta Gazette and thereupon will have the force of law under their by third of Victoria. Chapter III.

1. This Regulation shall extend to the districts named in the preamble, and shall come into force on the 1st of November 1873.

2. It shall be lawful for the local Government of Bengal with the previous sanction of the Governor-General-in-Council to prescribe, and from time to time after by notification in the Calcutta Gazette, a line to be called "The Inner Line" in each or any of the above named districts. The Local Government by notification in the Calcutta Gazette, prohibit all British subjects, or any class of British subjects, or any persons, sending in or passing through, such districts, from going beyond such line without a pass under the hand and seal of the executive officer to such district of such officer as he may authorise to grant such pass; and the Local Government may from time to time cancel or vary such prohibition.

3. Any British subject or other person so prohibited who goes beyond 'the Inner Line' fixed in accordance with section 2 of the Regulation after its notification in the Calcutta Gazette, without a pass shall be liable, on conviction before a Magistrate to a fine not exceeding Rs. 100/- for the first offence, and to a fine of not exceeding Rs. 500/- or to simple or rigorous imprisonment for a term of not exceeding three months, or to both for each subsequent offence.

4. The Local Government may from time to time, prescribe, by notification in the Calcutta Gazette, a form of pass for each district, and may in such form of pass fix such restrictions or conditions a Local Government may deem fit, and may require the payment of such dues and fees for such passes as to the Local Government may seem proper. Any holder of such pass shall on breach of any such restriction or condition be liable on conviction to a fine not exceeding Rs. 100 for a first offence and to a fine not exceeding Rs. 500, or to simple or rigorous imprisonment which may extend to seven months, or to both, for each subsequent offence.

5. Any rubber, wax, ivory, or other jungle product found in possession of any person convicted of an offence under this Regulation may be confiscated to the Government by an order to be passed at the time of conviction by the Magistrate.

6. The chief executive officer of any district comprised in any notification as aforesaid may subject to the approval of the Local Government authorise, by a written instrument under his hand, any public servant to arrest and bring before him with the least practicable delay.

Firstly—Any person prohibited from crossing the Inner Line prescribed for such district if such person, shall be found beyond the line and when asked to produce his pass shall refuse or be unable to do so.

Secondly—Any person to whom a pass may have been granted, and who has committed any infraction of its conditions.

7. It shall not be lawful for any British subject, or other persons not being native of the district comprised in the preamble of this Regulation to acquire any interest in the land or the product of land beyond the said Inner Line without the sanction of the Local Government as such officer as the Local Government shall appoint in this behalf. Any interest so acquired

may be dealt with as the Local Government or if said officer shall direct. The Local Government may also by notification, in the Local Gazette, extend the prohibition contained in this section to any class of persons natives of the said districts, and may from time to time in like manner cancel or vary such extension.

8. Whenever, without the written permission of the officer authorised by the Local Government to grant such permission will or captures or attempts to kill or capture, or abets the killing or capturing of, a wild elephant in any of the districts to which this Regulation extends, shall be liable to a fine not exceeding Rs. 200 for each elephant so killed or captured, and any elephant so killed or captured shall be confiscated to Government provided that no person who kills or abets the killing of, an elephant in protection of himself, his houses or his crops shall be liable to punishment; and provided also that every person who in the like case captures, or abets the capture of an elephant shall not be liable to fine, but shall be bound to surrender such captured elephant to the Government, or to pay such royalty thereon as the Local Government, may from time to time direct.

9. It shall be competent for the Local Government to make rules for the issue of licences to kill or capture elephant, and for all purposes connected with the capture of elephants.

10. The prosecution for every offence punishable under section 8 of the Regulation shall be commenced within 6 months after the offence is committed.

11. Offences against this Regulation may be tried by Magistrates of the first or second class and shall be bailable.

2. THE SCHEDULED DISTRICTS ACT, 1874

An Act to ascertain the enactments in force in various parts of British India, and for other purposes.

Whereas various parts of British India have never been brought within, or have from time to time been removed from, the operation of the general Acts and Regulations and the jurisdiction of the ordinary Courts of Judicature;

And whereas doubts have arisen in some cases as to which Acts or Regulations are in force in such parts and in other cases as to what are the boundaries of such parts; And whereas among such parts are the territories specified in the first schedule hereto annexed, and it is expedient to provide readier means than now exist for ascertaining the enactments in force in such territories and the boundaries thereof, and for administering the law therein;

And whereas it is expedient to declare that certain Acts are in force in a tract of land lying between the Railway Station at Satna and the eastern boundary of the Jabalpur Division;

(It is hereby enacted as follows):

Short Title—(1) This Act may be called the Scheduled Districts Act, 1874.

This Act extends in the first instance to the whole of British India other than the territories mentioned in the first schedule hereto annexed, and it shall come into force in each of the Scheduled Districts on the issue of a notification under section 3 relating to such district.

1. In this Act the term "Scheduled Districts" means the territories mentioned in the first schedule hereto annexed; and from the date fixed in the resolution next hereinafter mentioned, it shall also include any other territory to which the Secretary of State for India, by resoultion in Council may declare the provisions of the 33rd of Victoria, chapter 3, section I, to be applicable.

2. *Repeal of Enactments*—The enactments mentioned in the second schedule hereto annexed shall be repealed.

3. *Notification of Enactments in force in Scheduled Districts*—The Local Government . . . . . . may, from time to time, by notification . . . . . . in the local Gazette . . . . . .

(a) declare what enactments are actually in force in any of the Scheduled Districts, or in any part of any such district,

(b) declare of any enactment that it is not actually in force in any of the districts or in any part of any such district,

(c) correct any mistake of fact in any notification issued under this section.

Provided that a declaration once made under clause (a) or clause (b) of this section shall not be altered by any subsequent declaration other than a declaration under clause (c) of this section.

4. *Effect of Notification under Section 3.*—On the issue, under section 3, of a notification declaring what enactments are in force, or not in force in any Scheduled District, the enactments so notified shall be deemed to be in force or not in force, according to the tenor of the notification, in such district, and every such notification shall be binding on all courts of law.

5. *Power to extend Enactments to Scheduled District.*—The Local Government . . . . . . may, from time to time, by notification . . . . . . in the local Gazette . . . . . . extend to any of the Scheduled Districts or to any part of any such district, any enactment which is in force in any part of British India at the date of such extension.

5A. *Modification of Enactments in their application to Scheduled District.*—In declaring an enactment in force in a Scheduled District or part thereof under section 3 of this Act, or in extending an enactment to a Scheduled District or part thereof under Section 5 of this Act, the Local Government . . . . . . may declare the operation of the enactment to be subject to such restrictions and modifications as that Government thinks fit.

6. *Appointment of Officers and Regulation of their Procedure:* The Local Government may from time to time:

(a) appoint officers to administer civil and criminal justice and to suprintend the settlement and collection of the public revenue, and all matters relating to rent and otherwise to conduct the administration, within the Scheduled District;

(b) regulate the procedure of the officers so appointed; but not so as to restrict the operation of any enactment for the time being in force in any of the said districts;

(c) direct by what authority any jurisdiction, powers or duties incident to the operation of any enactment for the time being in force in such district shall be exercised or performed.

7. *Continuance of existing Rules and Officers.*—All rules heretofore prescribed by the Governor-General-in-Council or the Local Government for the guidance of officers appointed within

any of the Scheduled Districts for all or any of the purposes mentioned in section 6, and in force at the time of the passing of this Act, shall continue to be in force unless and until the Governor-General-in-Council or the Local Government, as the case may be, otherwise directs.

All existing officers so appointed previous to the date on which this Act comes into force in such districts shall be deemed to have been appointed hereunder.

8. *Settlement of Questions as to Boundary.*—Whenever any question arises as to the line of boundary between any of the Scheduled Districts and other territory such officer as the Local Government or (where the said district and the the other territory are not subject to the same Local Government) as the Governor-General-in-Council from time to time appoints, may consider and determine such line of boundary; and the order made thereon by such officer, if confirmed by the Government which appointed him, shall be conclusive in all Courts of Justice.

9. *Place of Imprisonment or Transportation.*—Any person liable to be imprisoned or to be transported beyond sea under any order or sentence passed by any officer appointed under section 6 may (subject to such rules as the Local Government may from time to time prescribe in this behalf) be imprisoned in such jail or transported to such place as the Local Government directs.

10. *Extension to Satna strip of Acts relating to Public Gambling and Salt.*—Acts No. III of 1867, . . . and No. XXV of 1869 are hereby declared to be in force in the tract of land ceded to the British Government in the year 1863 and lying between the Railway Station at Satna and the eastern boundary of the Jabalpur District.

11. *Saving of Criminal Jurisdiction over European British Subjects, and savings of other Laws.*—Nothing contained in this Act or in any notifications issued under the power hereby conferred shall be deemed;

(a) to affect the criminal jurisdiction of any Court over European British subjects, or

(b) to affect any law other than laws contained in Acts or Regulations or in Rules made in exercise of powers conferred by such Acts or Regulations.

THE FIRST SCHEDULE

(See Section 1)

Part I

Scheduled Districts, 5 Madras

1—In Ganjam

Part X

The Chief Commissionership of Assam

The Second Schedule

(See Section 2)

Number and year	Title
3 * * *	
4 XXXVII of 1855	An Act to remove from the operation of the General Laws and Regulations certain districts inhabited by Santhals and others, and to place the same under the superintendence of an officer to be specially appointed for that purpose.

Scheduled Districts (1874: Act XIV)

Presidency or Province	Scheduled Districts	No. and date of Notification	Gazette in which the Notification is published
Assam	The Chief Commissionership of Assam	1651, dated 3rd November, 1877 dated 7th Nov., 1877	India 1877 pt. I p. 662 Assam, 1877 pt. I. p. 383
	The Lushai Hills (formerly known as the North and South Lushai Hills) and Rutton Puiya's villages, including Demagiri, in the Chittagong Hills Tracts	921 p., dated 1st April 1898	India, 1898 pt. II, p. 345 Assam, 1898 pt. I, p. 379

APPENDIX B

Territories which have become Scheduled Districts by virtue of the concluding portion of the third paragraph of section 1 of the Scheduled Districts Act, 1874 namely, those to which the Secretary of State for India has, by resolution in Council, declared the provisions of the Government of India Act, 1870 (33 Vict., c. 3) section 1, to be applicable.

Presidency or Province	Territories	Date from which Resolution took effect	Gazette of India in which the Resolution is published
Assam	The North Lushai Hills The South Lushai Hills	6th September, 1895	1895, Pt. I, p. 935

3. THE ASSAM FRONTIER TRACTS REGULATION, 1880[1]

Whereas it is expedient to provide for the removal of certain frontier tracts in Assam inhabited or frequented by barbarous or semi-civilized tribes from the operation of enactments in force therein; It is hereby enacted as follows :

1. *Local extent.*—This Regulation extends to such frontier tract in Assam as the Governor-General-in-Council may, by notification, direct (see s. I) and may similarly be extended by him to the Garo Hills District, the Khasi and Jaintia Hills District and any portion of the Nowgong District (see Reg. III of 1884 s. I post).

The Regulation has been extended by such notifications to the districts of the Garo Hills, the Khasi and Jaintia Hills and the Lushai Hills (including the areas transferred from the Cachar District in 1904), the Mikir Hills Tract (in the Nowgong District), the North Cachar Hills, the Sadiya, Balipara and Lakhimpur Frontier Tracts, the area added to the Lakhimpur Frontier Tract by Notification No. 2847-A.P. dated 12th August 1929, the Naga Hills District, the Melomi Primi area added to the Naga Hills District, by Notification No. 6492-A.P., dated 23rd November 1927, the area transferred to the Balipara Frontier Tract by Notification No. 1470-A.P., dated 26th February 1931, see Vol. III Appendix II Table C.

The Regulation has (with the exception of the second and third paragraphs of section 1, the words "in manner hereinbefore prescribed" in section 2, and the words "as aforesaid" in section 3) been extended to the Mokokchang Sub-division (including the area added to it by Notification No. 68-P, dated 1st February 1910) of the Naga Hills District by Notification under the Scheduled District Act, 1874 (XIV of 1874).

1. *Short Title and Commencement*—This regulation may be called the Assam Frontier Tracts Regulation, 1880.

It extends to such frontier tracts within the territories (for the time being)[2] administered by the Chief Commissioner of Assam (as he)[3] may, by notification in the (local Gazette)[4] from time to time direct.

It shall come into force in each of such tracts on such day as (he) in like manners directs in this behalf.

[5]2. *Power to direct that enactments shall cease to be in force*—Wh n this Regulation has been extended in manner here-inbefore prescribed to any tract, the Chief Commissioner may from time to time[6] . . . . by notification in the local Gazette, direct that any enactment in force in such tract shall cease to be in force therein,[7] but not so as to affect the criminal jurisdiction of any Court over European British Subjects.

3. *Settlement of Question as to Boundary*—Whenever any question arises as to the line of boundary between any tract to which the provisions of this Regulation have been extended as aforesaid and the adjoining territory in British India, such officer as the Chief Commissioner of Assam from time to time appoints may consider and determine such line of boundary;

2. The words in brackets were inserted by Assam Frontier Tracts Regulation (1880) Amendment Regulation, 1898 (II of 1898).

3. Substituted for the words "the Governor-General in Council by section 2 of the Devolution Act XXXVIII of 1920.

4. Substituted for the words "Gazette of India" by Act XXXVIII of 1920.

5. The concluding paragraph of s. 1 which was repealed by the Assam Frontier Tracts Regulation (1880) Amendment Regulation, 1898 (II of 1898 s. 2 (2) is omitted. It ran thus :

"Every notification extending this Regulation to any tract shall specify the boundaries by which such tract is separated from the adjoining territory in British India".

6. The words "with the previous sanction of the Governor-General-in-Council" were omitted by Act XXXVIII of 1920.

7. For a list of enactments which have been barred in areas to which this Regulation extends, see Manual of Local Rules and Orders in force in Assam see Vol. III, Appendix II, Table C.

For reference to rules under the Scheduled Districts Act, 1874 (XIV of 1874) for the administration of the said areas and of the Eastern Duars in the Goalpara district, Manual of Local Rules and Orders in force in Assam see Vol. III. Appendix I, Table 1.

and the order made thereon by such officer, if confirmed by the said Chief Commissioner, shall be conclusive.

4. RULES FOR THE ADMINISTRATION OF JUSTICE IN THE DIBRUGARH FRONTIER TRACT, 1886

(Amended up to 1913)

I. General

1. The administration of the Dibrugarh Frontier Tract is vested in the Chief Commissioner of Assam, the Political Officer, Central and Eastern Sections, North-East Frontier, his Assistants, and the native village authorities, or such other officer or officers as the Chief Commissioner may see fit from time to time to appoint in that behalf, subject to the restrictions and rules hereinafter recorded.

2. The Political Officer shall nominate and appoint the village authorities, if any, subject to the confirmation of the Chief Commissioner, and shall assign to them their respective functions under these rules, and define, so far as may be necessary the local limits within which such duties shall be exercised by each, respectively, and may cancel or modify any such order. When no village authorities have been so nominated and appointed, the powers and duties assigned to them by these rules shall be exercised and performed by the Political Officer or by such other officers as he may depute for this purpose.

II. Police

3. The ordinary duties of police in respect of crime will be discharged by the village authorities. They shall arrest all criminals and maintain peace and order within their respective local limits.

4. It shall be the duty of the village authorities to report to the Political Officer or such other officer as may be authorised by him in that behalf, at the earliest practicable moment, all crimes, violent deaths, and serious accidents occurring within their respective local limits, and all occurrences, whether within or beyond such limits, which may come to their knowledge and which are likely to affect the public peace; and to deliver up

offenders as soon as may be to the officer authorised to try them.

5. The village authorities shall watch and report, or apprehend and deliver up, all vagrants or bad and suspicious characters found within their respective local limits.

6. On the occurrence of any heinous crime* or of offences under the Arms Act or Excise Act within their local limits, the inhabitants of the village shall at once, if possible, apprehend the offender, and in any case shall at once inform the chief village authority, who, if the offender has not been apprehended, shall proceed without delay to the place where the crime occurred, and enquire into the matter. He shall further, as soon as possible, report any such offence to the Political Officer or such other officer as may be duly authorised by him in that behalf, whether the offender has been apprehended or not.

7. The village authorities may pursue an offender fleeing beyond their jurisdiction and arrest him, but shall not ordinarily attempt to arrest an offender beyond their own jurisdiction without the cognizance and co-operation of the village authorities within whose limits the offender has fled. When an offender is traced from one jurisdiction to another, it will be sufficient to point him out to the village authorities within whose limits he may be found, aiding them, if required, to effect his capture.

8. When the village authorities are unable to arrest an offender, they shall apply to the Political Officer or such other officer as may be duly authorised by him in this behalf for the aid of the regular police.

9. All inhabitants of the tract are bound to aid the village authorities when required to do so for the maintenance of order or apprehending offenders, and are liable to fine for failing to give such assistance; the fine to be adjudged by the chief village authority to the extent of his powers in criminal cases, or by the Political Officer or his Assistants. And if it appears that the community is to blame, and that particular offenders cannot

*Heinous crimes are :

Arson, Cattle stealing, Counterfeiting coin or passing it, Dacoity, Forgery, House breaking, Murder, Rape, Rebellion, Robbery, Riot, Wounding to the danger of life or limb.

be discovered, a fine may be imposed upon the community, but by the Political Officer only.

10. Misconduct on the part of the village authorities in police matters shall be punishable by fine which may extend to Rs. 500, or by simple imprisonment to the extent which would be awardable under the Penal Code or other law for a like offence, or by both. Imprisonment may be awarded in lieu of fine in accordance with the provisions of the Penal Code or any other law in force.

11. An appeal shall lie from all orders of the chief village authority in police matters to an Assistant Political Officer authorised by the Political Officer in that behalf, and from him to the Political Officer, whose orders are final; but the Chief Commissioner may at any time call for the proceedings, and modify or reverse any order of the Political Officer.

III. Criminal Procedure

12. Criminal justice shall be ordinarily administered by the Political Officer and his Assistants and by the chief village authority duly authorised in this behalf.

13. The Political Officer shall be competent to pass sentence of death, transportation, or imprisonment up to the maximum amount provided for the offence, of whipping and of fine up to any amount : Provided that all sentences of death or transportation or imprisonment for a term of seven years and upwards shall be subject to the confirmation of the Chief Commissioner.

The Chief Commissioner or Political Officer may call for the proceedings of any officer subordinate to him and reduce, enhance or cancel any sentence passed or remand the case for retrial; but no offence shall be punished by a sentence exceeding that awardable under the Indian Penal Code. The Assistant Political Officers shall exercise such powers not exceeding those of a Magistrate of the first class as defined in the Criminal Procedure Code, as they may be invested with by the Chief Commissioner.

14. The chief village authorities may themselves dispose of the cases of persons residing within their jurisdiction charged with the following offences :

Theft.
Injury to property of whatever kind.
Injury to person not endangering life or limb.
House-trespass.
Affronts of whatever kind.

15. The chief village authorities may impose a fine for any offence which they are competent to try up to a limit of Rs. 50 and may award restitution or compensation to the extent of the injury sustained. Fines may be enforced by distraint of the property of the offender.

16. The chief village authorities may not decide in cases :

(a) where their father, mother, son, daughter, their wife, or the children, husbands, or wives of any of these are concerned; or

(b) where the defendant does not reside within their jurisdiction;

(c) where the offence is one against the State or of causing death or danger to life or limb, or of robbery of any sort with violence or of arson or of making or passing counterfeit coins or of making fraudulent documents, or offences under the Arms Act or Excise Act, and generally any offences of a heinous nature.

17. The chief village authorities shall decide all cases in open Darbar in the presence of at least three witnesses and of the complainant and accused whose attendance they are empowered to compel.

18. The chief village authority may carry out his decision as soon as pronounced, unless the accused person appeals. If the sentence is fine, and the accused person does not pay, he shall be sent to the Political Officer or any Assistant authorised by him in that behalf to be dealt with while the fine is being realised.

19. Either party may appeal from the decision of the chief village authority at the time the decision is pronounced. The case shall then be tried *de novo*.

20. An appeal shall lie from the decision of an Assistant Political Officer to the Political Officer if preferred within thirty days.

21. No appeal shall lie as a matter of right from any sentence passed by the Political Officer involving less than three years' imprisonment. An appeal shall lie to the Chief Commissioner against sentences of three years' imprisonment and upwards, and from all sentences of death or transportation. Appeals must be presented within thirty days of the date of the order appealed against excluding the time required for procuring copy of the order : Provided that an appeal from a sentence of death shall be preferred within seven days from the date of the sentence.

22. The Political Officer and the Assistant Political Officers shall be guided in regard to procedure by the principles of the Code of Criminal Procedure so far as they are applicable to the circumstances of the district and consistent with these rules. The chief exceptions are :

(a) Verbal orders of notice only shall be requisite in any case except when the regular police are employed, or when the person concerned is not a resident of or in the tract at the time; but orders or summonses shall in every case before a fixed day, and the order shall be made known to the person concerned or to some adult member of his family, and failing this shall be openly proclaimed at the place where he is, or was last known to be, in sufficient time to allow him, if he sees fit, to appear.

(b) The proceedings of the chief village authorities need not be recorded in writing nor shall it be necessary that examinations before the Political Officer and the Assistant Political Officers be signed by the parties examined; but the Political Officer may require the chief village authorities to report their proceedings in any way which appears to him suitable.

(c) There shall be no preliminary enquiries by regular or village police unless the Political Officer or Assistant Political Officers see fit to direct one.

(d) Recognizance to appear shall not be taken unless it appears necessary to the Political Officer or Assistant Political Officers.

(e) Examinations and proceedings generally shall be recorded in English only.

(f) Oaths shall be administered to parties and witnesses in cases where the accused is charged with murder, but not in other cases unless the Court or either party so require. It is, however, at all times optional with the Court to put witnesses on oath ; but witnesses, whether on oath or not, shall be punishable for giving false evidence. In all cases where oaths are administered, all persons shall be sworn in the mode most binding on their conscience.

IV. Civil Procedure

23. The administration of civil justice in the Dibrugarh Frontier Tract shall be conducted by the Political Officer, the Assistant Political Officers and the chief village authorities.

24. The chief village authorities may try cases in which plaintiff and defendant are living in their jurisdiction without limit as to amount, but with the following reservations.

25. The chief village authorities may not try suits in which their fathers, mothers, sons or daughters, uncles or aunts, sisters or brothers, the children of any of the foregoing, their wives, or persons in the above relationship to a wife, or any near relative, are concerned.

26. All suits shall be decided in open Darbar in the presence of the parties, and at least three respectable witnesses.

27. The chief village authorities shall have power to compel attendance of parties to any suit and witnesses, and to fine up to a limit of Rs. 50, persons failing to attend when ordered to do so. They have power to award all costs, also compensation to defendants for unfounded or vexatious suits brought against them.

28. All proceedings shall be viva voce, but the Political Officer may require the chief village authorities to report their proceedings in any way which may appear to him suitable. After hearing both parties and their witnesses, if any, they shall, with or without the opinion of assessors, as they may see fit, forthwith pronounce a decision.

29. The chief village authorities may carry out their decisions at once, if necessary, by distraint of any property belonging to the person found liable, to pay (unless appeal is made, or security given to the chief village authorities satisfaction); but if an appeal is made at the time of decision, the chief village authority shall send up the parties and their witnesses to the Political Officer or any other officer authorised by him in that behalf forthwith, as soon as may be. He shall either accompany them himself or send at least one respectable person who has been present at the trial with them.

30. The Political Officer and the Assistant Political Officers shall not ordinarily hear any suits triable by the chief village authorities; but suits which under these rules the chief village authority cannot try shall be tried by the Political Officer or an Assistant Political Officer.

31. The Political Officer and the Assistant Political Officers shall in all cases coming before them, in which the parties are indigenous inhabitants of the frontier tract, endeavour to induce them to submit their case to a Panchayat. In that event, each party shall name an equal number of arbitrators, and the Court shall either choose, or leave the arbitrators to choose, an umpire. The name and residence of the arbitrators and umpire and the matter in dispute shall be recorded before their proceedings commence, and the Court shall direct the chief village authority, or some other person, to assemble the panchayat and witnesses within such reasonable period as the Court may fix. When the case has been decided, the umpire shall appear with the parties before the Court, which shall proceed to record the decision and enforce it as its own. From such decision there shall be no appeal.

32. On appeals to the Political Officer from a decision of the chief village authority, a record shall be made of the matter in dispute, and of the decision of the chief village authority, if necessary, the Court shall examine the parties, and, if the decision appears to be just, it shall be affirmed and enforced by the Court as its own. If, on the other hand, the Court sees grounds to doubt the justice of the decision, it shall try the case *de novo*, or refer it to a Panchayat, as provided above.

33. Decrees against persons resident beyond the jurisdiction of the Court in the Dibrugarh Frontier Tract, if satisfaction cannot be obtained within the Dibrugarh Frontier Tract, shall be transferred for execution to the Court having jurisdiction.

34. Houses, needful clothing, or cooking utensils, or implements whereby the owner or his family subsists, shall not be attached, sold, or transferred in execution of a decree, unless the house or other things above exempted is the actual subject-matter of the suit. Land may be sold or temporarily transferred where custom admits of individual right in it being recognized.

35. There shall be no imprisonment for debt, excepting when the Political Officer is satisfied that fraudulent disposition or concealment of property has taken place. In such case the debtor may be detained for a period not exceeding six months.

36. The Chief Commissioner or Political Officer may, on application or otherwise, call for the proceedings of any case decided by any officer subordinate to him and pass such orders as he may deem fit.

An appeal shall lie to the Political Officer against any decision of an Assistant Political Officer, and to the Chief Commissioner against an original decision of the Political Officer, if the value of the suit be rupees five hundred or over, or if the suit involve a question of tribal rights or customs, or of right to, or possession of, immovable property: Provided that the petition of appeal accompanied by a copy of the order appealed against by a clear statement of the grounds of appeal be filed within thirty days from the date of decision, excluding the time required for obtaining a copy of the decision. An appeal which lies to the Chief Commissioner may be pretended to the Political Officer, who shall, if it be in order and presented in due time, endorse upon it the date of receipt and transmit it with the records of the case to the Chief Commissioner.

The decree of the appellate Court shall be transferred to the Court passing the original order for execution as a decree of its own.

37. The Courts of the Chief Commissioner, Political Officer and Assistant Political Officers, shall be guided by the spirit, but not be bound by the letter, of the Code of Civil Procedure.

38. No professional pleader or mukhtar shall be allowed to appear in any case except with the sanction of the Court. Near relatives may appear for persons incapacitated by age, sex, or sickness.

39. Oaths shall not be administered to parties or witnesses in suits unless the Court or either party to a suit so require.

In all cases where oaths are administered, all persons shall be sworn in the manner most binding on their consciences. It is at all times optional with the Court to put witnesses on oath; but witnesses, whether on oath or not, shall be punishable for giving false evidence.

40. The Political Officer is empowered to try suits up to any amount. The Assistant Political Officers shall hear and decide original civil suits up to a value of Rs. 1,000, and shall hear and decide appeals from the decision of the chief village authorities up to a value of Rs. 500.

5. GOVERNMENT OF INDIA ACT, 1919

13(52A) 1. The Governor-General in Council may, after obtaining an expression of opinion from the local Government and the local Legislature affected, by notification, with the sanction of His Majesty previously signified by the Secretary of State in Council, constitute a new Governor's province or place part of a Governor's province under the administration of a Deputy Governor to be appointed by the Governor-General, and may in such case apply, with such modifications as appear necessary or desirable, all or any of the provisions of this Act relating to Governor's provinces, or provinces under a Lieutenant-Governor or Chief Commissioner to any such new province or part of a province.

2. The Governor-General-in-Council may declare any territory in British India to be a "Backward Tract" and may, by notification, with such sanction as aforesaid, direct that this Act shall apply to that territory subject to such exceptions and modification as may be prescribed in the notification.

Where the Governor-General-in-Council has, by notification, directed as aforesaid, he may, by the same or subsequent notification, direct that any Act of the Indian Legislature shall not apply to the territory in question or any part thereof, or shall apply to the territory or any part thereof subject to such exceptions or modifications as the Governor-General thinks fit, or may authorize the Governor in Council to give similar directions as respects any act of the local Legislature.

6. GOVERNMENT OF INDIA ACT, 1935

91.1. In this Act the expressions "Excluded Area" and "Partially Excluded Area" mean respectively such areas as His Majesty may by order in Council declare to be excluded areas or partially excluded areas.

The Secretary of State shall lay the draft of the order which it is proposed to recommend His Majesty to make under this sub-section before Parliament within six months from the passing of this Act.

2. His Majesty may at any time by Order in Council :

(a) direct that the whole or any specified part of an Excluded Area shall become, or become part of a Partially Excluded Area;
(b) direct that the whole or any specified part of a Partially Excluded area shall cease to be a Partially Excluded Area or a part of such an area;
(c) alter, but only by way of rectification of boundaries, any excluded or Partially Excluded Area;
(d) on any alteration of the boundaries of a province or the creation of a new province, declare any territory not previously included in any province to be, or to form part of, an Excluded Area or a Partially Excluded Area, and any such order may contain such incidental and consequential provisions as appear to His Majesty to be necessary and proper, but save as aforesaid the Order in Council made under sub-section (1) of the section shall not be varied by any subsequent order.

92. 1. The executive authority of a province extends to Excluded and Partially Excluded areas therein but, notwithstanding anything in this Act, no Act of the Federal Legislature or of the Provincial Legislature, shall apply to an Excluded Area or Partially Excluded Area unless the Governor in giving such a direction with respect to any Act may direct that the Act shall in its application to the area, or to any specified part thereof, have effect subject to such exceptions or modifications as he thinks fit.

2. The Governor may make regulations for the peace and

good government of any area in a province which is for the time being an excluded area, or a partially excluded area, and any regulations so made may repeal or amend any Act of the Federal Legislature or of the Provincial Legislature, or any existing Indian law, which is for the time being applicable to the area in question.

Regulations made under this sub-section shall be submitted forthwith to the Governor-General and until assented to by him in his discretion shall have no effect and the provisions of this part of this Act with respect to the power of His Majesty to disallow Act shall apply in relation to any such regulations assented to by the Governor-General as they apply in relation to Acts of a Provincial Legislature assented to by him.

3. The Governor shall, as respects any area in a province which is for the time being an excluded area, exercise his functions in his discretion.

7. THE GOVERNMENT OF INDIA (EXCLUDED AND PARTIALLY EXCLUDED AREAS) ORDER, 1936

Whereas by sub-section (1) of section ninety-one of the Government of India Act, 1935 (hereafter in this order referred to as "the Act"), His Majesty in Council is empowered to declare what areas are to be Excluded Areas and Partially Excluded Areas within the meaning of the Act:

And whereas draft of this Order has been laid before Parliament in accordance with the provisions of sub-section (1) of section three hundred and nine of the Act and an Address has been presented to His Majesty by both Houses of Parliament praying that an Order may be made in the terms of this order:

Now, therefore, His Majesty, in the exercise of the powers conferred on him as aforesaid and of all other powers enabling him in that behalf, is pleased by and with the advice of his Privy Council to order, and it is hereby ordered as follows:

1. This order may be cited as "The Government of India (Excluded and Partially Excluded Areas) Order, 1936".

2. The areas specified in Part I of the Schedule to this Order shall be the Excluded Areas, and the areas specified in Part II of that Schedule the Partially Excluded Areas, within the meaning of the Act.

3. Any reference in the said Schedule to any district, administration area or estate shall be construed as a reference to that district, area or estate as existing on the first day of January nineteen hundred and thirty six.

M.P.A. HANKEY

Assam

The North-East Frontier (Sadiya, Balipara and Lakhimpur) Tracts
The Naga Hills District
The Lushai Hills District
The North-Cachar Hills Sub-division of the Cachar District.

8. THE INDIA (PROVISIONAL CONSTITUTION) ORDER, 1947

And whereas by paragraph (c) of sub-section (1) of section 9 of the said Act it is provided that the Governor-General shall by order make such provision as appears to him to be necessary or expedient for making omissions or additions to, and adaptations and modifications of, the Government of India Act, 1935, in its application to the separate new Dominions :

* * * *

3. (2) The following expressions shall be omitted wherever they occur, namely "in his discretion", "acting in his discretion" and "exercising his individual judgement."

9. CONSTITUTIONAL PROVISION FOR NEFA

240. *Powers of President to make Regulations for certain Union Territories* : (1) The President may make regulations for the peace, progress and good government of the Union Territory of :

(a) the Andaman and Nicobar Islands
(b) the Laccadive, Minicoy and Amindivi Islands
(c) Dadra and Nagar Haveli
(d) Goa, Daman, and Diu
(e) Pondicherry

(1) Provided that when any body is created under article 239A to function as a Legislature for the Union Territory of Goa, Daman and Diu or Pondicherry, the President shall not make any Regulation for the peace, progress and good government of that Union Territory with effect from the date appointed for the first meeting of the Legislature.

(2) Any Regulation so made may repeal or amend any Act made by Parliament or any existing law which is for the time being applicable to the Union Territory and, when promulgated by the President, shall have the same force and effect as an Act of Parliament which applies to that Territory.

SIXTH SCHEDULE

18. In application of the provisions of this Schedule to areas specified in Part B of the table appended to paragraph 20.—(1) the Governor may :

(a) subject to the previous approval of the President, by public notification, apply all or any of the foregoing provisions of this Schedule to any tribal area specified in Part B of the table appended to paragraph 20 of this Schedule or any part of such area and thereupon such area or part shall be administered in accordance with such provisions, and

(b) with like approval, by public notification, exclude from the said table any tribal area specified in Part B of that table or any part of such area.

(2) Until a notification is issued under sub-paragraph (1) of this paragraph in respect of any tribal area specified in Part B of the said table or any part of such area, the administration of such area or part thereof, as the case may be, shall be carried on by the President through the Governor of Assam as his agent and the provisions of Art. 240 shall apply thereto as if such area or part thereof were a Union Territory specified in that article.

(3) In the discharge of his functions under sub-paragraph (2) of this paragraph as the agent of the President the Governor shall act in his discretion.

20. *Tribal areas.*—(1) The areas specified in Parts A and

B of the table below shall be tribal areas within the State of Assam.

(2) The United Khasi Jaintia Hills District shall comprise the territories which before the commencement of this Constitution were known as the Khasi States and the Khasi and Jaintia Hills District, excluding any areas for the time being comprised within the cantonment and municipality of Shillong, but including so much of the area comprised within the municipality of Shillong as formed part of the Khasi State or Mylliem.

Provided that for the purposes of clauses (e) and (f) of sub-paragraph (1) of paragraph 3, paragraph 4, paragraph 5, paragraph 6, sub-paragraph (2) clauses (a), (b) and (d) of sub-paragraph (3) and sub-paragraph (4) of paragraph 8, and clause (d) of sub-paragraph (2) of paragraph 10 of this Schedule no part of the area comprised within the municipality of Shillong shall be deemed to be within the District.

(2A) The Mizo District shall comprise the area which at the commencement of this Constitution was known as the Lushai Hills District.

(3) Any reference in the table below to any District (other than the United Khasi Jaintia Hills District and the Mizo District) or administrative area shall be construed as a reference to that district or area at the commencement of this Constitution.

Provided that the tribal areas specified in Part B of the table below shall not include any such areas in the Plain as may, with the previous approval of the President, be notified by the Governor of Assam in that behalf.

Table

Part-A

* * *

Part-B

* * *

10. REPRESENTATION OF THE PEOPLE ACT, 1950

Part II

ALLOCATION OF SEATS AND DELIMITATION OF CONSTITUENCIES

The House of the People

3. *Allocation of seats in the House of the People* : The allocation of Seats to the States in the House of the People and the number of seats, if any, to be reserved for the Scheduled Castes and for the Scheduled Tribes of each State shall be as shown in the First Schedule.

4. *Filling of seats in the House of the People and Parliamentary Constituencies* : (1) The seat allotted in the House of the People under section 3 to the Part B tribal areas shall be the seat to be filled by a person nominated by the President.

THE FIRST SCHEDULE

(See section 3)

Allocation of Seats in the House of the People

Name of the State/Union Territory or Area	Number of seats in the House as constituted on the 1st November, 1969			Number of seats in the House as subsequently constituted		
	Total	Reserved for the Scheduled Castes	Reserved for the Scheduled Tribes	Total	Reserved for the Scheduled Castes	Reserved for the Scheduled Tribes
1	2	3	4	5	6	7
III—AREA						
North-East Frontier Tract	1	...	1	...	...	...

11. THE NORTH-EAST FRONTIER AREAS (ADMINISTRATION) REGULATION, 1954

A Regulation to provide for the readjustment of the administrative units of the North-East Frontier Tract specified in Part B of the table annexed to the Sixth Schedule to the Constitution, and for certain matters incidental thereto.

In exercise of the powers conferred by clause (2) of article 243 of the Constitution, read with sub-paragraph (2) of paragraph 18 of the Sixth Schedule to the Constitution, the President is pleased to promulgate following Regulation made by him.

1. *Short title and commencement* : This Regulation may be

called the North-East Frontier Areas (Administration) Regulation, 1954.

2. It shall come into force on such date as the Governor of Assam may, be notification in the official gazette appoint.

3. *Re-adjustment of administrative units* : On and from the commencement of this Regulation

(a) The North-East Frontier Tract, including the Balipara Frontier Tract, the Tirap Frontier Tract, the Abor Hills District, the Mishmi Hills District shall be known as the North-East Frontier Agency.

(b) The Balipara Frontier Tract shall be divided into two separate units of administration called the Subansiri Frontier Division and the Kameng Frontier Division, each comprising the areas set out in Schedules I and II respectively.

(c) Each of the areas specified in column 1 of the table below shall be known by the name mentioned in the entry corresponding thereto in column 2 thereof.

Existing name of area	New name
Tirap Frontier Tract	Tirap Frontier Division
Abor Hills District	Siang Frontier Division
Mishmi Hills District	Lohit Frontier Division

4. *Construction of certain references in existing laws* : Any reference in any existing law

(a) to the Balipara Frontier Tract shall be construed as a reference to the Subansiri Frontier Division and the Kameng Frontier Division; and

(b) to any of the areas specified in column 1 of the table annexed to section 2 shall be construed as a reference to the area specified in the entry corresponding thereto in column 2 of the said table.

Explanation.—In this section "existing law" means any law, ordinance, order, bye-law, or regulation passed or made before the commencement of this Regulation by any Legislature, authority or person having power to make such law, ordinance, order, bye-law, rule or regulation.

SCHEDULE I

See section 2(b)

Areas in the Subansiri Frontier Division

North : The McMahon Line...

East and South : From the point where the Subansiri river cuts the McMahon Line on the India-Tibet Frontier the boundary runs down the midstream of the Subansiri river till it meets the Inner Line of the Balipara Frontier Tract at the junction of the Siplu and Subansiri rivers at Siplumukh; thence along the Inner Line of the Balipara Frontier Tract to the point where it meets the Burai river south of Somna Parbat...

West : From the point where the Inner Line of the Balipara Frontier Tract meets the Burai river the boundary runs in a north-westerly direction along the hill ridge that forms the watershed between the Papum and Dessing rivers to the hill top with height 6980 ; thence in a north-easterly direction along the hill ridge between the Papum and Pakkui rivers to the hill top with height 7590 ; thence in a north-westerly direction along the hill ridge between the Pakkui and Par rivers to the hill top with height 7510 ; thence in a northerly and then in a north-westerly, and westerly direction over the hill tops with height 11710, 12390, 11579, 12127, 10004, 11320 and among the main hill ridge that forms the watershed between the river Kameng and its tributaries on the west and the river Panir and Khru in the east. . . .

SCHEDULE II

See section 2(b)

Areas in the Kameng Frontier Division

North : The McMahon Line.......................

East : The western boundary of the Subansiri Frontier Division as set out in the First Schedule, from the McMahon Line on the north to the Innner Line of the Balipara Frontier Tract to the south.

South : From the south-western corner of the Subansiri Frontier Division on the Burai river westwards along the Inner Line of the Balipara Frontier Tract as defined in the Assam

Government Notification No. 6778-AP, dated the 2nd November, 1934 to the point at which the boundary between the India and Bhutan leaves Inner Line and turns northwards.

West : Along the boundary between India and Bhutan from the point where it leaves the Inner Line of the Balipara Frontier Tract to the McMahon Line.

RAJENDRA PRASAD
President

No. GA. 140/50/122.—In pursuance of sub-section (2) of section I of the North-East Frontier Areas (Administration) Regulation, 1954 (Regulation I of 1954), the Governor of Assam is pleased to appoint the 26th January, 1954, as the date on which the said Regulation shall come into force.

N.K. RUSTOMJI
Adviser to the Governor of Assam

12. NORTH-EAST FRONTIER AGENCY (ADMINISTRATION) REGULATION, 1965

Promulgated by the President in the Sixteenth Year of the Republic of India.

A Regulation to make further provision for the administration of the North-East Frontier Agency and for certain matters connected therewith.

In exercise of the powers conferred by Article 240 of the Constitution, read with sub-paragraph (2) of paragraph 18 of the Sixth Schedule to the Constitution, the President is pleased to promulgate the following Regulation made by him.

1. *Short title and Commencement* : (1) This Regulation may be called the North-East Frontier Agency (Administration) Regulation, 1965.

(2) It shall come into force on such date as the Central Government may, by notification in the Official Gazette, appoint.

2. *Definition* : In this Regulation

(a) "Division" means any of the Frontier Division referred to in section 2 of the North-East Frontier Areas (Administration) Regulation, 1954.

(b) "Existing law" means any law, ordinance, regulation, order, bye-law, rule, scheme, notification or other instrument having the force of law in India or any part thereof.

(c) "North-East Frontier Agency" shall have the meaning assigned to it in the North-East Frontier Areas (Administration) Regulation, 1954.

3. *Change of names of administrative units of the North-East Frontier Agency*: On and from the commencement of this Regulation, each of the Divisions of the North-East Frontier Agency specified in column 1 of the table below shall be known by the name mentioned in the entry corresponding thereto in column 2 thereof.

Table

Existing name of Division 1	New Name 2
Kameng Frontier Division	Kameng District
Subansiri Frontier Division	Subansiri District
Siang Frontier Division	Siang District
Lohit Frontier Division	Lohit District
Tirap Frontier Division	Tirap District

4. *Construction of certain references in existing laws*: Any reference in any existing law to any of the Division specified in column 1 of the table annexed to section 3 shall be construed as a reference to the District specified in the entry corresponding thereto in column 2 of the said table.

5. *Amendment of existing laws*: Whenever an expression mentioned in column 1 of the table below occurs in any existing law as applicable to the North-East Frontier Agency, there shall be substituted therefor the expression set opposite to it in column 2 of the said table, and there shall also be made

Table

1	2
Political Officer	Deputy Commissioner
Additional Political Officer	Additional Deputy Commissioner
Assistant Political Officer	Assistant Commissioner

in any sentence in which the expression occurs such consequential amendments as the rules of grammar may require.

Sd/- S. RADHAKRISHNAN,
President

Sd/- R.C.S. SARKAR,
Secretary to the Government of India

13. THE NORTH-EAST FRONTIER AGENCY PANCHAYAT RAJ REGULATION, 1967

Promulgated by the President in the Eighteenth year of the Republic of India.

A Regulation to provide for the constitution of Anchal Samitis, Zilla Parishads and Agency Council in the North-East Frontier Agency and for matters connected therewith.

In exercise of the powers conferred by article 240 of the Constitution, read with sub-paragraph (2) of Paragraph 18 of the Sixth Schedule to the Constitution, the President is pleased to promulgate the following Regulation made by him.

CHAPTER I

Preliminary

1. *Short title, extent and commencement* : (1) This Regulation may be called the North-East Frontier Agency Panchayat Raj Regulation, 1967.

(2) It extends to the whole of the North-East Frontier Agency.

(3) It shall come into force on such date as the Governor may, by notification, appoint, and different dates may be appointed for different provisions of this Regulation and for different areas.

2. *Definitions*: In this Regulation, unless the context otherwise requires

(i) "Agency Council" means the Agency Council constituted under section 57 ;

(ii) "Anchal Samiti" means an Anchal Samiti constituted under Section 4 ;

(iii) "Block" means such area as may be declared by the Governor under section 3 to be a Block ;

(iv) "Deputy Commissioner" means the Deputy Commissioner of a District ;

(v) "District" means a District of the North-East Frontier Agency ;

(vi) "Governor" means the Governor of Assam ;

(vii) "Gram Panchayat" means a village authority constituted under the Assam Frontier (Administration of Justice) Regulation, 1845, by whatever name called ;

(viii) "North-East Frontier Agency" shall have the meaning assigned to it in the North-East Frontier Areas (Administration) Regulation, 1954 ;

(ix) "Notification" means a notification published in the official Gazette ;

(x) "Prescribed" means prescribed by rules made under this Regulation ;

(xi) "Sub-Divisional Officer" means the Additional Deputy Commissioner or the Assistant Commissioner in charge of a Sub-division ;

(xii) "Village" means an area recognized to be a village at the commencement of this Regulation and includes any area which the Governor may, by notification, declare to be a village ;

(xiii) "Zilla Parishad" means a Zilla Parishad constituted under section 51.

CHAPTER II

Anchal Samitis

3. *Declaration of Blocks* : The Governor may, by notification, declare such contiguous areas in a District as he deems a Block for the purposes of this Regulation and may specify the Gram Panchayats in the Block :

Provided that no area included in a municipality, town committee or cantonment constituted under any law for the time being in force shall be included in a Block.

4. *Constitution of Anchal Samitis and their incorporation* : (1) The Governor may, be notification, constitute an Anchal Samiti for a Block with effect from such date as may be specified therein.

(2) Every Anchal Samiti shall, by the name of the Block for

which it is constituted, be a body corporate having perpetual succession and a common seal with power to acquire, hold and dispose of property and to enter into contracts and shall by its corporate name sue and be sued.

5. *Alteration in area of Block.* (1) The Governor may, after consultation with an Anchal Samiti or Samitis concerned, at any time by notification—

(a) include any village or part of a village within the limits of a Block;

(b) exclude any village or part of a village from the limits of a Block; or

(c) amalgamate two or more Blocks into a single Block.

(2) Where, by a notification under sub-section (1), any village or part of a village is included within the limits of a Block, the jurisdiction of the Anchal Samiti established for that Block shall extend to such village or part which shall, unless the Governor otherwise directs, become subject to all notifications, rules, bye-laws and orders made under this Regulation or any other law in force in that Block.

(3) Where by a notification under sub-section (1), any village or part of a village is excluded from the limits of a Block, the jurisdiction of the Anchal Samiti established for that Block over such village or part shall thereupon cease and all notifications, rules, bye-laws and orders made under this Regulation or any other law in force in that Block shall cease to apply to that village or part, as the case may be.

(4) Where, by a notification under sub-section (1), two or more Blocks are amalgamated into a single Block, the Governor may make such incidental and consequential orders as may be necessary for effecting such amalgamation.

6. *Composition of Anchal Samiti* : (1) Every Anchal Samiti shall consist of—

(i) One representative elected in the prescribed manner, by the members of each Gram Panchayat falling within its jurisdiction:

Provided that where the number of villages in any Block exceeds twenty-five, the Deputy Commissioner may, by notification, divide such Block, in the prescribed manner, into not more than twenty-five constituencies, each consisting of one or more villages, and the members of Gram Panchayats included in each constituency shall elect, in the prescribed manner, one representative to the Anchal Samiti:

Provided further that, if at any time there is no Gram Panchayat in any village or as the case may be, in any of the villages included in a constituency, or the members of the Gram Panchayat or Panchayats in a village or constituency, the Deputy Commissioner may nominate a person ordinarily resident in that village or constituency, as the case may be, to be a member of the Anchal Samiti representing that village or constituency;

(ii) one representative elected, in the prescribed manner, by the chairman of the co-operative societies situated within the Block from amongst themselves, ex-officio :

Provided that where there is only one co-operative society in a Block, the chairman of that society shall be a member of the Anchal Samiti;

(iii) not more than five persons nominated by the Deputy Commissioner from the members of their tribes which have not secured representation in the Anchal Samiti under clause (i) or clause (ii);

(iv) the Sub-divisional Officer of the sub-division in which the Block is situated, ex-officio:

Provided that if the area of a Block extends to two or more sub-divisions, the Sub-divisional Officer of any one of the sub-divisions specified by the Deputy Commissioner in this behalf shall be a member of the Anchal Samiti constituted for that Block.

(2) The Deputy Commissioner may appoint such officers as ex-officio members of an Anchal Samiti as may be deemed necessary:

Provided that the officers so appointed shall have the right to attend the meetings of the Anchal Samiti and take part in the proceedings thereof but shall not be entitled to vote.

7. *Disqualifications for membership* : A person shall be disqualified for being chosen as, and for being a member of an Anchal Samiti, if he

(a) is not a citizen of India; or
(b) is not twenty-five years of age; or
(c) has been dismissed from the service of Government or an Anchal Samiti or any other local authority for

misconduct unless a period of five years has elapsed from such dismissal; or

(d) holds any office of profit under the Government of an Anchal Samiti or any other local authority; or

(e) has directly or indirectly any share or monetary interest in any work done by, or to, the Anchal Samiti or in any contract or employment with, under, or by, or on behalf of, the Anchal Samiti; or

(f) is an undischarged insolvent; or

(g) is of unsound mind and stands so declared by a competent court; or

(h) has been convicted by a criminal court of any offence involving moral turpitude and sentenced to imprisonment for not less than six months and five years have not elapsed since his release :

Provided that the disqualifications specified in clauses (d) and (e) shall not apply to an ex-officio member.

8. *President and Vice-President* : (1) The Sub-divisional Officer who is a member of an Anchal Samiti shall be its President.

(2) In the first meeting of an Anchal Samiti, the members shall elect from among themselves a Vice-President in the manner prescribed.

9. *Term of office of, and vacancies among, members of Anchal Samiti* : (1) Subject to the provisions of this section, the members of an Anchal Samiti shall hold office for a term of three years:

Provided that the Governor may, by or er in writing and for reasons to be recorded therein, extend the said term by a period or periods not exceeding one year in the aggregate, and every such order shall be notified in the official gazette.

(2) The term of office of the members of an Anchal Samiti shall be deemed to commence on the date of the first meeting of the Anchal Samiti which shall be held on a date fixed by the Deputy Commissioner.

(3) The term of office of outgoing members shall be deemed to extend to and expire with the date preceding the date of the first meeting of the newly constituted Anchal Samiti.

(4) The term ot office of an ex-officio member shall continue so long as he holds the office by virtue of which he is such a member.

(5) The Vice-President of an Anchal Samiti shall hold such office as long as he is a member of the Anchal Samiti.

(6) A member (other than an ex-officio member) shall be deemed to have vacated his seat if he is absent without excuse, sufficient in the opinion of the Anchal Samiti, from three consecutive ordinary meetings of the Anchal Samiti.

(7) An outgoing member shall be eligible for re-nomination or re-election.

10. *Resignation of office and filling up of casual vacancies* : (1) The Vice-President of an Anchal Samiti or any member thereof, not being an ex-officio member, may resign his office by giving notice in writing to that effect to its President and such resignation shall take effect from the date of its receipt by the President.

(2) A casual vacancy in the office of the Vice-President or any member shall be filled by election or nomination in accordance with the provisions of this Regulation or the rules made thereunder :

Provided that a member elected or nominated under this sub-section shall hold office for the remainder of the term of the member in whose place he is elected or nominated.

11. *Oath of office* : (1) Every member of an Anchal Samiti shall before taking his seat make and subscribe before such officer as the Governor may specify in this behalf, an oath or affirmation in the form set out in the first Schedule.

(2) A member who has not complied with the requirements of sub-section (1), shall not vote, take part in the proceedings of any meeting of the Anchal Samiti nor shall he be included as a member of any committee constituted by the Anchal Samiti.

12. *Officers and employees of Anchal Samiti* : (1) The Governor shall appoint an Executive Officer for every Anchal Samiti.

(2) The Executive Officer shall act as the Secretary of the Anchal Samiti and shall, subject to the control of the President, carry out the resolutions and directions of the Anchal Samiti and discharge such other functions as may be prescribed.

(3) Subject to such rules as may be made in this behalf, the Anchal Samiti may appoint such other officers and employees and in such number as may from time to time be necessary.

13. *Motion of no confidence* : (1) A motion of no confidence may be moved by any member of an Anchal Samiti against its Vice-President after giving at least seven days' notice in writing to the President of the Anchal Samiti, of his intention to move such a motion.

(2) If the motion is carried by a majority of not less than two-thirds of the total number of members of the Anchal Samiti the Vice-President shall cease to hold office.

(3) Notwithstanding anything contained in this Regulation, the Vice-President of an Anchal Samiti shall not preside at a meeting in which a motion of no confidence against him is under discussion, but he shall have the right to speak or otherwise take part in the proceedings of such meetings.

14. *Power of Governor to remove Vice-President or member of Anchal Samiti* : The Governor may, by order, remove from office the Vice-President or any other member of an Anchal Samiti, after giving him an opportunity of making a representation, if he

(a) incurs any of the disqualifications specified in section 7, or

(b) refuses to act or becomes incapable of acting, or

(c) is, in the opinion of the Governor, guilty of misconduct in the discharge of his duties, or

(d) is, in the opinion of the Governor, undesirable in the public interest to be continued in office, or

(e) has caused financial loss, waste or misappropriation of any money, or property belonging to the Anchal Samiti, by neglect or misconduct in the performance of his duties; and the Vice-President or member so removed shall not be eligible for re-election or renomination to the vacancy so created.

15. *Meetings of Anchal Samiti* : (1) The time and place of meetings of an Anchal Samiti and the procedure at such meetings (including the quorum thereat) shall be such as may be prescribed.

(2) A member of an Anchal Samiti may, at any meeting, move any resolution and put questions to the President or the

Vice-President on matters connected with the administration of the Anchal Samiti in the manner prescribed.

(3) No resolution of an Anchal Samiti shall be modified, amended, varied or cancelled by the Anchal Samiti within a period of three months from the date of passing thereof except by a resolution supported by two-thirds of the total number of members of the Anchal Samiti.

16. *Committees* : (1) Subject to such rules as may be made in this behalf, an Anchal Samiti may appoint from among its members as many committees as it thinks fit to assist it in the discharge of any specified functions and may delegate to such committees such of its powers as may be deemed necessary.

(2) The President and Vice-President of an Anchal Samiti shall be the Chairman and Vice-Chairman respectively of every committee appointed under sub-section (1) and the Executive Officer of the Anchal Samiti shall be an ex-officio member of every such committee.

(3) An Anchal Samiti may temporarily associate with any committee persons not being members of the Anchal Samiti, who have special experience and knowledge of any subject dealt with by a committee and any such person shall have the right to take part in the discussions of the committee but shall not have the right to vote and shall not be a member for any other purpose.

17. *Proceedings not to be invalid* : No act or proceeding of an Anchal Samiti or of any committee thereof shall be deemed to be invalid by reason only of the existence of any vacancy in, or defect in the constitution of, the Anchal Samiti or committee or of any informality in its proceedings.

18. *General meeting* : The President of an Anchal Samiti may convene a general meeting of all the members of the Gram Panchayats falling within its jurisdiction to review the action taken by the Anchal Samiti during the preceding year and to present the working plan of the Anchal Samiti for the succeeding year.

19. *Travelling and daily allowances of members of Anchal Samiti* : Every member of an Anchal Samiti who is not in the service of the Government shall be entitled to receive from the Anchal Samiti travelling and daily allowances for attending its committees at such rates as may be prescribed.

20. *Functions of Anchal Samiti* : (1) It shall be the duty of every Anchal Samiti so far as its fund and the resources at its disposal may allow, to make reasonable provision within its jurisdiction in regard to the matters specified in the second Schedule:

Provided that it may assign to any Gram Panchayat falling within its jurisdiction all or any of its functions relating to matters specified in Part I of the said Schedule.

(2) An Anchal Samiti may also make provision for carrying out within the area under its jurisdiction, any other work or measure which is likely to promote the health, safety, education, comfort, convenience or social or economic well-being of the residents of the area.

21. *Control of Anchal Samiti on certain properties* : (1) The Anchal Samiti, in respect of all roads, streets, bridges, culverts and other properties placed by the Governor under sub-section (1) of section 47 under its direction, management and control, may do all things necessary for the maintenance and repair thereof and in particular, may

(a) widen, open, enlarge or otherwise improve any such road, street, bridge or culvert and plant and preserve trees on the sides of such roads,

(b) deepen or otherwise improve any water course and other property mentioned in clause (c) of sub-section (1) of section 47, and

(c) cut any hedge or branch of any tree projecting on any such public road or street.

(2) The Anchal Samiti shall also have control of all roads, streets, waterways, bridges and culverts which are situated within its jurisdiction, not being private property or not being the property for the time being under the control of the Government, and may do all things necessary for the improvement, maintenance and repair thereof, and in particular, may

(a) lay out and make new roads, and

(b) construct new bridges and culverts.

22. *Transfer of any work or management of any institution to or from Anchal Samiti* : (1) Subject to such rules as may be made in this behalf, and to such conditions as may be agreed upon an Anchal Samiti may take over the execution, maintenance or repair of any work or the management of any institution within its jurisdiction on behalf of the Government or any local authority.

(2) Subject to such rules as may be made in this behalf, an Anchal Samiti may, with the consent of a local authority or any person, make over to such authority or person, the execution, maintenance or repair of any work or the management of any institution within its jurisdiction.

23. *Public charitable dispensaries and hospitals* : (1) The Governor may, with the consent of an Anchal Samiti, by notification, direct that any public charitable dispensary or hospital falling within its jurisdiction shall be placed under the control and administration of the Anchal Samiti.

(2) On the publication of the notification referred to in sub-section (1), the Anchal Samiti shall subject to such rules as may be made in this behalf, be charged with the control and administration of the dispensary or hospital and the construction, repair and maintenance of all buildings connected therewith.

24. *Establishment and maintenance of dispensaries and hospitals* : Subject to such rules as may be made in this behalf, an Anchal Samiti may

(a) establish and maintain, within its jurisdiction, dispensaries, hospitals, asylums and places for the reception of the sick or destitute or contribute towards the cost of establishment and maintenance of such institutions;

(b) provide for the employment of medical practitioners and for payment of allowances to such practitioners for services rendered;

(c) provide medicines or medical assistance for persons resident within its jurisdiction or take such measures as may appear to it to be necessary during the prevalence of any disease;

(d) with the previous sanction of the Governor, contribute such annual or other sums as may be agreed upon, towards the establishment or maintenance of any dispensary, hospital, asylum or place for the reception of the sick or destitute which is situated outside its jurisdiction, but is, or may be ordinarily used by persons resident within its jurisdiction.

25. *Improvement of sanitation* : (1) If an Anchal Samiti is of opinion that it is necessary so to do for the promotion of public health or for the prevention of danger to life or property, it may, by a notice in writing and within such period as may be specified therein, direct the owner or occupier of any building or land

(i) to remove huts or privies wholly or partly; or
(ii) to remove, alter or construct private drains; or
(iii) to remove, alter or construct any public drain; or
(iv) to fill up, clean or deepen any water-course, well, pool, ditch, tank, pond or any place containing, or used for the collection of, drainage or filth, to drain out stagnant water which appears to be injurious to health or offensive to the neighbourhood or to take such action as may be deemed necessary; or
(v) to clear any land of thick vegetation, undergrowth or jungle.

(2) If any work required to be done under sub-section (1) is not executed within the period specified in the notice, the Anchal Samiti may itself cause such work to be executed or done and the cost incurred thereon may be recovered from the owner or occupier in the prescribed manner.

(3) Any person who wilfully disobeys any direction issued under sub-section (1) shall be liable to a fine which may extend to ten rupees.

(4) If the Anchal Samiti considers that the owner or occupier or any other person has suffered loss as a result of any action taken under this section, not being due to his fault it may award such compensation as it may deem adequate from its own funds.

26. *Power to do certain acts in the event of an epidemic* : On the outbreak of an epidemic or an infectious disease, an Anchal Samiti shall have power to take all or any of the following measures for controlling and preventing the spread of the epidemic or disease in the area within its jurisdiction, namely :

(i) restriction of the movement of infected person or goods within its jurisdiction;
(ii) provision for vaccination or inoculation, as the case may be;
(iii) seizure of any polluted food-stuffs:
(iv) disinfection of wells, tanks or other sources of water supply; and
(v) doing of such other acts as may be necessary.

27. *Disinfection of buildings and articles* : (1) If the Anchal Samiti is of opinion that the cleansing or disinfecting of a building or any part thereof, or any article therein, which is likely to retain infection, will tend to prevent or check the spread of any disease, it may, by notice require the occupier, or where there is no occupier, the owner thereof, to cleanse or disinfect the same in the manner and within the time specified in the notice.

(2) If

(a) within the time specified as aforesaid, the person on whom the notice is served fails to have the building or part thereof or the article cleansed or disinfected, or
(b) such person gives his consent, the Anchal Samiti may at his cost cause the building or part thereof or the article to be cleansed and disinfected :

Provided that the Anchal Samiti may, in its discretion, pay the whole or any part of such cost.

28. *Removal of patients suffering from infectious or contagious diseases to hospital* : If any person suffering from any infectious or contagious disease is found, within the jurisdiction of any such Anchal Samiti as may be specified by the Governor by notification, to be :

(a) without proper lodging or accommodation, or
(b) living in a sarai or other public place, the Anchal Samiti or any person authorised by it in this behalf may, on the advice of a medical officer not below in

rank to that of an Assistant Surgeon, Grade I, remove the said person to any hospital or place at which persons suffering from such diseases are received for medical treatment and may take all reasonable measures to effect such removal.

29. *Power to close markets* : (1) An Anchal Samiti may by order, with a view to preventing the spread of any infectious or contagious disease, close any market or shop within its jurisdiction for such period as may be specified in the said order and may also forbid any person from entering such market or shop.

(2) An order under sub-section (ii) shall be published in such manner and at such places as the Anchal Samiti may direct and notice thereof shall also be served on the owner or occupier of the market or shop, as the case may be.

(3) The owner or occupier of the market or shop may, after complying with the provisions of the order, appeal against it to the Deputy Commissioner and the decision of the Deputy Commissioner thereon shall be final.

(4) When an order has been published under sub-section (2) and has not been set aside by the Deputy Commissioner under sub-section (3) the owner or occupier of a market or shop who fails to close such market or shop shall be liable to a fine which may extend to five hundred rupees and any person who enters such market or shop in contravention of the provisions of the order shall be liable to a fine which may extend to fifty rupees.

30. *Licensing of market* : (1) An Anchal Samiti may, by order, direct that no place other than markets established by, or under the control or administration of, the Anchal Samiti shall be used as a market except in accordance with the terms and conditions of a licence granted by it.

(2) The Anchal Samiti may grant a licence under the provisions of this section subject to such conditions as it may think fit as to supervision and inspection, sanction and water supply, weights and measures to be used, rents and fees to be charged and such other matters as may be specified in the bye-laws to be framed for the purpose.

(3) The Anchal Samiti may at any time suspend, cancel or

modify a licence granted under sub-section (2) for contravention of any of the conditions thereof.

(4) Any person aggrieved by an order of the Anchal Samiti under sub-section (3) may appeal against such order to the Deputy Commissioner who may, after giving such person an opportunity to represent his case, modify, annul or confirm the order.

(5) The Anchal Samiti or any officer authorised by it may close any place used as a market without a licence or the licence for which has been suspended or cancelled.

31. *Water supply* : (1) An Anchal Samiti may take such action as may be necessary for poorer and sufficient supply of water to any area within its jurisdiction and for this purpose may construct, repair and maintain water works, wells or tanks.

(2) The Anchal Samiti may, by order set apart convenient tanks, springs, wells or part of rivers, streams, channels or water-courses, for the supply of water for drinking or for culinary purposes.

32. *Compulsory vaccination*: An Anchal Samiti shall take such action as may be necessary for the enforcement of vaccination in the area within its jurisdiction.

33. *Power to make contributions to Gram Panchayats*: Subject to such conditions as may be prescribed, an Anchal Samiti may make annual or other contributions to any Gram Panchayat falling within its jurisdiction to whom any of its powers or functions are assigned under section 20.

34. *Power to protect crops*: An Anchal Samiti may by itself or in association with any Gram Panchayat or any other Anchal Samiti take such steps as may be necessary to scare away monkeys, squirrels, elephants, birds, locusts or other pests in order to save crops from being damaged.

35. *Power of entry of Anchal Samiti officers* : A member of an Anchal Samiti and any officer or other employee of the Anchal Samiti authorised by it in this behalf may enter into or upon any house, building or land with or without assistants or workmen to make any inspection or execute any work required under any of the provisions of this Regulation:

Provided that

(a) no such entry shall be made between sun-set and sunrise; and

(b) no entry into a dwelling house may be made except with the consent of the occupier thereof and without giving the said occupier at least twenty-four hours' previous notice of the intention to make such entry signed by the President or the Vice-President of the Anchal Samiti; and due regard shall always be paid to the social and religious customs and usages of the occupants of the house so entered.

36. *Other powers of Anchal Samiti* : An Anchal Samiti may, within its jurisdiction,

(a) establish and maintain bungalows and sarais for the use of travellers and charge therefor such fees as it thinks fit; and

(b) offer rewards at such scales as may be approved by the Governor for the destruction of unclaimed or diseased dogs and animals.

37. *Anchal Samiti Fund*: (1) There shall be an Anchal Samiti Fund for each Anchal Samiti and the same shall be utilised for discharging its function under this Regulation.

(2) The following shall be credited to and form part of, the Anchal Samiti Fund, namely :

(i) the proceeds of any tax, fees, licence fees, cess and surcharge levied under this Regulation;

(ii) the collection charges referred to in section 46;

(iii) any grants and contributions made by the Governor or any local authority or other persons;

(iv) all sums received by way of loan or gift;

(v) the income from, or the sale proceeds of, any property of the Anchal Samiti;

(vi) the sale proceeds of all dust, dirt, dung or refuse collected by the employees of the Anchal Samiti;

(vii) all sums received in aid of, or for expenditure on, any institution or service, maintained, managed or financed by the Anchal Samiti;

(viii) any other sums paid to the Anchal Samiti.

(3) The amount in the Anchal Samiti Fund shall be kept in such custody as may be prescribed.

38. *Raising of loans and formation of a Sinking Fund* : Subject to such rules as may be made in this behalf, and subject to the provisions of any law for the time being in force relating to the raising of loans by local authorities, an Anchal Samiti may raise loans for discharging its functions under this Regulation, and for the repayment of such loans from a Sinking Fund.

39. *Application of Anchal Samiti Fund* : The Anchal Samiti Fund shall be applied for payments in the following order namely :

(a) payment of interest on loans raised under section 38, and payments into the Sinking Fund, if formed;

(b) payment of the salaries, allowances and other remuneration of the officers and other employees of the Anchal Samiti;

(c) payment of expenses incurred by the Anchal Samiti in the discharge of its functions under this Regulation;

(d) payment of such other administrative expenses of the Anchal Samiti as may be prescribed.

40. *Powers of taxation* : (1) Subject to approval by the Governor and subject to such rules as may be prescribed, an Anchal Samiti may levy

(a) a tax on brick or concrete buildings;

(b) a tax on supply of drinking water, sale of fire-wood and thatch, conservance, lighting and slaughter-houses;

(c) a tax on cultivable land lying fallow for two consecutive years;

(d) a tax on fisheries allotted to the Anchal Samiti;

(e) a fee on the registration of cattle sold within its jurisdiction;

(f) a licence fee in respect of

(i) tea stalls, hotels, sweetmeat shops, restaurants, bakeries and confectioneries;

(ii) collection of hides and bones;

(iii) cinema halls, circuses, professional variety shows and fairs;
(iv) brick and tile kilns;
(v) oil and rice mills;
(vi) *hats* and bamboo stall;
(vii) carts, carriages, cycles and boats;
(viii) saw mills and timber depots;

(g) a cess for the supply of water for irrigation;
(h) a surcharge on duty for the transfer of immovable property.

(2) The taxes, fees and surcharge shall be imposed, assessed, and realised at such times and in such manner as may be prescribed.

41. *Recovery of taxes and other duties* : (1) When any tax or fee or other sum due to an Anchal Samiti has become payable, the Anchal Samiti shall, with the least practicable delay, cause to be sent to the person liable for the payment thereof, a demand notice in the prescribed form for the amount due from him and require him to pay the amount within a date to be specified in such notice.

(2) Every notice of demand under sub-section (1) shall be served in such manner as may be prescribed.

(3) If the sum for which a notice of demand has been served is not paid within the date specified therein, the Anchal Samiti may recover the same in the prescribed manner.

42. *Appeal against levy of tax etc.* : Any person aggrieved by the assessment, levy or imposition of any tax, fee or surcharge may appeal to the Deputy Commissioner within thirty days of the date of the order imposing such tax, fee or surcharge, and the decision of the Deputy Commissioner thereon shall be final :

Provided that an appeal may be admitted after the expiration of the period specified in this section, if the appellant satisfies the Deputy Commissioner that he had sufficient cause for not preferring the appeal within that period.

43. *Objections to assessment*: No objection shall be taken to any assessment made under this Regulation, nor shall the liability of any person so assessed be questioned otherwise than in accordance with the provisions of this Regulation of the rules made thereunder.

44. *Suspension of levy of tax etc.* : The Governor may, by notification, suspend the levy or imposition of any tax, fee or surcharge and may at any time in like manner rescind such suspension.

45. *Power of Governor to increase taxation* : (1) If, in the opinion of the Governor, the regular income of an Anchal Samiti falls below what is required for the proper discharge of its functions under this Regulation he may require the said Anchal Samiti to take steps to increase its income to such extent and within such period as may be specified by him.

(2) If the Anchal Samiti fails to take adequate steps to increase its income to the extent required within the period specified, the Governor may direct the Anchal Samiti to levy any of the taxes or fees specified in section 40, or increase the rate at which any such tax or fee is levied.

(3) If an Anchal Samiti fails to levy a tax or fee or enhance the rate of any tax or fee as required under sub-section (2), the Governor may, by notification, levy, or increase the rate of, such tax or fee.

46. *Collection of tax or revenue due to Government*: An Anchal Samiti may, in the prescribed manner, collect any class of tax or revenue or fee or due payable to Government in respect of the area falling within its jurisdiction, being allowed a prescribed percentage of collection charges.

47. *Properties placed under the direction, management and control of Anchal Samiti* : (1) The Governor may, if he deems fit, place all or any of the following properties situated within the jurisdiction of the Anchal Samiti, under the direction, management and control of the Anchal Samiti, namely:

(a) open sites, waste, vacant and grazing lands, not being private property, and river beds;

(b) public roads and streets;

(c) public channels, watercourses, wells, ponds, tanks (except irrigation tanks under the control of the Government) public springs, reservoirs, cisterns, fountains aqueducts and any adjacent land (not being private property) appertaining thereto.

(d) public sewers, drains and drainage works, tunnels and culverts and things appertaining thereto and other conservancy works;

(e) sewage, rubbish and offensive matter deposited on streets or collected by the Anchal Samiti from streets, latrines, urinals, sewers, cesspools and other places; and

(f) Public lamps, lamp-posts and apparatus connected therewith or appertaining thereto.

(2) All markets and fairs or such portions thereof as are held upon public land shall be managed and regulated by the Anchal Samiti and shall receive to the credit of the Anchal Samiti Fund all dues levied or imposed in respect thereof.

48. *Accounts and Audits* : (1) Every Anchal Samiti and every Gram Panchayat receiving contributions from an Anchal Samiti under section 33 shall maintain accounts of its receipts and expenditure in such form, as may be prescribed.

(2) The accounts of every Anchal Samiti and the Gram Panchayat referred to in sub-section (1) shall be audited annually in such manner as may be prescribed.

49. *Preparation of budget estimate of Anchal Samiti* : (1) An Anchal Samiti shall prepare annually on or before such date and in such form as may be prescribed a budget estimate of its income and expenditure for the next financial year and may also prepare a supplementary budget estimate at any time during a financial year.

(2) The annual or supplementary budget estimate of an Anchal Samiti shall be submitted to the Deputy Commissioner and after being approved by him shall be binding on the Anchal Samiti.

(3) No expenditure shall be incurred by an Anchal Samiti unless it is included in the budget estimates which have been approved by the Deputy Commissioner under sub-section (2).

50. *Administration Report* : (1) Every Anchal Samiti shall submit annually to the Deputy Commissioner by such date as may be prescribed, a report on the administration of the Anchal Samiti during the previous year.

(2) The report shall be prepared by the Executive Officer and after it is approved by the Anchal Samiti shall be forwarded

to the Deputy Commissioner with a copy of the resolution of the Anchal Samiti thereon.

CHAPTER III

Zilla Parishads

51. *Constitution and composition of Zilla Parishads*: (1) The Governor may, by notification, constitute a Zilla Parishad for each District with effect from such date as may be specified therein.

(2) Every Zilla Parishad shall consist of

(i) the Vice-Presidents of all the Anchal Samitis in the District, ex-officio;

(ii) one representative of every Anchal Samiti in the District, to be elected by its members from amongst themselves in the prescribed manner;

(iii) not more than six persons to be nominated by the Governor from out of the tribes which have not secured representation on the Zilla Parishad:

Provided that no person shall be nominated or after having been nominated, remain member of a Zilla Parishad, if he suffers from any of the disqualifications specified in clauses (a) to (h) of section 7;

(iv) The Deputy Commissioner in charge of the District, ex-officio.

52. *Term of office of members of Zilla Parishad*: (1) A person who is a member of a Zilla Parishad by virtue of clause (i) or clause (ii) of sub-section (2) of section 51, shall cease to be such member on his ceasing to be a Vice-President or a member as the case may be, of the Anchal Samiti.

(2) The term of office of a person nominated under clause (iii) of sub-section (2) of section 51 shall be three years:

Provided that a member nominated to fill a casual vacancy shall hold office for the remainder of the term of the member in whose place he is nominated.

53. *President and Vice-President of Zilla Parishad*: (1) The Deputy Commissioner shall be the President of the Zilla Parishad.

(2) As soon as may be after a Zilla Parishad is constituted, the Zilla Parishad shall elect in the prescribed manner from amongst members a Vice-President which shall, subject to the other provisions of this Regulation, hold office for a period of three years.

(3) If a casual vacancy occurs in the office of the Vice-President of a Zilla Parishad, the persons elected in the manner specified in sub-section (2) to fill such vacancy shall hold office for the remainder of the term of the Vice-President in whose place he is elected.

54. *Resignation of Vice-President or member of Zilla Parishad*: The Vice-President, or any member other than an ex-officio member, of a Zilla Parishad may resign his office by intimating in writing his intention to do so to the President of the Zilla Parishad and such resignation shall take effect from the date of its receipt by the President.

55. *Functions of Zilla Parishad*: (1) The Zilla Parishad shall advise the Governor on all matters concerning the activities of the Gram Panchayats and Anchal Samitis situated within the District.

(2) In particular, it shall be the duty of the Zilla Parishad,

(a) to make recommendations to the Governor in respect of
- (i) the budget estimates of the Anchal Samitis;
- (ii) the coordination and consolidation of the plan proposed by the Anchal Samitis and drawing up of the District plan;
- (iii) the coordination of the work of the Gram Panchayats and Anchal Samitis; and
- (iv) land settlement and raising of revenues for the Anchal Samitis.

(b) to review the working of the Anchal Samiti from time to time;

(c) to advise on such other matters as may be referred to it by the Governor.

56. *Meetings*: (1) The Zilla Parishad shall meet as often as may be necessary and shall observe, subject to the provisions of sub-sections (2) and (3), such rules of procedure in regard to the transaction of business at its meetings as may be prescribed:

Provided that not more than six months shall elapse between one meeting of the Zilla Parishad and another.

(2) The President of the Zilla Parishad or in his absence, the Vice-President, or in the absence of both, any member nominated by the President in that behalf shall preside at any meeting of the Zilla Parishad.

(3) All questions at a meeting of the Zilla Parishad shall be decided by a majority of the votes of the members present and voting and in the case of equality of votes the President of the Zilla Parishad or in his absence, the person presiding shall have a second or casting vote.

CHAPTER IV

Agency Council

57. *Constitution of Agency Council*: The Governor may constitute an advisory body to be called the Agency Council consisting of :

(i) the Governor,
(ii) the Member of Parliament representing the North-East Frontier Agency;
(iii) the Vice-Presidents of all the Zilla Parishads;
(iv) three representatives from each of the Zilla Parishads to be elected by its members from amongst themselves in the prescribed manner;
(v) the Adviser to the Governor, ex-officio.

58. *Functions of Agency Council*: The Agency Council may be consulted by the Governor in regard to

(a) matters of administration involving general questions of policy relating to the North-East Frontier Agency in the State field;
(b) the Five Year Plan and the annual plan proposals for the development of the North-East Frontier Agency;

(c) the estimated receipts and expenditure pertaining to the North-East Frontier Agency to be credited to, and to be made from, the Consolidated Fund of India;

(d) proposals for undertaking legislation with respect to any of the matters enumerated in the State List in the Seventh Schedule to the Constitution;

(e) any other matters which the Governor may refer to it for advice.

59. *Meetings of Agency Council*: (1) The Agency Council shall meet as often as may be necessary and not more than one year shall elapse between one meeting of the Agency Council and another meeting.

(2) The Governor shall preside at the meetings of the Agency Council.

(3) Meetings of the Agency Council shall be regulated by such procedure as may be prescribed.

(4) Subject to rules regulating the procedure of the Agency Council, and subject to the discretion of the Governor to refuse to give information or to allow discussion on any subject in the public interest, a member of the Agency Council shall have the right to ask questions on matters of public interest relating to the North-East Frontier Agency.

CHAPTER V

Control of Gram Panchayats and Anchal Samitis

60. *Powers of inspection, supervision and control of Governor etc.* : The Governor, and such officers as are empowered by him in this behalf, shall have the powers of inspection, supervision and control over the performance of the functions of Gram Panchayats and Anchal Samitis and without prejudice to the generality of the foregoing powers, may

(a) enter and inspect any immovable property in the occupation or control of, or any work in progress under the direction of, a Gram Panchayat or an Anchal Samiti;

(b) call for and inspect any document which is in the possession or control of a Gram Panchayat or an Anchal Samiti;

(c) require by an order in writing, a Gram Panchayat or an Anchal Samiti to furnish such reports, statements, accounts or proceedings as are necessary;

(d) give such advice in writing in respect of the functions and proceedings of a Gram Panchayat or an Anchal Samiti as they think fit;

(e) institute an inquiry in respect of any matter relating to a Gram Panchayat or an Anchal Samiti and rectify any of its acts or omissions.

61. *Inspection of construction work etc. by members of Anchal Samiti* : With the previous sanction of the President of the Anchal Samiti, a member of an Anchal Samiti may inspect

(a) any work or institution constructed or maintained in whole or in part at the expense of the Anchal Samiti, or

(b) any register, books, accounts, or other documents belonging to, or in the possession of, the Anchal Samiti.

62. *Inspector of Local Works* : (1) The Governor may appoint an officer of Government to be Inspector of Local Works for one or more Sub-divisions.

(2) The Inspector of Local Works shall

(a) advise with regard to the construction or repairs of any Gram Panchayat or Anchal Samiti and may for this purpose enter and inspect any immovable property and every such Gram Panchayat or Anchal Samiti shall furnish such statements, estimates and reports as he may require; and

(b) perform such other functions and exercise such other powers as may be prescribed.

(3) A report of every inspection made under this section shall be prepared and a copy thereof shall be forwarded to the Gram Panchayat or Anchal Samiti concerned.

(4) Every Gram Panchayat or Anchal Samiti shall in all matters of technical details be guided by the report of the Inspector of Local Works.

63. *Default in performance of duty by Anchal Samiti members, officer etc.* : (1) If at any time it appears to the Deputy Commissioner or any officer authorised by him in this behalf that an Anchal Samiti or any member, officer or employee thereof has made wilful or persistent default in the performance of any duty imposed under this Regulation, the Deputy Commissioner or officer may, by order in writing, fix a period for the performance of that duty, and if the duty is not performed within the period so fixed, the Deputy Commissioner or the officer may, by order, appoint any person to perform the said duty and direct that the expenses of the performance of the duty shall be paid by the defaulting Anchal Samiti within such period as he may think fit.

(2) The Deputy Commissioner or the officer exercising the power under sub-section (1) shall call for the explanation of the Anchal Samiti concerned for any default under sub-section (1) and shall forthwith report to the Governor who may, after giving notice to the Anchal Samiti officer or employee and after making such inquiry as he deems fit, rescind, modify or confirm the order.

64. *Suspension of execution of order or resolution of Anchal Samiti* : (1) If, in the opinion of the Deputy Commissioner or any officer authorised by him in this behalf the execution of any order or resolution of an Anchal Samiti or the doing of an act, which is about to be done or is being done by, or on behalf of an Anchal Samiti, is causing or is likely to cause injury or annoyance to the public or to lead to a breach of the peace or is unlawful, he may, by order in writing, suspend the execution of that order or resolution or prohibit the doing of that act.

(2) When the Deputy Commissioner or the officer makes an order under sub-section (1), he shall forthwith send to the Anchal Samiti affected thereby a copy of the order together with a statement of the reasons for making it.

(3) The Deputy Commissioner or the officer shall also forthwith submit to the Governor a report of the circumstances in which the order is made under this section and the Governor may, after giving notice to the Anchal Samiti and making such inquiry as he deems fit, rescind, modify or confirm the order.

65. *Power of Deputy Commissioner to call for records relating to tax or fees and make suggestions*: The Deputy Commissioner

may at any time, call for the records of an Anchal Samiti relating to taxes or fees levied within its area and may make suggestions for alteration, addition or modification of any tax or fee so levied or the rate thereof.

(2) On receipt of a suggestion under sub-section (1), the Anchal Samiti shall reconsider the matter in a meeting and a copy of the resolution adopted shall be sent to the Deputy Commissioner.

66. *Dissolution of an Anchal Samiti* : (1) If in the opinion of the Governor, an Anchal Samiti

(a) exceeds or abuses its powers; or
(b) is competent to perform, or make wilful and persistent default in the discharge of the functions imposed on it by, or under, this Regulation or any other law for the time being in force; or
(c) persistently disobeys the order of the Deputy Commissioner or the officer under sub-section (1) of section 63, the Governor may, by order in writing, dissolve the Anchal Samiti and direct that it shall be reconstituted in the manner provided in this Regulation.

(2) No order under sub-section (1) shall be passed by the Governor without giving to the Anchal Samiti a reasonable opportunity to render an explanation.

(3) When an Anchal Samiti is dissolved under sub-section (1),

(a) all the members of the Anchal Samiti shall, from the date specified in the order, vacate their offices as members,
(b) all the functions of the Anchal Samiti shall, during the period of dissolution, be discharged by such person or persons as the Governor may appoint in this behalf.

67. *Disputes between local authorities* : If any dispute arises between two or more Anchal Samitis or between an Anchal Samiti and a Gram Panchayat or between two or more Gram Panchayats, it shall be referred to the Governor and his decision thereon shall be final.

68. *Governor's power to call for proceedings* : Notwithstanding anything contained in this chapter, the Governor may call for and examine the records relating to any order passed by any officer or Anchal Samiti for the purpose of satisfying himself as to the legality or propriety of the order passed and may revise or modify the order as he may deem fit.

CHAPTER VI

Miscellaneous

69. *Bar of action against Anchal Samiti etc. and previous notice before institution* : (1) No suit or prosecution shall lie against any member, officer, employee or agent of a Gram Panchayat or an Anchal Samiti, in respect of anything done or intended to be done in good faith under this Regulation or any rule or bye-law made thereunder.

(2) No suit or other legal proceeding shall be instituted against any Gram Panchayat or Anchal Samiti or any member, officer, employee or agent thereof for anything done or purporting to be done under this Regulation or any rule or bye-law made thereunder, until the expiration of two months next after notice in writing has been left or delivered at the office of the Gram Panchayat or Anchal Samiti, as the case may be and also at the residence of the member, officer, employee, or agent thereof against whom such suit or proceeding is intended to be instituted, and the notice shall state the cause of action, the nature of the relief sought, the amount of compensation claimed and the name and place of abode of the person who intends to institute the suit or proceedings.

(3) Every suit or proceeding referred to in sub-section (2) shall be instituted within six months after the date on which the cause of action arose.

70. *Liability of members for loss, waste or misapplication* : (1) Every member of an Anchal Samiti shall be personally liable for the loss, waste or misapplication of any money or other property of the Anchal Samiti to which he has been a party or which has been caused or facilitated by his misconduct or wilful neglect of duty as a member amounting to fraud.

(2) If, after giving the member concerned a reasonable opportunity for showing cause to the contrary, the Deputy

Commissioner or any officer authorised by him in this behalf, is satisfied, aftar such inquiry as he deems fit, that the loss, waste or misapplication of any money or other property of the Anchal Samiti is a direct consequence of the misconduct or wilful neglect on the part of such member, he shall, by order in writing, direct such member to the Anchal Samiti before a fixed date the amount required to reimburse it for such loss, waste or misapplication :

Provided that no such order shall be made for bonafide or technical irregularities or mistakes of a member.

(3) If the amount is not so paid, the Deputy Commissioner or the officer authorised by him in that behalf shall recover it in the prescribed manner.

(4) An order of the Deputy Commissioner or the officer under sub-section (2) shall be subject to an appeal to the Governor if made within thirty days of the date of the order.

71. *Members etc. to refrain from taking part at sales* : A member of an Anchal Samiti or any officer thereof having a duty to perform in connection with any sale or contract under this Regulation shall not directly or indirectly bid for, or accept a contract work.

72. *Penalty for obstructing Anchal Samiti or officers from doing anything under this Regulation etc.* : (1) Whoever obstructs an Anchal Samiti or any member, employee or agent thereof, or prevents or attempts to prevent any such member, employee or agent from doing anything which he is empowered or required to do under the provisions of this Regulation or any rule or bye-law made thereunder; or

(2) Without lawful authority removes or destroys, defaces or otherwise obliterates any notice, materials, lamp-post, direction post, stand post or any other property exhibited or erected by the Anchal Samiti or under its authority, shall be punishable with fine which may extend to fifty rupees.

73. *Penalty for encroachment of road etc.*: Whoever encroaches upon any land, road, site, public drain, sewer aqueduct, watercourse or other property placed under the control of an Anchal Samiti under section 47, by making any excavation or by erecting any wall, fence, rail, post, projection or other obstruction or by depositing any movable property shall for every such offence, be punishable with fine which may

extend to fifty rupees, and, in the case of a continuing encroachment, with an additional fine which may extend to ten rupees for every day after the first during which he has persisted in the encroachment.

74. *Intimation to be given of infectious diseases* : If a medical practitioner who is aware of the existence of any infectious or contagious disease in any place other than a public hospital or dispensary fails to intimate forthwith the existence of such a disease to such officers as the Anchal Samiti may specify, or gives false information about the existence of such a disease, he shall be punishable with fine which may extend to fifty rupees.

75. *Power to compound cases* : (1) The Anchal Samiti may, either before or after the institution of criminal proceedings under this Regulation, compound any offence against this Regulation or any rule or bye-law made thereunder on payment of such sum in cash to the Anchal Samiti Fund as may be agreed upon.

76. *Penalty for contravention of Regulation etc.* : Whoever contravenes any of the provisions of this Regulation or any rule made thereunder shall, if no other penalty is provided elsewhere in this Regulation for such contravention, be punishable with fine which may extend to two hundred rupees and in the case of a continuing contravention, with an additional fine which may extend to ten rupees for every day after the first during which he has persisted in the contravention.

77. *Power to delegate* : (1) The Governor may, by notification and subject to such restrictions and conditions as may be specified therein, authorise any officer subordinate to him to exercise in respect of Anchal Samitis, any of the powers which may be exercised by the Governor under this Regulation or rules framed thereunder, except the power to make rules under section 83.

(2) The Governor may also, by notification, authorise any officer subordinate to him to perform all or any of the functions of the Deputy Commissioner under this Regulation or rules framed thereunder.

(3) The Deputy Commissioner may delegate all or any of his powers under this Regulation or rules framed thereunder to any officer subordinate to him.

78. *Cooperation with Government officers* : The Anchal Samiti shall, so far as practicable, act in cooperation with and shall

assist, every Government officer who works for the welfare of the rural population within its area.

79. *Powers and duties of police in respect of offences and assistance to Anchal Samiti etc.* : Every police officer shall give immediate information to the Anchal Samiti of an offence coming to his knowledge which has been committed against this Regulation or any rule or bye-law made thereunder within its jurisdiction, and shall assist the members and employees of the Anchal Samiti in the exercise of their lawful authority.

80. *Members etc. of Anchal Samiti to be public servants* : Every member, officer or other employee of an Anchal Samiti shall be deemed to be a public servant within the meaning of section 21 of the Indian Penal Code.

81. *Inspection and copies of records* : Every Anchal Samiti shall on application made to it by any person interested, allow inspection of its records and grant certified copies thereof on payment of the prescribed fee.

82. *Removal of difficulties* : If any difficulty arises in giving effect to the provisions of this Regulation, the Governor may, by order published in the official gazette, make such provision, not inconsistent with the provisions of this Regulation, which appears to him to be necessary or expedient for the purpose of removing the difficulty.

83. *Power to make rules* : (1) The Governor may, after previous publication, make rules to carry out the purposes of this Regulation.

(2) In particular, and without prejudice to the generality of the foregoing power, such rules may provide for

(i) the manner of election of members and the Vice-President of an Anchal Samiti;

(ii) the manner of division of a Block into constituencies for the purpose of election of members to an Anchal Samiti under clause (i) of sub-section (1) of section 6;

(iii) the functions to be discharged by the Executive Officer of an Anchal Samiti;

(iv) the appointment of the officers and employees of Anchal Samitis;

(v) the conduct of meeting of Anchal Samiti and the transaction of business thereat;

(vi) the appointment of committees of Anchal Samitis and their functions;

(vii) the travelling and other allowances to be paid to the members of the Anchal Samitis or any other person for attending meetings of Anchal Samitis or any of its Committees;

(viii) the establishment, control, administration and maintenance of dispensaries, hospitals, asylums and places for the reception of the sick or destitutes within the jurisdiction of the Anchal Samiti;

(ix) the custody and investment of the Anchal Samiti fund;

(x) the raising of loans by the Anchal Samitis and the conditions subject to which an Anchal Samiti may make annual or other contributions to Gram Panchayats;

(xi) the imposition and assessment of taxes, fees and surcharge and the realisation thereof;

(xii) the form of demand notices and the manner of their services;

(xiii) the manner of filing appeals under this Regulation and hearing of such appeals;

(xiv) the collection by Anchal Samitis of any tax, fee or other due on behalf of Government and payment of collection charges therefor;

(xv) the form of accounts to be maintained by the Anchal Samitis and the Gram Panchayats receiving contribution from an Anchal Samiti and the manner of audit of such accounts;

(xvi) the form of annual estimates of Anchal Samitis and the date before which they are to be prepared;

(xvii) the manner in which any moneys due to the Anchal Samiti may be recovered;

(xviii) the manner of election of members and the Vice-President of a Zilla Parishad;

(xix) the conduct of meetings of Zilla Parishads and the procedure to be followed thereat;

(xx) the allowances to be paid to the members of the Zilla Parishad and Agency Council for attending meetings;

(xxi) the manner of election of members to the Agency Council;

(xxii) the conduct of meetings of the Agency Council and the procedure to be followed thereat;

(xxiii) the powers and functions of Inspectors of Local Works;

(xxiv) the fees to be levied by Anchal Samiti for supply of copies of documents and the procedure to be followed in furnishing such copies;

(xxv) any other matter which has to be or may be prescribed:

Provided that the rules under clause (xxii) shall be made after consultation with the Agency Council.

84. *Power to make bye-laws* : (1) Subject to the provisions of this Regulation and the rules made thereunder, an Anchal Samiti may frame bye-laws

(a) to regulate the appointment, functions, powers, duties and conditions of services of its officers and employees ;

(b) to prohibit or regulate the discharge of water from any drain or premises on a public street or into a river, pond, tank, well or any other place ;

(c) to regulate sanitation, conservancy and drainage in the area within its jurisdiction;

(d) to prohibit or regulate the use of roads, public streets or other public places ;

(e) to regulate the terms and conditions subject to which licence may be granted for the running of markets by private persons, the fees to be charged therefor and other incidental matters;

(f) to regulate the manner in which tanks, ponds, cesspools, pasture lands, play-grounds, manure-pits, land for disposal of dead bodies and bathing places may be maintained and used; and

(g) to regulate any of its functions under this Regulation.

(2) Any bye-law made under sub-section (1) may provide that a contravention thereof shall be punishable with fine which may extend to twenty five rupees and in the case of a continuing contravention, with an additional fine which may extend to five rupees for each day during which the contravention continues.

(3) The power to make bye-laws conferred under sub-

section (1) is conferred subject to the condition of the bye-law so made shall not take effect until it has been approved by the Governor and published in the official gazette.

THE FIRST SCHEDULE

Form of Oath of Office

(see Section 11)

I, ...a member of the ....Anchal Samiti, do swear in the name of God/solemnly affirm that I will bear true faith and allegiance to the Constitution of India as by law established, that I will uphold the sovereignty and integrity of India, and that I will duly and faithfully to the best of my ability, knowledge and judgement perform the duties of my office without fear or favour or affection or ill will.

THE SECOND SCHEDULE

Matters within the Jurisdiction of Anchal Samitis

(see Section 20)

Part I

I. In the sphere of sanitation and health :

(1) Cleaning and lighting of streets.

(2) Sanitation and conservancy of the area within the jurisdiction of the Gram Panchayat and the prevention of public nuisance therein.

(3) Opening and regulation of burial and cremation grounds for the dead bodies of human beings and regulating places for disposal of dead animals and of other offensive matters.

(4) Supply of water for drinking and domestic use.

(5) Cleaning of public roads, drains, ponds, tanks, wells and other public places or works.

(6) Layout and maintenance of play-grounds for village children and of public gardens.

(7) Disposal of unclaimed corpses and unclaimed cattle.

(8) Construction and maintenance of public latrines.

(9) Taking of measures to prevent the outbreak, spread or recurrence of any infectious disease.

(10) Removal of rubbish heaps, jungle growth, the filling in of disused wells, insanitary ponds, pools, ditches, the prevention of water logging in irrigated areas and other improvements in sanitary conditions.

(11) Providing medical relief.

(12) Reclaiming unhealthy localities.

(13) Maternity and child welfare.

(14) Encouragement of vaccination in human beings and animals.

II. In the sphere of public works :

(1) Control, regulation and development of grazing grounds, village common and other community property.

(2) Controlling and maintaining buildings, institutions and property belonging to, or placed under the control of, the Anchal Samitis or which may be transferred to it for management.

(3) Planting of trees along the roads and public places and maintenance thereof.

(4) Establishment, maintenance and management of cattle ponds and to perform such functions as may be transferred to it by notification under section 31 of the Cattle Trespass Act, 1871 (1 of 1871).

(5) Destruction of stray and ownerless dogs.

(6) Removal of obstructions in public places and sites which are not private property.

(7) Construction, maintenance and repair of buildings, waterways, public roads, drains, embankments, bunds and bridges.

(8) Control, maintenance and regulation of fairs, minor hats or minor bazars and cart stands.

(9) Construction and maintenance of dharmasalas.

(10) Construction and maintenance of houses for the staff of the Anchal Samiti.

(11) Provision and maintenance of camping grounds.

(12) Extension of village sites and the regulation of buildings.

(13) Management of community lands.

(14) Excavation, cleaning and maintenance of ponds for supply of water to animals.

(15) Construction and maintenance of minor irrigation works.

(16) Construction and maintenance of warehouses.
(17) Land management.

III. In the sphere of education and culture :

(1) Maintenance of public radio sets for the benefit of rural population.
(2) Establishment and maintenance of library, reading room, club or other places of recreation and games.
(3) Popularisation of village sports, organisation and celebration of national and public festivals.
(4) Spread of education to Middle English and Middle Vernacular standards.
(5) Establishment and maintenance of youth clubs and other places of recreation.
(6) establishment and maintenance of theatres for promotion of art and culture.

IV. In the sphere of self-defence and village defence :

(1) Watch and ward of the village and of the crops therein, that the cost of watch and ward shall be levied and recovered from persons resident in the village.
(2) Rendering assistance in extinguishing fires and the protection of life and property in the event of fire.

V. In the sphere of administration :

(1) Maintenance of records relating to agricultural produce, census of village industries, population census, cattle census, spinning wheels and weaving machine census, census of unemployed persons or persons having no economic holding or such other statistics as may be necessary.
(2) Registration of births, deaths, marriages and maintenance of registers for the purpose.
(3) Distribution of such reliefs as may be granted by Government or other agencies.
(4) Supplying local information to the Government or any other statutory authority.
(5) Numbering of premises.

(6) Drawing up of programmes for increasing the output of agricultural and non-agricultural produce in the village.

(7) Preparation of a statement showing the requirements of the supplies and finance needed for carrying out rural development schemes.

(8) Control of cattle stands, threshing floors, grazing grounds and community waste-lands.

(9) Reporting to proper authorities complaints which are not removable by Anchal Samitis.

(10) Preparation of plans for the development of the village.

(11) Establishment, maintenance and regulation of fairs, pilgrimage and festivals.

VI. In the sphere of the welfare of the people :

(1) Propagation of ideas connected with improved housing, encouraging people to undertake improved housing, installation of smokeless *chullas* and ventilators.

(2) Organisation of welfare activities among women and children and among illiterate sections of the community.

(3) Welfare of the backward classes.

(4) Organising voluntary labour for community works and works for the uplift of the village.

VII. In the sphere of agriculture and preservation of forests :

(1) Construction and maintenance of places for the storage of cow-dung, oil cakes and other manure and regulating its collection, removal and disposal.

(2) Tethering and grazing of cattle and encouraging stall-feeding of cattle and growing feeder for the purpose.

(3) Improvement of agriculture.

(4) Establishment of granaries.

(5) Provision of agricultural finance with the assistance of Government, Co-operative and Agricultural Production.

(6) Bringing under cultivation waste and fallow land placed by the Governor with the Anchal Samiti.

(7) Ensuring minimum standards of cultivation in the village with a view to increasing agricultural production.

(8) Ensuring conservation of manurial resources, preparation of compost and selling of manures.

(9) Establishment and maintenance of nurseries for improved seeds and provision of implements and stores.

(10) Production and use of improved seeds.

(11) Promotion of co-operative farming.

(12) Crop experiments and crop protection.

VIII. In the sphere of breeding and protecting cattle :

Improvement of cattle and cattle breeding and general care of livestock.

IX. In the sphere of village industries :

Promotion, improvement and encouragement of cottage and village industries.

Part II

I. In the sphere of sanitation and health :

(1) Public health and sanitation including curative and preventive measures in respect of an epidemic.

(2) Medical relief including establishment and maintenance of hospitals and dispensaries.

(3) Taking anti-malarial and anti-kala azar measures.

II. In the sphere of public works :

(1) Maintenance and regulation of the use of public buildings, grazing lands, forest lands, including lands assigned under section 28 of the Indian Forest Act, 1927 (16 of 1927), tanks and wells placed under the control of the Anchal Samiti

(2) Control of major *hats*.

(3) Establishment and maintenance of works or provision of employment in time of scarcity.

III. In the sphere of self defence and village defence:

(1) Regulation of offensive and dangerous trades or practices.

IV. In the sphere of education and culture:

Spread of education above the Middle English and Middle Vernacular Standards.

V. In the sphere of administration:

(1) Collection of statistics and maintenance of records.
(2) General power over Gram Panchayats in respect of functions assigned to them.
(3) To act as agent of the Government for development works within the area where funds for specific purposes are provided.
(4) Acting as channel through which assistance given by the Governor or for any purpose reaches the village.

VI. In the sphere of the welfare of people:

Relief of distress caused by floods, drought, earthquake and scarcity conditions and other calamities.

VII. In the sphere of agriculture and preservation of forests:

(1) Development of agriculture and horticulture.
(2) Measures for encouraging soil conservation, land reclamation and plantation.
(3) Improvement of cattle and poultry including popularisation of the use of veterinary service, cattle inoculation facilities, castration on scientific lines and establishment of artificial insemination centres.

VIII. Any other function that may be assigned to it by the Governor.

ZAKIR HUSSAIN
President

V. N. BHATIA
Secretary to the Government of India

SECTION VI

1. SIXTH SCHEDULE*

[Articles 244(2) and 275(1)]

Provisions as to the administration of Tribal Areas (in the States of Assam and Meghalaya and in the Union territory of Mizoram).

1. *Autonomous districts and autonomous regions*: (1) Subject to the provisions of this paragraph, the tribal areas in each item of (Part I and II and in Part III) of the table appended to Paragraph 20 of this Schedule shall be an autonomous district.

(2) If there are different Scheduled Tribes in an autonomous district, the Governor may, by public notification, divide the area or areas inhabited by them into autonomous regions.

(3) The Governor may, by public notification,

(a) include any area in **(any of the Parts) of the said table,

(b) exclude any area from **(any of the Parts) of the said table,

(c) create a new autonomous district,

(d) increase the area of any autonomous district,

(e) diminish the area of any autonomous district,

(f) unite two of more autonomous districts or Parts thereof so as to form one autonomous district,[1] [alter the name of any autonomous district],

(g) define the boundaries of any autonomous district :

Provided that no order shall be made by the Governor under clauses (c), (d), (e) and (f) of this sub-paragraph execpt after

*Not applicable to the State of Jammu and Kashmir : Constitution (J&K) Order, 1954.

**Substituted by Act 81 of 1971.

1. Inserted by Act 55 of 1969.

consideration of the report of a Commission appointed under sub-paragraph (1) of Paragraph 14 of this Schedule.

[2][Provided further that any order made by the Governor under this sub-paragraph may contain such incidental and consequential provisions (including any amendment of paragraph 20 and of any item in any of the Parts of the said table) as appear to the Governor to be necessary for giving effect to the provisions of the order.]

2. *Constitution of District Councils and Regional Councils* : [3][(1) There shall be a District Council for each autonomous district consisting of not more than thirty members, of whom not more than four persons shall be nominated by the governor and the rest shall be elected on the basis of adult suffrage.]

(2) There shall be a separate Regional Council for each area constituted an autonomous region under sub-paragraph (2) of paragraph 1 of this Schedule.

(3) Each District Council and each Regional Council shall be a body corporate by the name respectively of "the District Council of (name of district)" and "the Regional Council of (name of Region)", shall have perpetual succession and a common seal and shall by the said name sue and be sued.

(4) Subject to the provisions of this Schedule, the administration of an autonomous district shall, in so far as it is not vested under this Schedule in any Regional Council within such district, be vested in the District Council for such district and the administration of an autonomous region shall be vested in the Regional Council for such region.

(5) In an autonomous district with Regional Councils, the District Council shall have only such powers with respect to the areas under the authority of the Regional Council as may be delegated to it by the Regional Council in addition to the powers conferred on it by this Schedule with respect to such areas.

(6) The Governor shall make rules for the first constitution of District Councils and Regional Councils in consultation with the existing Tribal Councils or other representative tribal organisations within the autonomous districts or regions concerned, and such rules shall provide for—

2. Inserted by Act 81 of 1971.
3. Substituted by Act 55 of 1969.

(a) the composition of the District Councils and Regional Councils and the allocation of seats therein;

(b) the delimitation of territorial constituencies for the purpose of elections to those Councils;

(c) the qualifications for voting at such elections and the preparation of electoral rolls therefor;

(d) the qualifications for being elected at such elections as members of such Councils;

(e) the term of office of members of [3](Regional Councils);

(f) any other matter relating to or connected with elections or nominations to such Councils;

(g) the procedure and the conduct of business [4](including the power to act notwithstanding any vacancy);

(h) the appointment of officers and staff of the District and Regional Councils.

[4][(6-A) The elected members of the District Council shall hold office for a term of five years from the date appointed for the first meeting of the Council after the general elections to the Council, unless the District Council is sooner dissolved under Paragraph 16 and a nominated member shall hold office at the pleasure of the Governor:

Provided that the said period of five years may, while a Proclamation of Emergency is in operation or if circumstances exist which, in the opinion of the Governor, render the holding of elections impracticable, be extended by the Governor for a period not exceeding one year at a time and in any case where a Proclamation of Emergency is in operation not extending beyond a period of six months after the proclamation has ceased to operate:

Provided further that a member elected to fill a casual vacancy shall hold office only for the remainder of the term of office of the member whom he replaces.]

(7) The District or the Regional Council may after its first constitution make rules [5](with the approval of the Governor) with regard to the matters specified in Sub-Paragraph (6) of this paragraph and may also make rules [5](with like approval) regulating—

4. Inserted by Act 55 of 1969.
5. Inserted by Act 55 of 1969.

(a) the formation of subordinate local Councils or Boards and their procedure and the conduct of their business; and

(b) generally all matters relating to the transaction of business pertaining to the administration of the district or region, as the case may be:

Provided that until rules are made by the District or the Regional Council under this sub-paragraph the rules made by the Governor under sub-paragaph (6) of this paragraph shall have effect in respect of elections to, the officers and staff of, and the procedure and the conduct of business in, each such Council:

(* * * * *)[6]

3. *Powers of the District Councils and Regional Councils to make laws* : (1) The Regional Council for an autonomous region in respect of all areas within such region and the District Council for an autonomous district in respect of all areas within the district except those which are under the authority of Regional Councils, if any, within the district shall have power to make laws with respect to—

(a) the allotment, occupation or use, or the setting apart, of land, other than any land which is reserved forest, for the purposes of agriculture or grazing or for residential or other non-agricultural purposes or for any other purpose likely to promote the interests of the inhabitants of any village or town:

Provided that nothing in such laws shall prevent the compulsory aquisition of any land, whether occupied or unoccupied for public purposes by the (Government of the State concerned)[7] in accordance with the law for the time being in force authorising such acquisition;

(b) the management of any forest not being a reserved forest;

(c) the use of any canal or water-course for the purpose of agriculture;

6. Omitted by Act 55 of 1969.
7. Substituted by Act 81 of 1971.

(d) the establishment of village or town committees or councils and their powers;

(e) any other matter relating to village or town administration, including village or town police and public health and sanitation;

(f) the appointment of succession of Chiefs or Headmen;

(g) the inheritance of property;

(h) (marriage and divorce)[8];

(i) social customs.

(2) In this paragraph, a "reserved forest" means any area which is a reserved forest under the Assam Forest Regulation, 1891, or under any other law for the time being in force in the area in question.

(3) All laws made under this paragraph shall be submitted forthwith to the Governor and, until assented to by him, shall have no effect.

4. *Administration of Justice in autonomous districts and autonomous regions* : (1) The Regional Council for an autonomous region in respect of areas within such region and the District Council for an autonomous district in respect of areas within the district other than those which are under the authority of the Regional Councils, if any within the district may constitute village councils or courts for the trial of suits and cases between the parties all of whom belong to Scheduled Tribes within such areas, other than suits and cases to which the provisions of sub-paragraph (1) of paragraph 5 of this Schedule apply, to the exclusion of any court in the State, and may appoint suitable persons to be members of such village councils or presiding officers of such courts, and may also appoint such officers as may be necessary for the administration of the laws made under paragraph 3 of this Schedule.

(2) Notwithstanding anything in this Constitution, the Regional Council for an autonomous region or any court constituted in that behalf by the Regional Council or, if in respect of any area within an autonomous district there is no Regional Council, the District Council for such district, or any court constituted in that behalf by the District Council, shall

8. Substituted by Act 55 of 1969.

exercise the powers of court of appeal in respect of all suits and cases triable by a village council or court constituted under sub-paragraph (1) of this paragraph within such region or area as the case may be, other than those to which provisions of sub-paragraph (1) of paragraph 5 of this Schedule apply, and no other court except the High Court and the Supreme Court shall have jurisdiction over such suits or cases.

(3) The High Court (* * * *)[9] shall have and exercise such jurisdiction over the suits and cases to which the provisions of sub-paragraph (2) of this paragraph apply as the Governor may from time to time by order specify.

(4) A Regional Council or District Council, as the case may be, may with the previous approval of the Governor make rules regulating :

(a) the constitution of village councils and courts and the powers to be exercised by them under this paragraph;

(b) the procedure to be followed by village councils or courts in the trial of suits and cases under sub-paragraph (1) of this paragraph;

(c) the procedure to be followed by the Regional or District Council or any court constituted by such Councils in appeals and other proceedings under sub-paragraph (2) of this paragraph;

(d) the enforcement of decisions and orders of such Councils and courts;

(e) all other ancillary matters for the carrying of the provisions of sub-paragraphs (1) and (2) of this paragraph;

[10][(5) On and from such date as the President may [10a](after consulting the Government of the State concerned) by notification appoint in this behalf, this paragraph shall have effect in relation to such autonomous district or region as may be specified in the notification, as if

(i) in sub-paragraph (1), for the words "between the parties all of whom belong to Scheduled Tribes within such areas, other than suits and cases to which the provisions

9. The words "of Assam" deleted by Act 81 of 1971.

10. Inserted by Act 55 of 1969.

10a. Substituted by Act 81 of 1971.

of sub-paragraph (1) of paragraph 5 of this Schedule apply," the words "not being suits and cases of the nature referred to in sub-paragraph (1) of paragraph 5 of this Schedule, which the Governor may specify in this behalf," had been substituted.

(ii) sub-paragraph (2) and (3) had been omitted.

(iii) in sub-paragraph (4) :

(a) for the words "A Regional Council or District Council, as the case may be, may with the previous approval of the Governor make rules regulating," the words "the Governor may make rules regulating" had been substituted; and

(b) for clause (a), the following clause had been substituted, namely :

"(a) the constitution of village councils and courts, the powers to be exercised by them under this paragraph and the courts to which appeals from the decisions of village councils and courts shall lie";

(c) for clause (c), the following clause had been substituted, namely :

"(c) the transfer of appeals and other proceedings pending before the Regional or District Council or any court constituted by such Council immediately before the date appointed by the President under sub-paragraph (5)"; and

(d) in clause (e), for the words, brackets and figures "sub-paragraphs (1) and (2)", the word, brackets and figure "sub-paragraph (1)" had been substituted.]

5. *Conferment of powers under the Code of Civil Procedure, 1908, and the Code of Criminal Procedure, 1898, on the Regional and District Councils and on certain courts and officers for the trial of certain suits, cases and offences*—(1) The Governor may, for the trial of suits or cases arising out of any law in force in any autonomous district or region being a law specified in that behalf by the Governor or for the trial of offences punishable with death, transportation for life, or imprisonment for a term

of not less than five years under the Indian Penal Code or under any other law for the time being applicable to such district or region, confer on the District Council or the Regional Council having authority over such district or region or on courts constituted by such District Council or on any officer appointed in that behalf by the Governor, such powers under the Code of Civil Procedure, 1908, or, as the case may be, the Code of Criminal Procedure, 1898, as he deems appropriate, and there upon the said Council, court or officer in exercise of the powers so conferred.

(2) The Governor may withdraw or modify any of the powers conferred on a District Council, Regional Council, court or officer under sub-paragraph (1) of this paragraph.

(3) Save as expressly provided in this paragraph, the Code of Civil Procedure, 1908, and the Code of Criminal Procedure, 1898, shall not apply to the trial of any suits, cases of offences in an autonomous district or in any autonomous region to which the provisions of this paragraph apply.

[11][(4) On and from the date appointed by the President under sub-paragraph (5) of paragraph 4 in relation to any autonomous district or autonomous region, nothing contained in this paragraph shall, in its application to that district or region, be deemed to authorise the Governor to confer on the District Council or Regional Council or on courts constituted by the District Council any of the powers referred to in sub-paragraph (1) of this paragraph.]

[12] [6. *Powers of the District Council to establish primary schools, etc.* : (1) The District Council for an autonomous district may establish, construct, or manage primary schools, dispensaries, markets, cattle pounds, ferries, roads, road transport and waterways in the district and may, with the previous approval of the Governor, make regulations for the regulation and control thereof and, in particular, may prescribe the language and the manner in which primary education shall be imparted in the primary schools in the district.

(2) The Governor may, with the consent of any District Council, entrust either conditionally or unconditionally to that Council or to its officers, functions in relation to agriculture,

11. Inserted by Act 55 of 1969.

12. Substituted by Act 55 of 1969.

animal husbandry, community projects, co-operative societies, social welfare, village planning or any other matter to which the executive power of the State [12a](* * *) extends.]

7. *District and Regional Funds* : (1) There shall be constituted for each autonomous district, a District Fund and for each autonomous region, a Regional Fund to which shall be credited all moneys received respectively by the District Council for that district and the Regional Council for that region in the course of the administration of such district or region, as the case may be, in accordance with the provisions of this Constitution.

[12a][(2) The Governor may make rules for the management of the District Fund, or, as the case may be, the Regional Fund and for the procedure to be followed in respect of payment of money into the said Fund, the withdrawal of moneys therefrom, the custody of moneys therein and any other matter connected with or ancillary to the matters aforesaid.

(3) The accounts of the District Council or, as the case may be, the Regional Council shall be kept in such form as the Comptroller and Auditor-General of India may, with the approval of the President, prescribe.

(4) The Comptroller and Auditor-General shall cause the accounts of the District and Regional Councils to be audited in such manner as he may think fit, and the reports of the Comptroller and Auditor-General relating to such accounts shall be submitted to the Governor who shall cause them to be laid before the Council.]

8. *Powers to assess and collect land revenue and to impose taxes* : (1) The Regional Council for an autonomous region in respect of all lands within such region and the District Council for an autonomous district in respect of all lands within the district except those which are in the areas under the authority of Regional Councils, if any, within the district, shall have the power to assess and collect revenue in respect of such lands in accordance with the principles for the time being followed [12b](by the Government of the State in assessing lands for the purpose of land revenue in the State of Assam generally.)

(2) The Regional Council for an autonomous region in

12a. Omitted by Act 81 of 1971.
12b. Substituted by Act 81 of 1971.

respect of areas within such region and the District Council for an autonomous district in respect of all areas in the district except those which are under the authority of Regional Council, if any, within the district, shall have power to levy and collect taxes on lands and buildings, and tolls on persons resident within such areas.

(3) The District Council for an autonomous district shall have the power to levy and collect all or any of the following taxes within such district, that is to say—

(a) taxes on professions, trades, callings and employments;
(b) taxes on animals, vehicles and boats;
(c) taxes on the entry of goods into a market for sale therein, and tolls on passengers and goods carried in ferries; and
(d) taxes for the maintenance of schools, dispensaries or roads.

(4) A Regional Council or District Council, as the case may be, may make regulations to provide for the levy and collection of any of the taxes specified in sub-paragraphs (2) and (3) of this paragraph [13](and every such regulation shall be submitted forthwith to the Governor and, until assented to by him, shall have no effect).

9. *Licences of leases for the purpose of prospecting for, or extraction of, minerals* : (1) Such share of the royalties accruing each year from licences or leases for the purpose of prospecting for, or the extraction of, minerals granted by [13a](the Government of the State) in respect of any area within an autonomous district as may be agreed upon between [13a](the Government of the State) and the District Council of such district shall be made over to that District Council.

(2) If any dispute arises as to the share of such royalties to be made over to a District Council, it shall be referred to the Governor for determination and the amount determined by the Governor in his discretion shall be deemed to be the amount payable under sub-paragraph (1) of this paragraph to the District Council and the decision of the Governor shall be final.

10. *Power of District Council to make regulations for the*

13. Inserted by Act 55 of 1969.
13a. Substituted by Act 81 of 1971.

control of money-lending and trading by non-tribals : (1) The District Council of an autonomous district may make regulations for the regulation and control of money-lending or trading within the district by persons other than Scheduled Tribes resident in the district.

(2) In particular and without prejudice to the generality of the foregoing power, such regulations may—

(a) prescribe that no one except the holder of a licence issued in that behalf shall carry on the business of money-lending;

(b) prescribe the maximum rate of interest which may be charged or be recovered by a money lender;

(c) provide for the maintenance of accounts by money-lenders and for the inspection of such accounts by officers appointed in that behalf by the District Council;

(d) prescribe that no person who is not a member of the Scheduled Tribes resident in the district shall carry on wholesale or retail business in any commodity except under a licence issued in that behalf by the District Council :

Provided that no regulations may be made under this paragraph unless they are passed by a majority of not less than three-fourths of the total membership of the District Council.

Provided further that it shall not be competent under any such regulations to refuse the grant of a licence to a money-lender or a trader who has been carrying on business within the district since before the time of the making of such regulations.

(3) All regulations made under this paragraph shall be submitted forthwith to the Governor and, until assented to by him, shall have no effect.

11. *Publication of laws, rules and regulations made under the Schedule* : All laws, rules and regulations made under this Schedule by a District Council or a Regional Council shall be published forthwith in the Official Gazette of the State and shall on such publication have the force of law.

12. [13b]*(Application of Acts of Parliament and of the Legislature*

13b. Substituted by Act 81 of 1971.

of the State of Assam to autonomous districts and autonomous regions in the State of Assam) : (1) Notwithstanding anything in this Constitution—

(a) no Act of the (Legislature of the State of Assam)[13c] in respect of any of the matters specified in paragraph 3 of this Schedule and matters with respect to which a (District Council or a Regional Council may make laws and no Act of the Legislature of the State of Assam)[13c] prohibiting or restricting the consumption of any non-distilled alcoholic liquor shall apply to any autonomous district or autonomous region unless in either case the District Council for such district or having jurisdiction over such region by public notification so directs, and the District Council in giving such direction with respect to any Act may direct that the Act shall in its application to such district or region or any part thereof have effect subject to such exceptions or modifications as it thinks fit;

(b) the Governor may, by public notification, direct that any Act of Parliament or of the (Legislature of the State of Assam)[13c] to which the provisions of clause (a) of this sub-paragraph do not apply shall not apply to an autonomous district or an autonomous region [13d](in the State), or shall apply to such district or region or any part thereof subject to such exceptions or modifications as he may specify in the notification.

(2) Any direction given under sub-paragraph (1) of this paragraph may be given so as to have retrospective effect.

[13e][12-A. *Application of Acts of Parliament and of the Legislature of the State of Meghalaya to autonomous districts and autonomous regions in the State of Meghalaya*: Notwithstanding anything in this Constitution,—

(a) if any provision of a law made by a District or Regional Council in the State of Meghalaya with respect to any matter specified in sub-paragraph (1) of paragraph 3 of

13c. Substituted by Act 81 of 1971.
13d. Inserted by Act 81 of 1971.
13e. Inserted by Act 81 of 1971.

this Schedule or if any provision of any regulation made by a District Council or if a Regional Council in that State under paragraph 8 or paragraph 10 of this Schedule, is repugnant to any provision of a law made by the Legislature of the State of Meghalaya with respect to that matter, then, the law or regulation made by the District Council or, as the case may be, the Regional Council whether made before or after the law made by the Legislature of the State of Meghalaya, shall, to the extent of repugnancy, be void and the law made by the Legislature of the State of Meghalaya shall prevail;

(b) the President may, with respect to any Act of Parliament, by notification, direct that it shall not apply to any autonomous district or an autonomous region in the State of Meghalaya, or shall apply to such district or region or any part thereof subject to such exceptions or modifications as he may specify in the notification and any such direction may be given so as to have retrospective effect.]

[14][**12-B.** *Application of Acts of Parliament and other Acts to autonomous districts and autonomous regions in the Union Territory of Mizoram* : Notwithstanding anything in this Constitution, the President may with respect to any Act, by notification, direct that it shall not apply to an autonomous district or an autonomous region in the Union Territory of Mizoram or shall apply to such district or region or any part thereof subject to such exceptions or modifications as he may specify in the notification and any such direction may be given so as to have retrospective effect.]

13. *Estimated receipts and expenditure pertaining to autonomous districts to be shown separately in the annual financial statement*: The estimated receipts and expenditure pertaining to an autonomous district which are to be credited to, or is to be made from, the Consolidated Fund of the State, [15](* * *) shall be first placed before the District Council for discussion and then after such discussion be shown separately in the

14. Inserted by Act 81 of 1971.
15. Omitted by Act 81 of 1971.

annual financial statement of the State to be laid before the Legislature of the State under Article 202.

14. *Appointment of Commission to inquire into and report on the administration of autonomous districts and autonomous regions* : (1) The Governor may at any time appoint a Commission to examine and report on any matter specified by him relating to the administration of the autonomous districts and autonomous regions in the State, including matters specified in clauses (c), (d), (e) and (f) of sub-paragraph (3) of paragraph 1 of this Schedule, or may appoint a Commission to inquire into an report from time to time on the administration of autonomous districts and autonomous regions in the State generally and in particular on—

(a) the provision of educational and medical facilities and communications in such districts and regions;

(b) the need for any new or special legislation in respect of such districts and regions; and

(c) the administration of the laws, rules and regulations made by the District and Regional Councils;

and define the procedure to be followed by such Commission.

(2) The report of every such Commission with the recommendations of the Governor with respect thereto shall be laid before the Legislature of the State by the Minister concerned together with an explanatory memorandum regarding the action proposed to be taken thereon by [15a](the Government of State).

(3) Allocating the business of the Government of the State among his Ministers, the Governor may place one of his Ministers specially in charge of the welfare of the autonomous districts and autonomous regions in the State.

15. *Annulment or suspension of acts and resolutions of District and Regional Councils* : (1) If at any time the Governor is satisfied that an act or resolution of a District or a Regional Council is likely to endanger the safety of India [15b](or is likely to be prejudiced to public order), he may annul or suspend such act or resolution and take such steps as he may consider necessary (including the suspension of the Council and the

15a. Substituted by Act 81 of 1971.
15b. Inserted by Act 55 of 1969.

assumption to himself of all or any of the powers vested in or exercisable by the Council) to prevent the Commission or continuance of such act, or the giving of effect to such resolution.

(2) Any order made by the Governor under sub-paragraph (1) of this paragraph together with the reasons therefor shall be laid before the Legislature of the State as soon as possible and the order shall, unless revoked by the Legislature of the State, continue in force for a period of twelve months from the date on which it was so made :

Provided that if and so often as a resolution approving the continuance in force of such order is passed by the Legislature of the State, the order shall unless cancelled by the Governor continue in force for a further period of twelve months from the date on which under this paragraph it would otherwise have ceased to operate.

16. *Dissolution of a District or a Regional Council.* : [16][(1) The Governor may on the recommendation of a Commission appointed under paragraph 14 of this Schedule by public notification order the dissolution of a District or a Regional Council and—

(a) direct that a fresh general election shall be held immediately for the reconstitution of the Council, or

(b) subject to the previous approval of the Legislature of the State assume the administration of the area under the authority of such Council himself or place the administration of such area under the Commission appointed under the said paragraph or any other body considered suitable by him for a period not exceeding twelve months :

Provided that when an order under clause (a) of this paragraph has been made, the Governor may take the action referred to in clause (b) of this paragraph with regard to the administration of the area in question pending the reconstitution of the Council on fresh general election:

Provided further that no action shall be taken under clause (b) of this paragraph without giving the District or the Regional Council, as the case may be, an opportunity of placing its view

16. Renumbered as substituted paragraph (1) by Act 55 of 1969.

before the Legislature of the State.

[17][( ) If at any time the Governor is satisfied that a situation has arisen in which the administration of an autonomous district or region cannot be carried on in accordance with the provisions of this Schedule, he may, by public notification, assume to himself all or any of the functions or powers vested in or exercisable by the District Council or, as the case may be, the Regional Council and declare that such functions or powers shall be exercisable by such person or authority as he may specify in this behalf, for a period not exceeding six months:

Provided that the Governor may by a further order or orders extend the operation of the initial order by a period not exceeding six months on each occasion.

(3) Every order made under sub-paragraph (2) of this paragraph with the reasons therefor shall be laid before the Legislature of the State and shall cease to operate at the expiration of thirty days from the date on which the State Legislature first sits after the issue of the order, unless, before the expiry of that period it has been approved by the State Legislature.]

17. *Exclusion of areas from autonomous districts in forming constituencies in such districts*: For the purposes of elections to the [17a](Legislative Assembly of Assam or Meghalaya), the Governor may by order declare that any area within an autonomous district [17b](in the State of Assam or Meghalaya, as the case may be) shall not form part of any constituency to fill a seat or seats in the Assembly reserved for any such district but shall form part of a constituency to fill a seat or seats in the Assembly not so reserved to be specified in the order.

18. (Omitted).[18]

19. *Transitional provisions*: (1) As soon as possible after the commencement of this constitution the Governor shall take steps for the constitution of a District Council for each autonomous district in the State under this Schedule and until a District Council is so constituted for an autonomous district, the administration of such district shall be vested in the Governor and the following provisions shall apply to the administra-

17. Added by Act 55 of 1969.
17a. Substituted by Act 81 of 1971.
17b. Added by Act 81 of 1971.
18. Omitted by Act 81 of 1971.

tion of the areas within such district instead of the foregoing provisions of this Schedule, namely:

(a) no Act of Parliament or of the Legislature of the State shall apply to any such area unless the Governor by public notification so directs; and the Governor in giving such a direction with respect to any Act may direct that the Act shall, in its application to the area or to any specified part thereof, have effect subject to such exceptions or modifications as he thinks fit;

(b) the Governor may make regulations for the peace and good government of any such area and any regulations so made may repeal or amend any Act of Parliament or of the Legislature of the State or any existing law which is for the time being applicable to such area.

(2) Any direction given by the Governor under clause (a) of sub-paragraph (1) of this paragraph may be given so as to give retrospective effect.

(3) All regulations made under clause (b) of sub-paragraph (1) of this paragraph shall be submitted forthwith to the President and, until assented to by him, shall have no effect.

20. *Tribal areas* : (1) The areas specified in Parts I, II and III of the table below shall retrospectively be the tribal areas within the State of Assam, the State of Meghalaya and the Union Territory of Mizoram.

(2) Any reference in the table below to any district shall be construed as a reference to the territories comprised within the autonomous district of that name existing immediately before the day appointed under clause (b) of Section 2 of the North-Eastern Areas (Reorganisation) Act, 1971:

Provided that for the purposes of clauses (e) and (f) of sub-paragraph (1) of paragraph 3, paragraph 4, paragraph 5, paragraph 6, sub-paragraph (2), clauses (a), (b) and (d) of sub-paragraph (3) and sub-paragraph (4) of paragraph 8 and clause (d) of sub-paragraph (2) of paragraph 10 of this Schedule, no part of the area comprised within the municipality of Shillong shall be deemed to be within the United Khasi-Jaintia Hills District.

TABLE

PART I

1. The North Cachar Hills District.
2. The Mikir Hills District.

PART II

1. The United Khasi-Jaintia Hills District.
2. The Jowai District.
3. The Garo Hills District.

PART III

The Mizo District.

20-A. *Interpretatian*: Subject to any express provision made in this behalf, the provisions of this Schedule shall, in their application to the Union Territory of Mizoram, have effect

(1) as if references to the Governor and Government of the State were references to the Administrator of the Union Territory appointed under article 239 and references to State (except in the expression "Government of the State") were references to the Union Territory of Mizoram,

(2) as if:

(a) in sub-paragraph (3) of paragraph 1,

(i) after clause (g), the following clause had been inserted, namely:

"(h) divide any autonomous region into two or more autonomous regions and define the boundaries thereof";

(ii) the first proviso had been omitted;

(b) in sub-paragraph (5) of paragraph 4 the provision for consultation with the Government of the State concerned had been omitted;

(c) in sub-paragraph (2) of paragraph 9, the words "in his discretion" had been omitted;

(d) paragraph 13 had been omitted;

(e) sub-paragraph (2) and (3) of paragraph 14 had been omitted;

(f) sub-paragraph (2) (including the proviso thereto) of paragraph 15 had been omitted;

(g) in paragraph 16,

(i) in sub-paragraph (1), in clause (d), the words "subject to the previous approval of the Legislature of the State" and the second proviso to that sub-paragraph had been omitted;

(ii) "sub-paragraph (3) had been omitted."

21. *Amendment of the Schedule*: (1) Parliament may from time to time by law amend by way of addition, variation or repeal any of the provisions of this Schedule and, when the Schedule is so amended, any reference to this Schedule in this Constitution shall be construed as a reference to such Schedule as so amended.

(2) No such law as is mentioned in sub-paragraph (1) of this paragraph shall be deemed to be an amendment of this Constitution for the purposes of Article 368.

2. THE STATE OF NAGALAND ACT, 1962

An Act to provide for the formation of the State of Nagaland and for matters connected therewith

(4th September, 1962)

Be it enacted by Parliament in the Thirteenth Year of the Republic of India as follows:

PART I

Preliminary

1. *Short title* : This Act may be called the State of Nagaland Act, 1962.

2. *Definitions* : In this Act, unless the context otherwise requires,—

(a) "appointed day" means the day which the Central Government may, by notification in the Official Gazette, appoint;

(b) "article" means an article of the Constitution;

(c) "assembly constituency" and "parliamentary constituency" have the same meanings as in the Representation of the People Act, 1950;

(d) "law" includes any enactment, ordinance, regulation, order, bye-law, rule, scheme, notification or other instrument or custom or usage having the force of law;

(e) "Naga Hills-Tuensang Area" means the Naga Hills-Tuensang Area specified in Part B of the Table appended to paragraph 20 of the Sixth Schedule to the Constitution, comprising the areas which at the commencement of the Constitution were known as the Naga-Hills District and the Naga Tribal Area;

(f) "regional council" means the regional council referred to in Article 371-A

PART II

Formation of the State of Nagaland

3. *Formation of State of Nagaland*: (1) As from the appointed day, there shall be formed a new State to be known as State of Nagaland comprising the territories which immediately before that day were comprised in the Naga Hills-Tuensang Area and thereupon the said territories shall cease to form part of the State of Assam.

(2) Without prejudice to the power of the State Government to alter after the appointed day, the name, extent or boundaries of any district, the State of Nagaland shall consist of three districts to be called the Kohima district, Mokokchung district and Tuensang district, each comprising the areas respectively set out in the Schedule.

4. *Amendment of First Schedule to the Constitution*: As from the apointed day, in the First Schedule to the Constitution under the heading "I. THE STATES"

(a) in the paragraph relating to the territories of the State of Assam, the following shall be added at the end, namely:

"and the territories specified in sub-section (1) of Section 3 of the State of Nagaland Act, 1962.";

(b) after Entry 15, the following entry shall be inserted namely:

"16. Nagaland . . . . . The territories specified in sub-section (1) of section 4 of the State of Nagaland Act, 1962".

5. *Amendment of Sixth Schedule to the Constitution:* As from the appointed day, in the Sixth Schedule to the Constitution,—

(a) in paragraph 20—

(i) sub-paragraph (2-B) shall be omitted;

(ii) in sub-paragraph (3) the brackets and words "(other than the Naga Hills-Tuensang Area)" shall be omitted;

(b) in the Table appended to paragraph 20, in Part B, the item "2. The Naga Hills-Tuensang Area" shall be omitted.

PART III

Representation in the Legislatures

THE COUNCIL OF STATES

6. *Representation in Council of States*: As from the appointed day—

(a) there shall be allotted one seat to the State of Nagaland in the Council of States;

(b) in the Fourth Schedule to the Constitution in the Table:

(i) Entries 16 to 19 shall be renumbered as Entries 17 to 20,

(ii) after Entry 15, the following entry shall be inserted namely:

"16. Nagaland . . . . 1",

(iii) at the end, for the figures "224", the figures "225" shall be substituted.

7. *Election to fill vacancy* : As soon as may be after the appointed day, there shall be held an election to fill the seat allotted to the State of Nagaland in the Council of States.

8. *Term of office* : The term of office of the member for the first time elected to fill the seat allotted to the State of Nagaland in the Council of States shall expire on the 2nd day of April, 1968.

THE HOUSE OF THE PEOPLE

9. *Representation in House of the People* : (1) As from the appointed day—

(a) there shall be allotted one seat to the State of Nagaland in the House of the People;

(b) in the First Schedule to the Representation of the People Act 1950 :

(i) the Entry "25. Naga Hills-Tuensang Area .... 1" shall be omitted;

(ii) Entries 16 to 24 shall be renumbered as Entries 17 to 25;

(iii) after entry 15, the following entry shall be inserted namely:

"16. Nagaland .... 1".

(2) The whole of the State of Nagaland shall form one parliamentary constituency to be called the parliamentary constituency of Nagaland for the purpose of filling the seat allotted to that State in the House of the People.

(3) For the period referred to in clause (2) of Article 371A, Section 13-D of the Representation of the People Act, 1950, shall apply in relation to the parliamentary constituency of Nagaland with the modification that it shall be necessary to prepare and revise separately the electoral roll for that part of the said parliamentary constituency which comprises the Tuensang District and the provisions of Part III of the Act shall apply in relation to the said part as they apply in relation to an assembly constituency.

10. *Provision as to sitting member* : The sitting member of the House of the People representing, immediately before the appointed day, the Naga Hills-Tuensang Area shall, as from that day, represent the State of Nagaland in that House and shall continue to do so until a person is elected in accordance with law to fill the seat allotted to the parliamentary constituency of Nagaland.

THE LEGISLATIVE ASSEMBLY

11. *Strength of Legislative Assembly :* (1) The total number of seats to be filled by persons chosen by direct election in the Legislative Assembly of Nagaland shall be 60:

Provided that for the period referred to in clause (2) of Article 371-A, the total number of seats in the Legislative Assembly of Nagaland shall be 46, of which—

(a) six seats shall be allocated to the Tuensang District and shall be filled by persons chosen by the members of the regional council from amongst themseleves in such manner as the Governor, after consulting that council may by notification in the Official Gazette specify, and

(b) the remaining forty seats shall be filled by persons chosen by direct election from assembly constituencies in the rest of the State of Nagaland.

(2) In the Representation of the People Act, 1950—

(a) in section 7, the following proviso shall be inserted at the end, namely:

"Provided that for the period referred to in clause (2) of Article 371-A, the total number of seats allotted to the Legislative Assembly of Nagaland shall be 46, of which—

(a) Six seats shall be allocated to the Tuensang District and shall be filled by persons chosen by the members of the regional council referred to in that article from amongst themselves in such manner as the Governor, after consulting that council, may by notification in the official Gazette, specify, and

(b) the remaining forty seats shall be filled by persons chosen by direct election from assembly constituencies in the rest of the State of Nagaland.,"

(c) in the Second Schedule, after Entry 14, the following entry shall be inserted, namely:
"15. Nagaland . . . . . . 60 (for the period referred to in clause (2) of Article 371-A, 46)."

(3) In the Representation of the People Act, 1951, in Section 5, in clause (c), the following proviso shall be inserted at the end, namely:

"Provided that for the period referred to in clause (2) of Article 371-A, a person shall not be qualified to be chosen to fill any seat allocated to the Tuensang District in the Legislative Assembly of Nagaland unless he is a member of the regional council referred to in that article."

(4) The Election Commission shall delimit the assembly constituencies in accordance with the provisions of the Constitution on the basis of the latest census figures, and in doing so

the Commission shall have regard to the following provisions, namely:

(a) all constituencies shall, as far as practicable, consist of geographically compact areas, and in delimiting them, regard shall be had to physical features, existing boundaries of administrative units, facilities of communication, public convenience and linguistic affinities of the people,

(b) all constituencies shall be single-member constituencies, and

(c) the population of each constituency shall not, as far as practicable, be more than six thousand.

(5) For the purpose of assisting the Election Commission in the performance of its functions under this section, the Commission shall associate with itself five persons of whom three shall be elected by the members of the Interim Body established under Section 3 of the Nagaland (Transitional Provisions) Regulation, 1961, from among themselves and two shall be nominated by the Central Government:

Provided that none of the said associate members shall have a right to vote or to sign any decision of the Election Commission.

(6) The Election Commission shall:

(a) formulate its proposals in regard to the matters mentioned in sub-section (4) and publish them in the Official Gazette of the State of Assam and in such other manner as the Commission may consider fit, together with a notice inviting objections and suggestions in relation to the proposals and specifying a date on or after which the proposals will be further considered by it;

(b) consider all objections and suggestions which have been received by it before the date so specified, and for the purpose of such consideration hold one or more public sittings at such place or places as it may think fit;

(c) after considering all objection and suggestions which have been received by it before the date specified, determine the matters mentioned in sub-section (4) by one or more final orders and cause such order or orders to be published in the Official Gazette of the State of Assam; and upon such publication the order or orders shall have the full force of law and shall not be called in question in any court;

(d) amend the Delimitation of Parliamentray and Assembly Constituencies Order, 1961, so as to include therein the Parliamentary constituency of Nagaland and the Assembly constituencies delimited under this section.

12. *Rules of Procedure*: The rules as to procedure and conduct of business in force immediately before the appointed day with respect to the Legislative Assembly of Assam shall until rules are made under clause (1) of Article 208, have effect in relation to the Legislative Assembly of Nagaland subject to such modifications and adaptations as may be made therein by the Speaker thereof.

PART IV

High Court

13. *Common High Court for Assam and Nagaland:* (1) As from the appointed day,

(a) there shall be a common High Court for the State of Assam and the State of Nagaland to be called the High Court of Assam and Nagaland (hereinafter referred to as the common High Court);

(b) the Judges of the High Court of Assam holding office immediately before that day shall, unless they have elected otherwise, become on that day Judges of the common High Court.

(2) Expenditure in respect of the salaries and allowances of the Judges of the Common High Court shall be allocated between the State of Assam and the State of Nagaland in such proportion as the President may by order determine.

14. *Provisions as to Advocates* : (1) As from the appointed day,

(a) in the Advocates Act, 1961, in section 3 in sub-section (1), for clause (b), the following clause shall be substituted, namely :

"(b) for the State of Assam and Nagaland and the Union territory of Manipur, to be known as the Bar Council of Assam and Nagaland",

(c) the Bar Council of Assam shall be deemed to be the Bar Council of Assam and Nagaland.

(2) Any person who immediately before the appointed day is an advocate entitled to practise in the High Court of Assam shall be entitled to practise as an advocate in the common High Court.

(3) All persons who immediately before the appointed day are advocates on the roll of the Bar Council of Assam shall as from the day become advocates on the roll of the Bar Council of Assam and Nagaland.

(4) The right of audience in the common High Court shall be regulated in accordance with the like principles as, immediately before the appointed day, are in force with respect to the right of audience in the High Court of Assam :

Provided that as between the Advocate-General of Assam and the Advocate-General of Nagaland the right of audience shall be determined with reference to their respective dates of enrolment as advocates.

15. *Practice and Procedure in common High Court* : Subject to the provisions of this part, the law in force immediately before the appointed day with respect to practice and procedure in the High Court of Assam shall, with necessary modifications, apply in relation to the common High Court.

16. *Custody of Seal of common High Court* : The law in force immediately before the appointed day with respect to the custody of the Seal of the High Court of Assam shall, with necessary modifications, apply with respect to the custody of the Seal of the Common High Court.

17. *Form of writs and other processes* : The law in force immediately before the appointed day with respect to the form of writs and other processes used, issued or awarded by the High Court of Assam shall, with necessary modifications, apply with respect to the form of writs and other processes used, issued or awarded by the common High Court.

18. *Power of Judges* : The law in force immediately before the appointed day with respect to the powers of the Chief

Justice, single Judges and division courts of the High Court of Assam and with respect to all matters ancillary to the exercise of those powers shall, with necessary modifications, apply in relation to the common High Court.

19. *Principal seat of common High Court* : The principal seat of the common High Court shall, unless otherwise determined by the Chief Justice after consultation with the Governors of Assam and Nagaland, be at the same place as the principal seat of the High Court of Assam immediately before the appointed day.

20. *Procedure as to appeals to Supreme Court* : The law in force immediately before the appointed day relating to appeals to the Supreme Court from the High Court of Assam and the Judges and division courts thereof shall, with necessary modifications, apply in relation to the common High Court.

21. *Pending suits, appeals and proceedings* : All suits, appeals and proceedings, civil, criminal or otherwise, pending in the High Court of Assam immediately before the appointed day shall, on that day, stand removed to the common High Court and the common High Court shall have jurisdiction to hear and determine the same, and the judgements, decrees, sentences and orders of the High Court of Assam delivered, passed or made before the appointed day shall have the same force and effect as if they had been delivered, passed or made by the common High Courts.

PART V

Financial Provisions

22. *Authorisation of expenditure pending its sanction by Legislature* : The President may, at any time before the appointed day, authorise such expenditure from the Consolidated Fund of the State of Nagaland as he deems necessary for a period of not more than six months beginning with the appointed day, pending the sanction of such expenditure by the Legislature of the State of Nagaland :

Provided that the Governor of Nagaland may, after the appointed day, authorise such further expenditure as he deems necessary from the Consolidated Fund of the State of Nagaland for any period not extending beyond the said period of six months.

23. *Distribution of revenues* : The President shall by order determine the grants-in-aid of the revenues of the State of Nagaland and the share of that State in the Union duties of excise, estate duty and taxes on income and for that purpose amend thereby the relevant provisions of the Union Duties of Excise (Distribution) Act, 1962, the additional Duties of Excise (Goods of Special Importance) Act, 1957, the Estate Duty (Distribution) Act, 1962, and the Constitution (Distribution of Revenues) Order 1962, in such manner as he thinks fit.

24. *Property, assets, rights, liabilities and obligations* : (1) All property and assets situated in, or used for, or in connection with the administration of the Naga Hills-Tuensang Area and vested in the Union immediately before the appointed day (other than any property or assets so vested for purposes of the Union) shall, as from that day, vest in the State of Nagaland :

Provided that the cash balances in the treasuries in the Naga Hills-Tuensang Area immediately before the appointed day shall as from that day vest in the State of Nagaland.

(2) All rights, liabilities and obligations of the Central Government, whether arising out of any contract or otherwise, which are, immediately before the appointed day, the rights, liabilities and obligations of the Central Government arising out of or in connection with the administration of the Naga Hills Tuensang Area shall, as from that day, be the rights, liabilities and obligations of the Government of the State of Nagaland.

25. *Arrears of Taxes* : The right to recover arrears of any tax or duty (being a tax or duty enumerated in the State List in the Seventh Schedule to the Constitution) which have fallen due in the Naga Hills-Tuensang Area shall pass to the State of Nagaland.

PART VI

Legal and Miscellaneous Provisions

26. *Continuance of existing laws and their adaptation*: (1) All laws in force, immediately before the appointed day, in the Naga Hills-Tuensang Area shall continue to be in force in the

State of Nagaland until altered, repealed or amended by a competent Legislature or other competent authority.

(2) For the purpose of facilitating the application in relation to the State of Nagaland of any law made before the appointed day, appropriate Government may, within two years from that day, by order make such adaptations and modifications of the law, whether by way of repeal or amendment, as may be necessary or expedient and thereupon every such law shall have effect subject to the adaptations and modifications so made until altered, repealed or amended by a competent Legislature or other competent authority.

Explanation : In this section, the expression "appropriate Government" means, as respects any law relating to a matter enumerated in the Union List in the Seventh Schedule to the Constitution, the Central Government, and as respects any other law, the Government of Nagaland.

27. *Power to construe laws* : Notwithstanding that no provision or insufficient provision had been made under Section 26 for the adaptation of a law made before the appointed day any court, tribunal or authority required or empowered to enforce such law may for the purpose of facilitating its application in relation to the State of Nagaland construe the law in such manner not affecting the substance as may be necessary or proper in regard to the matter before the court, tribunal or authority, as the case may be.

28. *Provisions as to continuance of courts and of officers, etc.* : (1) All courts and tribunal and all authorities discharging lawful functions throughout the Naga Hills-Tuensang Area or any part thereof immediately before the appointed day shall, unless their continuance is inconsistent with the provision of this Act or until other provision is made by a competent Legislature or other competent authority, continue to exercise their respective functions.

(2) Every person who, immediately before the appointed day, is holding or discharging the duties of any post or office in connection with the administration of the Naga Hills-Tuensang Area or any part thereof shall, except where by virtue or in consequence of the provisions of this Act such post or office ceases to exist on that day continue to hold the same post or office in the State of Nagaland, and shall be deemed, as from

that day, to have been duly appointed to such post or office by the Government or other appropriate authority in, such State.

(3) Nothing in sub-section (2) shall be deemed to prevent a competent authority, after the appointed day, from passing in relation to any such person any order affecting his continuance in such post or office.

29. *Amendment of Act 37 of 1956* : As from the appointed day, in Section 15 of the States Re-organisation Act, 1956, in clause (c), for the words, "and Assam" the words "Assam and Nagaland" shall be substituted.

30. *Effect of Provisions of Act inconsistent with other laws* : The provisions of this Act shall have effect notwithstanding anything inconsistent therewith contained in any other law.

31. *Power to remove difficulties* : (1) If any difficulty arises in giving effect to the provisions of this Act, the President may, by order, do anything not inconsistent with such provisions which appears to him to be necessary or expedient for the purpose of removing the difficulty.

(2) Every order made under this section shall be laid before each House of Parliament.

32. Every rule made under this section shall be laid as soon as may be after it is made, before each House of Parliament while it is in session for a total period of thirty days which may be comprised in one session or two or more successive sessions, and if, before the expiry of the session in which it is so laid or the successive sessions aforesaid, both Houses agree in making any modification in the rule or both Houses agree that the rule should not be made, the rule shall thereafter have effect only in such modified form or be of no effect, as the case may be,. so however that any such modification or annulment shall be without prejudice to the validity of anything previously done under that rule.

33. *Regulation 2 of 1961* : As from the appointed day, the Nagaland (Transitional Provisions) Regulation, 1961, shall stand repealed.

THE SCHEDULE

[(See Section 3(2)]

1. Kohima	The areas which immediately before the 1st day of December, 1957, were comprised in the Naga Hills District excluding the areas in Mokokchung District as specified in item No. 2.
2. Mokokchung	The areas which immediately before the 1st day of December, 1957, were comprised in the Mokokchung sub-division of the Naga Hills District.
3. Tuensang	The areas which immediately before the 1st day of December, 1957, were comprised in the Tuensang Frontier Division of the North-East Frontier Agency.

3. THE CONSTITUTION (TWENTY-SECOND AMENDMENT) ACT, 1969[1]

An Act further to amend the Constitution of India.

Be it enacted by Parliament in the Twentieth Year of the Republic of India as follows :

1. *Short title* : This Act may be called the Constitution (Twenty-second Amendment) Act, 1969.

2. *Insertion of new article 244A* : In Part X of the Constitution, after article 244, the following article shall be inserted, namely :

"244A. *Formation of an autonomous State comprising certain tribal areas in Assam and creation of Local Legislature of Council of Ministers or both therefor* : (1) Notwithstanding anything in this Constitution, Parliament may, by law, form within the State of Assam an autonomous State comprising (whether wholly or in part) all or any of the tribal areas specified in part A of the table appended to paragraph 20 of the Sixth Schedule and create therefor :

1. Received the assent of the President on 25.9.1969, Gazette of India, Pt.II.S. 1, Ext. p. 373.
For Statement of Objects and Reasons, see Gazette of India, dated 10.4.1969, Pt. II. S. 2, Ext., p. 406.

(a) a body, whether elected or partly nominated and partly elected, to function as a Legislature for the autonomous State, or

(b) a Council of Ministers, or both with such constitution, powers and functions, in each case, as may be specified in the law.

(2) Any such law as is referred to in clause (1) may, in particular,—

(a) specify the matters enumerated in the State List or the Concurrent List with respect to which the Legislature of the autonomous State shall have power to make laws for the whole or any part thereof, whether to the exclusion of the Legislature of the State of Assam or otherwise;

(b) define the matters with respect to which the executive power of the autonomous State shall extend;

(c) provide that any tax levied by the State of Assam shall be assigned to the autonomous State in so far as the proceeds thereof are attributable to the autonomous State;

(d) provide that any reference to a State in any article of this Constitution shall be construed as including a reference to the autonomous State; and

(e) make such supplemental, incidental and consequential provisions as may be deemed necessary.

(3) An amendment of any such law as aforesaid in so far as such amendment relates to any of the matters specified in sub-clause (a) or sub-clause (b) of clause (2) shall have no effect unless the amendment is passed in each House of Parliament by not less than two-thirds of the members present and voting.

(4) Any such law as is referred to in this article shall not be deemed to be an amendment of this Constitution for the purposes of article 368 notwithstanding that it contains any provision which amends or has the effect of amending this Constitution."

3. *Amendment of article 275* : In article 275 of the Constitution, after clause (1), the following clause shall be inserted, namely :

"(1A) On and from the formation of the autonomous State under article 244A,—

(i) any sums payable under clause (a) of the second proviso to clause (1) shall, if the autonomous State comprises as the tribal areas referred to therein, be paid to the autonomous State, and, if the autonomous State comprises only some of those tribal areas, be apportioned between the State of Assam and the autonomous State as the President may, by order specify;

(ii) these shall be paid out of the Consolidated Fund of India as grants-in-aid of the revenues of the autonomous State sums, capital and recurring, equivalent to the costs of such schemes of development as may be undertaken by the autonomous State with the approval of the Government of India for the purpose of raising the level of administration of that State to that of the administration of the rest of the State of Assam."

4. *Insertion of new article 371B* : After article 371A of the Constitution, the following article shall be inserted, namely :

"371B. *Special provision with respect to the State of Assam* : Notwithstanding anything in this Constitution, the President may, by order made with respect to the State of Assam, provide for the constitution and functions of a committee of the Legislative Assembly of the State consisting of members of the Assembly elected from the tribal areas specified in Part A of the table appended to paragraph 20 of the Sixth Schedule and such number of other members of that Assembly as may be specified in the order and for the modifications to be made in the rules of procedure of that Assembly for the constitution and proper functioning of such committee."

4. THE NORTH-EASTERN AREAS (REORGANISATION) ACT, 1971

An Act

to provide for the establishment of the States of Manipur and Tripura and to provide for the formation of the State of Meghalaya and of the Union territories of Mizoram and Arunachal Pradesh by reorganisation of the existing State of Assam and for matters connected therewith.

Be it enacted by Parliament in the Twenty-second Year of the Republic of India as follows :

PART I

Preliminary

1. *Short title* : This Act may be called the North-Eastern Areas (Reorganisation) Act, 1971.

2. *Definitions* : In this Act, unless the context otherwise requires—

(a) "Administrator" means the administrator of a Union territory appointed by the President under article 239 of the Constitution;

(b) "appointed day" means the day which the Central Government may, by notification in the Official Gazette, appoint;

(c) "article" means an article of the Constitution;

(d) "common High Court" means the Gauhati High Court (the High Court of Assam, Nagaland, Meghalaya, Manipur and Tripura) referred to in clause (b) of sub-section (1) of section 28;

(e) "Election Commission" means the Election Commission appointed by the President under article 324;

(f) "existing State of Assam" means the State of Assam as existing immediately before the appointed day;

(g) "law" includes any enactment, ordinance, regulation, order, bye-law, rule, scheme, notification or other instrument having, immediately before the appointed day, the force of law in the whole or any part of the existing State of Assam or the autonomous State of Meghalaya or the Union territory of Manipur or the Union territory of Tripura, as the case may be;

(h) "sitting member", in relation to either House of Parliament or the Legislative Assembly of the existing State of Assam, means a person who, immediately before the appointed day, is a member of that House or that Assembly;

(i) "successor State", in relation to the existing State of Assam, means the State of Assam or Meghalaya, and includes also the Union in relation to the Union territory of Mizoram;

(j) "treasury" includes a sub-treasury.

PART II

Establishment of the States of Manipur and Tripura and formation of the State of Meghalaya and of the Union territories of Mizoram and Arunachal Pradesh.

3. *Establishment of the State of Manipur* : On and from the appointed day, there shall be established a new State, to be known as the State of Manipur, comprising the territories which immediately before that day, were comprised in the Union territory of Manipur.

4. *Establishment of the State of Tripura* : On and from the appointed day, there shall be established a new State, to be known as the State of Tripura, comprising the territories which immediately before that day were comprised in the Union territory of Tripura.

5. *Formation of the State of Meghalaya* : On and from the appointed day, there shall be formed a new State, to be known as the State of Meghalaya, comprising,—

(a) the territories which immediately before that day were comprised in the autonomous State of Meghalaya formed under section 3 of the Assam Reorganisation (Meghalaya) Act, 1969 (55 of 1969), and

(b) so much of the territories comprised within the cantonment and municipality of Shillong as did not form part of that autonomous State,

and thereupon the said territories shall cease to form part of the existing State of Assam.

6. *Formation of the Union territory of Mizoram* : On and from the appointed day, there shall be formed a new Union territory, to be known as the Union territory of Mizoram, comprising the territories which immediately before that day were comprised in the Mizo District in the existing State of Assam and thereupon the said territories shall cease to form part of the existing State of Assam.

7. *Formation of the Union territory of Arunachal Pradesh* : On and from the appointed day, there shall be formed a new Union territory, to be known as the Union territory of Arunachal Pradesh comprising the territories which immediately before that day were comprised in the tribal areas specified in

Part B of the table appended to paragraph 20 of the Sixth Schedule to the Constitution (but excluding the areas covered by Notification No. TAD/R/35/50/109, dated the 23rd February, 1951 issued by the Governor of Assam under the proviso to sub-paragraph (3) of the said paragraph 20) and known as the North-East Frontier Agency and thereupon the said territories shall cease to form part of the existing State of Assam.

8. *Territories of the State of Assam* : On and from the appointed day, the State of Assam shall comprise the territories of the existing State of Assam other than those specified in sections 5, 6 and 7.

9. *Amendment of First Schedule to the Constitution* : On and from the appointed day, in the First Schedule to the Constitution,

(a) under the heading "I. THE STATE"—

(i) in the paragraph relating to the territories of the State of Assam, the following shall be added at the end, namely,—

"and the territories specified in sections 5, 6 and 7 of the North-Eastern Areas (Reorganisation) Act, 1971";

(ii) after entry 18, the following entries shall be inserted, namely :—

"19. Manipur: The territory which immediately before the commencement of the Constitution was being administered as if it were a Chief Commissioner's Province under the name of Manipur.

20. Tripura: The territory which immediately before the commencement of the Constitution was being administered as if it were a Chief Commissioner's Province under the name of Tripura.

21. Meghalaya: The territories specified in section 5 of the North-Eastern Areas (Reorganisation) Act, 1971".

(b) under the heading "II. THE UNION TERRITORIES":

(i) entries 2 and 3 shall be omitted and entries 4 to 9 shall be re-numbered as entries 2 to 7 respectively;

(ii) after entry 7 as so re-numbered, the following entries shall be inserted, namely :

"8. Mizoram: The territories specified in section 6 of the North-Eastern Areas (Reorganisation) Act 1971.

9. Arunachal Pradesh: The territories specified in section 7 of the North-Eastern Areas (Reorganisation) Act 1971."

PART III

REPRESENTATION IN THE LEGISLATURES

The Council of States

10. *Amendment of Fourth Schedule to the Constitution* : On and from the appointed day, in the Fourth Schedule to the Constitution, in the Table—

(a) for entries 19 to 22, the following shall be substituted namely :

"19	Manipur	1
20	Tripura	1
21	Meghalaya	1
22	Delhi	3
23	Pondicherry	1
24	Mizoram	1
25	Arunachal Pradesh	1"

(b) for the figures "226" the figures "232" shall be substituted.

11. *Allocation of sitting members representing the existing Union territories of Manipur and Tripura*: On and from the appointed day, the sitting members of the Council of States representing the existing Union territories of Manipur and Tripura shall be deemed to have been duly elected under clause (4) of article 80 to fill the seat allotted to each of the States of Manipur and Tripura respectively in that Council and the term of office of such sitting members shall remain unaltered.

12. *Election to fill the seats allotted to the State of Meghalaya and the Union territories of Mizoram and Arunachal Pradesh:* As soon as may be after the appointed day, steps shall be taken to fill the seats in the Council of States allotted to the State of Meghalaya and the Union territories of Mizoram and Arunachal Pradesh.

13. *Amendment of section 27A of Act 43 of 1950:* On and from the appointed day, in section 27A of the Representation of the People Act, 1950,—

(a) in sub-section (1), for the words "For the purpose of filling any seat" the words, brackets and figure "Subject to the provisions of sub-section (5) for the purpose of filling any seat" shall be substituted;

(b) in sub-section (4), for the words "The electoral college for each of the Union territories of Manipur, Tripura and Pondicherry", the words "The electoral college for the Union territory of Pondicherry" shall be substituted;

(c) after sub-section (4), the following sub-section shall be inserted, namely:

"(5) The seat allotted in the Council of States to each of the Union territories of Mizoram and Arunachal Pradesh shall be filled by a person nominated by the President in this behalf."

The House of the People

14. *Allocation of seats in the existing House of the People:* (1) On and from the appointed day and until the dissolution of the existing House of the People, the allocation of seats to the States of Assam, Manipur, Tripura and Meghalaya and the Union territories of Mizoram and Arunachal Pradesh in the House of the People and the number of seats, if any, to be reserved for the Scheduled Castes and for the Scheduled Tribes of each State and Union territory shall be as specified in the Table below and the First Schedule to the Representation of the People Act, 1950 (43 of 1950); shall be deemed to have been amended accordingly.

The Table

Name of the State/ Union territory	Number of seats in the existing House of the People		
	Total	Reserved for the Scheduled Castes	Reserved for the Scheduled Tribes
I. State			
1. Assam	14	1	2
2. Manipur	2	—	1
3. Tripura	2	—	1
4. Meghalaya	2	—	2
II. Union Territories			
1. Mizoram	1	—	1
2. Arunachal Pradesh	1	—	1

(2) On and from the appointed day and until the dissolution of the existing House of the People, Part A of Schedule II to the Delimitation of Parliamentary and Assembly Constituencies Order, 1966 shall stand amended as directed in the First Schedule.

15. *Parliamentary constituencies of the States of Manipur and Tripura and provision as to sitting members*: (1) On and from the appointed day and until the dissolution of the existing House of the People,—

(a) the two parliamentary constituencies of the existing union territory of Manipur shall be deemed to be the two parliamentary constituencies of the State of Manipur; and

(b) the two parliamentary constituencies of the existing Union territory of Tripura shall be deemed to be the two parliamentary constituencies of the State of Tripura;

and the Delimitation of Parliamentary and Assembly Constituencies Order 1966 shall be construed accordingly.

(2) Every sitting member of the House of the People representing parliamentary constituency which on the appointed day, by virtue of the provisions of sub-section (1), becomes a parliamentary constituency of the State of Manipur or Tripura, as the case may be, shall, as from that day be deemed to have

been elected under sub-clause (a) of clause (1) of article 81 to the House of the People from that constituency.

16. *Provision as to sitting members representing Cachar and Dhubri parliamentary constituencies in the House of the People and the election of representative from Diphu parliamentary constituency*: (1) The sitting member of the House of the People representing the Cachar parliamentary constituency which on the appointed day, by virtue of the provisions of sub-section (2) of section 14, stands altered shall, as from that day, be deemed to have been elected under sub-clause (a) of clause (1) of article 81 to the House of the People from the constituency as so altered.

(2) The sitting member of the House of the People representing the Dhubri parliamentary constituency which on the appointed day, by virtue of the provisions of sub-section (2) of section 14, stands altered shall, as from that day, be deemed to have been elected under sub-clause (a) of clause (1) of article 81 to the House of the People from that constituency so altered.

(3) As soon as may be after the appointed day election shall be held to the House of the People to elect a representative from the Diphu parliamentary constituency as if the seat of the member elected to the House of People from that constituency has become vacant and the provisions of section 149 of the Representation of the People Act, 1951 (43 of 1951), shall so far as may be, apply in relation to such election.

17. *Parliamentary constituencies of the State of Meghalaya and provision as to sitting member representing the Autonomous Districts parliamentary constituency in the House of the People and the election of representative from Tura parliamentary constituency*: (1) There shall be two parliamentary constituencies in the State of Meghalaya to be called the Shillong parliamentary constituency and the Tura parliamentary constituency.

(2) The area falling within the Garo Hills District as it exists immediately before the appointed day shall form the Tura parliamentary constituency and the remaining area in the State of Meghalaya shall form the Shillong parliamentary constituency and the said two parliamentary constituencies shall be deemed to have been delimited accordingly.

(3) The sitting member of the House of People representing immediately before the appointed day the Autonomous District

parliamentary constituency shall as from that day, be deemed to have been elected under sub-clause (a) of clause (1) of article 81 to the House of the People from the Shillong parliamentary constituency.

(4) As soon as may be after the appointed day election shall be held to the House of the People to elect a representative from the Tura parliamentary constituency as if the seat of the member elected to the House of the People from that constituency has become vacant and the provisions of section 149 of the Representation of the People Act, 1951 (43 of 1951) shall, so far as may be, apply in relation to such election.

18. *Parliamentary constituency of the Union territory of Mizoram*: The whole of the Union territory of Mizoram shall form one parliamentary constituency to be called the Mizoram parliamentary constituency and as soon as may be after the appointed day election shall be held to the House of the People to elect a representative from that constituency, as if the seat of the member elected to the House of the People from that constituency has become vacant and the provisions of section 149 of the Representation of the People Act, 1951 (43 of 1951) shall, so far as may be, apply in relation to such election.

19. *Provision as to the member to represent Arunachal Pradesh in the House of the People*: The sitting member nominated to fill the seat allotted in the House of the People to the Tribal Areas of Assam specified in Part B of the Table appended to paragraph 20 of the Sixth Schedule to the Constitution, known as the North-East Frontier Agency, shall on and from the appointed day, be deemed to have been nominated to fill the seat allotted to the Union territory of Arunachal Pradesh in the House of the People.

The Legislative Assemblies

20. *Allocation of seats in the Legislative Assemblies*: (1) On and from the appointed day, the total number of seats in the Legislative Assembly of the State of Assam, to be filled by persons chosen by direct election from territorial constituencies, shall be reduced from one hundred and twenty-six to one hundred and fourteen; and every sitting member of Legislative Assembly representing a constituency which ceases to be a constituency in the State of Assam by virtue of the provisions of sub-section (3) as from the appointed day, cease to be a member of that Legislative Assembly.

(2) The total number of seats in the Legislative Assembly of the State of Manipur, to be constituted at any time after the appointed day, to be filled by persons chosen by direct election from territorial constituencies shall be sixty, out of which one seat shall be reserved for the Scheduled Castes and nineteen seats shall be reserved for the Scheduled Tribes.

(3) The total number of seats in the Legislative Assembly of the State of Tripura, to be constituted at any time after the appointed day, to be filled by persons chosen by direct election from territorial constituencies shall be sixty, out of which six seats shall be reserved for the Scheduled Castes and nineteen seats shall be reserved for the Scheduled Tribes.

(4) The total number of seats in the Legislative Assembly of the State of Meghalaya, to be constituted at any time after the appointed day, to be filled by persons chosen by direct election from territorial constituencies shall be sixty, out of which fifty seats shall be reserved for the Scheduled Tribes.

(5) On and from the appointed day, Part B of Scheduled II to the Delimitation of Parliamentary and Assembly Constituencies Order, 1966 shall stand amended as directed in the First Schedule.

21. *Amendment of Second Schedule to Act 43 of 1950*: (1) In the Second Schedule to the Representation of the People Act, 1950—

(i) under the heading "I. STATES" :—

(a) in item 2 relating to Assam, for the figures "126", the figures "114" shall be substituted;

(b) after item 17 and the entries relating thereto the following shall be inserted, namely:

"18. Manipur	...	60	1	19
19. Tripura	...	60	6	19
20. Meghalaya	...	60	—	50";

(ii) under the heading "II. UNION TERRITORIES" items 3 and 5 and the entries relating thereto shall be omitted.

(2) The amendment made by clause (i) (a) of sub-section (1) shall have effect on and after the appointed day in relation to

the Legislative Assembly of the State of Assam and the amendments made by clause (i) (b) and clause (ii) of sub-section (1) shall have effect in relation to the Legislative Assemblies of the States of Manipur, Tripura and Meghalaya to be constituted at any time after the appointed day.

22. *Delimitation of constituencies*: (1) The Election Commission shall, in the manner herein provided, distribute, whether before or after the appointed day, the seats assigned to the Legislative Assemblies of the States of Manipur, Tripura and Meghalaya under section 20 to single member territorial constituencies and delimit them on the basis of the latest census figures having regard to the provisions of the constitution and to the following provisions:

(a) all constituencies shall, so far as practicable be geographically compact areas and in delimiting them, regard shall be had to physical features, existing boundaries of administrative units, facilities of communication and public convenience;

(b) every assembly constituency shall be so delimited as to fall only within one parliamentary constituency;

(c) constituencies in which seats are reserved for the Scheduled Castes shall be distributed in different parts of the States and located, as far as practicable, in those areas where the proportion of their population to the total population is comparatively large; and

(d) constituencies in which seats are reserved for the Scheduled Tribes shall, as far as practicable, be located in those areas where the proportion of their population to the total population is the largest.

Explanation: In this section "latest census figures" mean the census figures with respect to the State concerned ascertainable from the latest census of which the finally published figures are available.

(2) For the purpose of assisting in the performance of its functions under sub-section (1), the Election Commission shall associate with itself as associate members:

(a) in respect of the State of Manipur, all the sitting members of the House of the People representing the Union territory of Manipur or, as the case may be the State of Manipur under sub-section (2) of section 15, and such six persons who were members of the Legislative Assembly of the Union territory of Manipur immediately before its dissolution by order of the President published in the Gazette of India, dated 16th October, 1969 with notification No. S.O. 4223, dated 16th October, 1969 of the Government of India in the Ministry of Home Affairs, as the President may, by order, nominate;

(b) in respect of the State of Tripura, all the sitting members of the House of the People representing the Union territory of Tripura or, as the case may be, the State of Tripura under sub-section (2) of section 15, and such six persons, being members of the Legislative Assembly of the Union territory of Tripura as it functioned immediately before the 1st November, 1971, as the President may, by order, nominate;

(c) in respect of the State of Meghalaya, the member of the House of the People representing the Autonomous Districts parliamentary constituency or, as the case may be, the Meghalaya parliamentary constituency under section 17, and such of the six members of the Legislative Assembly of the Autonomous State of Meghalaya constituted under section 62 of the Assam Reorganisation (Meghalaya) Act, 1969 (55 of 1969) or, as the case may be, of the Provisional Legislative Assembly of the State of Meghalaya referred to in section 27, as the President may, by order, nominate;

Provided that none of the associate members shall have a right to vote or to sign any decision of the Election Commission.

(3) If owing to death or resignation, the office of an associate member falls vacant, it shall be filled, if practicable, in accordance with the provisions of sub-section (2).

(4) A member of any Legislative Assembly nominated under clause (b) or clause (c) shall continue to be an associate member notwithstanding that he ceases to be a member of such Legislative Assembly, otherwise than consequent on the incurring of any disqualification.

(5) The Election Commission shall:

(a) publish its proposals for the delimitation of constituencies, together with the dissenting proposals, if any, of any associate member who desires publication thereof, in the Official Gazette and in such other manner as the Commission may consider fit, together with a notice inviting objections and suggestions in relation to the proposals and specifying a date on or after which the proposals will be further considered by it;

(b) consider all objections and suggestions which may have been received by it before the date so specified;

(c) after considering all objections and suggestions which may have been received by it before the date so specified, determine by one or more orders the delimitation of constituencies and cause such order or orders to be published in the Official Gazette; and upon such publication, the order or orders shall have the full force of law and shall not be called in question in any court.

(6) As soon as may be after such publication, every such order shall be laid before the Legislative Assembly of the concerned State.

23. *Power of Election Commission to maintain delimitation orders up-to-date* : (1) The Election Commission may, from time to time, by notification in the Official Gazette:—

(a) correct any printing mistake in any order made under section 22 or any error arising therein from inadvertent slip or omission;

(b) where the boundaries or name of any territorial division mentioned in any such order or orders are or is altered, make such amendment as appear to it to be necessary or expedient for bringing such order up-to-date.

(2) Every notification under this section shall be laid, as soon as may be after it is issued, before the Legislative Assembly of the concerned State.

24. *Validation of acts done previous to the commencement of the Act*: All things done, and all steps taken, before the commencement of this Act with a view to delimiting the territorial constituencies of the States of Manipur, Tripura and Meghalaya for the purpose of elections to the Legislative Assemblies of those States shall, in so far as they are in conformity with the provisions of sections 22 and 23, be deemed to have been done or taken under those sections as if those sections were in force at the time such things were done or such steps were taken.

25. *Amendment of Scheduled Castes Orders*: (1) On and from the appointed day, the Constitution (Scheduled Castes) Order, 1950 shall stand amended as directed in the Second Schedule.

(2) On and from the appointed day, the Constitution (Scheduled Castes) (Union Territories) Order, 1951 shall stand amended as directed in the Third Schedule.

26. *Amendment of Scheduled Tribes Orders* : (1) On and from the appointed day, the Constitution (Scheduled Tribes) Order, 1950 shall stand amended as directed in the Fourth Schedule.

(2) On and from the appointed day, the Constitution (Scheduled Tribes) (Union Territories) Order, 1951 shall stand amended as directed in the Fifth Schedule.

27. *Provisions as to provisional Legislative Assembly of the State of Meghalaya and as to Rules of Procedure and Conduct of Business of the Legislative Assemblies of the States of Meghalaya, Manipur and Tripura* : (1) On and from the appointed day and until the Legislative Assembly of the State of Meghalaya has been duly constituted and summoned to meet for the first session under the provisions of the Constitution, the Provisional Legislative Assembly of the Autonomous State of Meghalaya, excluding the members nominated thereto, constituted under section 62 of the Assam Reorganisation (Meghalaya) Act, 1969 (55 of 1969), and functioning immediately before the appointed day, shall be the Provisional Legislative Assembly of the State of Meghalaya and that Assembly shall exercise all the powers and perform all the duties conferred by the provisions of the Constitution on the Legislative Assembly of that State :

Provided that for the purposes of this sub-section, the member representing the autonomous District of United Khasi-Jaintia Hills in the said Provisional Legislative Assembly of the autonomous State of Meghalaya shall be deemed also to represent the territories specified in clause (b) of section 5.

(2) The term of office of the members of the Provisional

Legislative Assembly of the State of Meghalaya shall, unless the said Legislative Assembly is sooner dissolved, expire immediately before the first meeting of the Legislative Assembly of the State of Meghalaya.

(3) The persons who, immediately before the appointed day, are the Speaker and the Deputy Speaker of the Provisional Legislative Assembly of the autonomous State of Meghalaya shall be the Speaker and the Deputy Speaker respectively of the Provisional Legislative Assembly of the State of Meghalaya.

(4) The Rules of Procedure and Conduct of Business of the Provisional Legislative Assembly of the autonomous State of Meghalaya, as in force immediately before the appointed day, shall, until rules are made under clause (1) of article 208, be the Rules of Procedure and Conduct of Business of the Provisional Legislative Assembly of the State of Meghalaya, and of the Legislative Assembly of the State of Meghalaya duly constituted under the provisions of the Constitution, subject to such adaptations as may be made therein by the Speaker of the Legislative Assembly, concerned.

(5) The Rules of Procedure and Conduct of Business of the Legislative Assembly of the Union territory of Manipur, as in force immediately before its dissolution by order of the President published in the Gazette of India, dated the 16th October 1969 with notification NO. S.O. 4223, dated the 16th October 1969 of the Government of India in the Ministry of Home Affairs, shall until rules are made under clause (1) of article 208, be the Rules of Procedure and Conduct of Business of the Legislative Assembly of the State of Manipur, subject to such modifications and adaptations as may be made therein by the Governor of that State.

(6) The Rules of Procedure and Conduct of Business of the Legislative Assembly of the Union territory of Tripura as in force immediately before the 1st November, 1971, shall, until rules are made under clause (1) of article 208, be the Rules of Procedure and Conduct of Business of the Legislative Assembly of the State of Tripura subject to such modifications and adaptations as may be made therein by the Governor of that State.

PART IV

High Court

28. *Common High Court for Assam, Nagaland, Meghalaya, Manipur and Tripura*: (1) On and from the appointed day,—

(a) the High Court of Assam and Nagaland shall cease to function and is hereby abolished;

(b) there shall be a common High Court for the States of Assam, Nagaland, Meghalaya, Manipur and Tripura to be called the Gauhati High Court (the High Court of Assam, Nagaland, Meghalaya, Manipur and Tripura);

(c) the Judges of the High Court of Assam and Nagaland holding office immediately before that day shall, unless they have elected otherwise, become on that day the Judges of the common High Court.

(2) Nothing in clause (a) of sub-section (1) shall prejudice or affect the continued operation of any notice served, injunction issued, direction given or proceedings taken before the appointed day by the High Court of Assam and Nagaland under the powers then conferred upon that Court.

29. *Jurisdiction of the common High Court*: On and from the appointed day, the common High Court shall have, in respect of the territories comprised in the States of Assam, Manipur, Meghalaya, Nagaland and Tripura, all such jurisdiction, powers and authority as under the law in force immediately before the appointed day, are exercisable in respect of those territories by the High Court of Assam and Nagaland or the Court of the Judicial Commissioner for Manipur, or the Court of the Judicial Commissioner for Tripura, as the case may be.

30. *Abolition of certain Courts*: (1) On and from the appointed day, the Courts of Judicial Commissioners for Manipur and Tripura shall cease to function and are hereby abolished.

(2) Nothing in sub-section (1) shall prejudice or affect the continued operation by any notice served, injunction issued, direction given or proceedings taken before the appointed day

by any of the Courts abolished by that sub-section, under the powers then conferred upon that court.

31. *Principal seat and other places of sitting of the common High Court* : (1) The principal seat of the common High Court shall be at the same place at which the principal seat of the High Court of Assam and Nagaland is located immediately before the appointed day.

(2) The President may be notified order provide for the establishment of a permanent bench or benches of the common High Court at one or more places within the territories to which the jurisdiction of the High Court extends, other than the principal seat of the High Court, and for any matters connected therewith :

Provided that before issuing any order under this sub-section, the President shall consult the Chief Justice of the common High Court and the Governor of the State in which the bench or benches is or are proposed to be established.

(3) Notwithstanding anything contained in sub-section (1) or sub-section (2), the Judges and division courts of the common High Court may also sit at such other place or places in the State of Assam, Manipur, Meghalaya, Nagaland or Tripura as the Chief Justice may, with the approval of the Governor of the State concerned, appoint.

32. *Extension of jurisdiction of the common High Court to the Union territories of Mizoram and Arunachal Pradesh* : On and from the appointed day, the jurisdiction of the common High Court shall extend to the Union territories of Mizoram and Arunachal Pradesh.

33. *Allocation of expenditure of the common High Court* : The expenditure in respect of salaries and allowances of the Judges of the common High Court shall be allocated amongst the States of Assam, Manipur, Meghalaya, Nagaland and Tripura and the Union in such proportion as the President may, by order, determine.

34. *Special provisions relating to advocates and Bar Council* : (1) Subject to any rule made or direction given by the common High Court in this behalf, any person, who immediately before the appointed day, is an advocate entitled to practise in the High Court of Assam and Nagaland or in the Court of the Judicial Commissioner for Manipur or in the Court of the

Judicial Commissioner for Tripura, shall be entitled to practise as an advocate in the common High Court.

(2) The right of audience in the common High Court shall be regulated in accordance with the like principles as, immediately before the appointed day, are in force with respect to the right of audience in the High Court of Assam and Nagaland :

Provided that as among the Advocates-General of the States of Assam, Manipur, Meghalaya, Nagaland and Tripura, the right of audience shall be determined with reference to their dates of enrolment as advocates.

(3) On and from the appointed day, in the Advocates Act 1961 (25 of 1961) (hereafter in this Part referred to as the Advocates Act), in section 3—

(a) in sub-section (1),—

(i) for clause (b), the following shall be substituted, namely :

"(b) for the States of Assam, Manipur, Meghalaya, Nagaland and Tripura and the Union territories of Mizoram and Arunachal Pradesh, to be known as the Bar Council of Assam, Nagaland, Meghalaya, Manipur and Tripura.",

(ii) in clause (e) for the words "Union territories of Tripura and the Andaman and Nicobar Islands," the words "Union territory of the Andaman and Nicobar Islands" shall be substituted;

(b) in sub-section (2), in clause (b), for the words "Bar Council of Assam", the words "Bar Council of Assam, Nagaland, Meghalaya, Manipur and Tripura" shall be substituted.

(4) The provisions of section 17 of the Advocates Act shall have effect in respect of the roll of the Bar Council of Assam, Nagaland, Meghalaya, Manipur and Tripura subject to the modifications that,—

(a) for clause (a) of sub-section (1) of the said section 17, the following clause shall be substituted, namely :

"(a) all persons who were entered as advocates,—

(i) on the roll of the Bar Council of Assam and Nagaland immediately before the day appointed under clause (b) of section 2 of the North-Eastern Areas (Reorganisation) Act 1971;

(ii) on the roll of the Bar Council of West Bengal immediately before that day and who, within three months from that day, express in such manner as the Bar Council of India may, by rules, prescribe their intention in writing to practise, within the jurisdiction of the Bar Council of Assam, Nagaland, Meghalaya, Manipur and Tripura,";

(b) in clause (a) of sub-section (3) of the said section 17, for the words and figures "with his date of enrolment under the Indian Bar Councils Act, 1926 (38 of 1926)" the words "with his seniority on the roll of the Bar Council of Assam and Nagaland or, as the case may be, the Bar Council of West Bengal" shall be substituted.

(5) Notwithstanding anything contained in the Advocates Act, as amended or modified by sub-sections (3) and (4);—

(a) in the case of the first Bar Council of Assam, Nagaland, Meghalaya, Manipur and Tripura under that Act, the fifteen members required to be elected under clause (b) of sub-section (2) of section 3 of that Act, shall be nominated by the Chief Justice of the common High Court from amongst the advocates who are entitled as of right to practise in that High Court and are ordinarily practising within the territories comprised in the States of Assam, Manipur, Meghalaya, Nagaland and Tripura and the Union territories of Mizoram and Arunachal Pradesh and the term of office of the members so nominated shall be one year from the date of the first meeting of the Council or until their successors are duly elected in accordance with the provisions of the said Act, whichever is earlier;

(b) the names of persons entered on the roll of the Bar Council of Assam, Nagaland, Meghalaya, Manipur and Tripura from the roll of the Bar Council of West Bengal in accordance with the provisions of clause (a) of sub-section (1) of section 17 of the Advocates Act, as modified by sub-section (4), shall, as from the date or dates on which the names are so entered, stand removed from the roll of the Bar Council of West Bengal;

(c) any proceedings which were pending or which may be instituted against any person before or by the Bar Council of Assam and Nagaland or by the Bar Council of West Bengal immediately before his name is entered in the roll of the Bar Council of Assam, Nagaland, Meghalaya, Manipur and Tripura in accordance with the provisions of clause (a) of sub-section (1) of section 17 of the Advocates Act, as modified by sub-section (4), may after such entry, be continued or instituted before or by the Bar Council of Assam, Nagaland, Meghalaya, Manipur and Tripura;

(d) every person who, immediately before his name stands removed from the roll of the Bar Council of West Bengal in accordance with the provisions of clause (b), is a member of the Bar Council of West Bengal, shall cease to be a member of that Council as from the date on which his name stands so removed from the roll of that Bar Council;

(e) the rules made or deemed to have been made by the Bar Council of Assam and Nagaland and in force immediately before the date on which the first Bar Council of Assam, Nagaland, Meghalaya, Manipur and Tripura is duly constituted in accordance with the provisions of clause (a), shall, subject to such modifications and adaptations as may be made therein by the Chairman of the Bar Council of Assam, Nagaland, Meghalaya, Manipur and Tripura, be deemed to be the rules made by that Bar Council and shall have effect accordingly.

(6) (a) As from the appointed day, the assets and liabilities of the Bar Council of Assam and Nagaland shall pass to the Bar Council of Assam, Nagaland, Meghalaya, Manipur and Tripura.

(b) The assets and liabilities of the Bar Council of West Bengal shall be apportioned between that Bar Council and the Bar Council of Assam, Nagaland, Meghalaya, Manipur and Tripura in such manner and proportion as may be agreed upon by the Bar Councils and in default of agreement with reference to any matter, the matter shall be referred to the Chairman of the Bar Council of India and his decision thereon shall be final.

Explanation : Expressions used in this section but not defined in this Act shall have the meanings assigned to them respectively in the Advocates Act.

35. *Practice and procedure in the common High Court* : Subject to the provisions of this Part, the law in force immediately before the appointed day with respect to practice and procedure in the High Court of Assam and Nagaland shall, with the necessary modifications apply in relation to the common High Court.

36. *Custody of seal of the common High Court* : The law in force immediately before the appointed day with respect to the custody of the seal of the High Court of Assam and Nagaland shall, with the necessary modifications, apply with respect to the custody of the seal of the common High Court.

37. *Form of writs and other processes* : The law in force immediately before the appointed day with respect to the form of writs and other processes used, issued or awarded by the High Court of Assam and Nagaland shall, with the necessary modifications, apply with respect to the form of writs and other processes used, or awarded by the common High Court.

38. *Powers of Judges* : The law in force immediately before the appointed day with respect to the powers of the Chief Justice single Judges and division courts of the High Court of Assam and Nagaland and with respect to all matters ancillary to the exercise of those powers shall, with the necessary modifications, apply in relation to the common High Court.

39. *Procedure as to appeals to Supreme Court* : The law in force immediately before the appointed day relating to appeals to the Supreme Court from the High Court of Assam and Nagaland and the Judges and division courts thereof shall, with

the necessary modifications, supply in relation to the common High Court.

40. *Transfer of proceedings from the High Court of Assam and Nagaland and the Courts of the Judicial Commissioners to the common High Court* : (1) All proceedings pending in the High Court of Assam and Nagaland and in the Courts of the Judicial Commissioners for Manipur and Tripura immediately before the appointed day shall, from such day, stand transferred to the common High Court.

(2) Every proceeding transferred under sub-section (1) shall be disposed of by the common High Court as if such proceeding was entertained by that High Court.

(3) Any order made before the appointed day by the High Court of Assam and Nagaland or by the Court of the Judicial Commissioner for Manipur or by the Court of the Judicial Commissioner for Tripura shall, for all purposes, have effect not only as an order of that High Court or, as the case may be, of that Court but also as an order of the common High Court.

41. *Interpretation* : For the purposes of section 40 :

(a) proceedings shall be deemed to be pending in a court until that court has disposed of all issues between the parties, including any issues with respect to the taxation of the costs of proceedings and shall include appeals, applications for leave to appeal to the Supreme Court, applications for review, petitions for revision and petitions for writs; and

(b) references to a High Court shall be construed as including references to a Judge or division court thereof, and references to an order made by a court or a Judge shall be construed as including references to a sentence, judgment or decree passed or made by that court or Judge.

42. *Right to appear or act in proceedings transferred to the common High Court* : Any person who, immediately before the appointed day, is an advocate entitled to practise in the High Court of Assam and Nagaland or in the Court of the Judicial Commissioner for Manipur or in the Court of the Judicial Commissioner for Tripura and was authorised to appear or to act in any proceedings transferred from the said High Court or

Courts of the Judicial Commissioners to the common High Court under section 40, shall have the right to appear or to act, as the case may be, in the common High Court in relation to those proceedings.

43. *Savings* : Nothing in this Part shall effect the application to the common High Court of any provisions of the Constitution, and this Part shall have effect subject to any provision that may be made on after the appointed day with respect to that High Court by any Legislature or other authority having power to make such provisions.

PART V

Authorisation of Expenditure and Distribution of Revenues

44. *Authorisation of expenditure pending sanction by Legislatures* : (1) The President may, at any time before the appointed day authorise by order of such expenditure from the Consolidated Fund of the State of Manipur or of the State of Tripura as he deems necessary for a period of not more than six months beginning with the appointed day pending the sanction of such expenditure by the Legislative Assembly of the State of Manipur or the State of Tripura, as the case may be :

Provided that the Governor of Manipur or of Tripura may, after the appointed day, authorise by order such further expenditure as he deems necessary from the Consolidated Fund of the State of Manipur or, as the case may be, of the State of Tripura for any period not extending beyond the said period of six months.

(2) The President, or as the case may be, the Governor of the concerned State shall make separate orders under sub-section (1) in respect of periods falling in different financial years.

(3) The Governor of Assam, exercising the functions as Governor in relation to the autonomous State of Meghalaya by virtue of the Assam Reorganisation (Meghalaya) Act, 1969, (55 of 1969) may at any time, before the appointed day, authorise by order such expenditure from the Consolidated Fund of the State of Meghalaya as he deems necessary for a period of not more than six months beginning with the appointed day pending the sanction of such expenditures by the Legislative Assembly of Meghalaya :

Provided that the Governor of Meghalaya may, after the appointed day, authorise such further expenditure as he deems necessary from the Consolidated Fund of the State of Meghalaya for any period not extending beyond the said period of six months.

(4) The Governors referred to in sub-section (3) shall make separate orders under that sub-section in respect of periods falling in different financial years.

(5) The President may, at any time, before or after the appointed day authorise by order such expenditure from the Consolidated Fund of India as he deems necessary for a period of not more than six months beginning with the appointed day for the administration of the affairs of the Union territory of Mizoram pending the sanction of such expenditure by Parliament.

(6) The President shall make separate orders under sub-section (5) in respect of periods falling in different financial years.

45. *Appropriation of moneys for expenditure to the Union territory of Arunachal Pradesh* : Any Act passed by Parliament for the appropriation of any money out of the Consolidated Fund of India to meet the expenditure in respect of any part of the financial year 1971-72 in, or for the purposes of the tribal areas of Assam specified in Part B of the Table appended to paragraph 20 of the Sixth Schedule to the Constitution shall, on and from the appointed day, have effect also in relation to the Union territory of Arunachal Pradesh and it shall be lawful for the President to spend any amount in, or for the purposes of, that Union territory out of the amounts authorised by such Act to be expended in, or for the purposes of, the said tribal areas.

46. *Reports relating to the accounts of the Union territories of Manipur and Tripura* : (1) The reports of the Comptroller and Auditor-General of India referred to in section 49 of the Government of Union Territories Act, 1965 (20 of 1965) relating to the accounts of the Union territory of Manipur or of the Union territory of Tripura in respect of any period prior to the appointed day shall be submitted to the Governor of Manipur or of Tripura, as the case may be, who shall cause them to be laid before the Legislative Assembly of the State of Manipur or of the State of Tripura, as the case may be.

(2) The Governor of Manipur or of Tripura, as the case may be, may, by order,—

(a) declare any expenditure incurred out of the Consolidated Fund of the Union territory of Manipur or of Tripura on any service in respect of any period prior to the appointed day during the financial year 1971-72, or in respect of any earlier financial year in excess of the amount granted for that service and for that year as disclosed in the reports referred to in sub-section (1) to have been duly authorised, and

(b) provide for any action to be taken on any matter arising out of the said reports.

47. *Reports relating to the accounts of the autonomous State of Meghalaya* : (1) The reports of the Comptroller and Auditor-General of India relating to the accounts of the autonomous State of Meghalaya in respect of any period prior to the appointed day shall be submitted to the Governor of Meghalaya who shall cause them to be laid before the Legislative Assembly of the State of Meghalaya.

(2) The Governor of Meghalaya may, by order,—

(a) declare any expenditure incurred out of the Consolidated Fund of the autonomous State of Meghalaya on any service in respect of any period prior to the appointed day during the financial year 1971-72 or in respect of any earlier financial year in excess of the amount granted for that service and for that year as disclosed in the reports referred to in sub-section (1) to have been duly authorised, and

(b) provide for any action to be taken on any matter arising out of the said reports.

48. *Allowances and privileges of the Governors of Assam, Manipur, Meghalaya and Tripura* : The allowances and privileges of the Governors of Assam, Manipur, Meghalaya and Tripura shall, until provision in that behalf is made by Parliament by law under clause (3) of article 158, be such as the President may, by order, determine.

49. *Distribution of revenues* : The President shall, by order, determine the grants-in-aid of the revenue of the States of Assam, Manipur, Meghalaya, and Tripura and the share of each such State in the Union duties of excise, estate duty and taxes on income and for that purpose amend thereby the relevant provisions of the Union Duties of Excise (Distribution) Act, 1962 (3 of 1962), the Additional Duties of Excise (Goods of Special Importance) Act, 1957 (58 of 1957), the Estate Duty (Distribution) Act, 1962 (9 of 1962) and the Constitution (Distribution of Revenues) Order, 1969 (G.O. 87) in such manner as he thinks fit.

PART VI

Assets and Liabilities

50. *Property, assets, rights, liabilities, obligations, etc., of the States of Manipur and Tripura* : (1) All such property and assets within the Union territory of Manipur or of Tripura as are held immediately before the appointed day by the Union for purposes of governance of that Union territory shall, on and from that day, pass to the State of Manipur or of Tripura, as the case may be, unless the purposes for which such property and assets are so held are Union purposes :

Provided that the cash balance in the treasuries in the Union territory of Manipur or of Tripura before the appointed day shall, as from that day, vest in the State of Manipur or of Tripura, as the case may be.

(2) All rights, liabilities and obligations (other than those relatable to, or in connection with, a Union purpose), whether arising out of any contract or otherwise, which are, immediately before the appointed day,—

(a) the rights, liabilities and obligations of the Central Government arising out of, or in connection with, the governance of the Union territory of Manipur or of Tripura; or

(b) the rights, liabilities and obligations of the Administrator of the Union territory of Manipur or of Tripura in his capacity as such or of the Government of the Union territory of Manipur or of Tripura, shall, on and from the appointed day, be the rights, liabilities and obligations of the Government of the State of Manipur or of Tripura, as the case may be.

(3) The right to recover arrears of—

(a) any tax or duty being a tax or duty enumerated in the State List in the Seventh Schedule to the Constitution, or

(b) any duty referred to in article 268, or

(c) any tax under the Central Sales Tax Act, 1956 (74 of 1956) which having fallen due in Union territory of Manipur or of Tripura immediately before the appointed day shall, on and from that day, pass to the State of Manipur or of Tripura, as the case may be.

(4) The provisions of this section shall not apply to or in relation to,

(a) any institution, undertaking or project the expenditure in relation to which is, immediately before the appointed day, met from and out of the Consolidated Fund of India;

(b) any property which has been placed by the Union at the disposal of the administration of the Union territory of Manipur or of Tripura subject to the condition that the ownership thereof will continue to vest in the Union.

Explanation : For the purposes of this section,—

(a) "liability" includes liability in respect of any civil deposit, local fund deposit, charitable or other endowment, provident fund account, pension or actionable wrong;

(b) "Union purposes" means the purposes of Government relatable to any of the matters mentioned in the Union List in the Seventh Schedule to the Constitution.

51. *Assets and liabilities of the State of Meghalaya* : (1) All rights, liabilities and obligations whether arising out of any contract or otherwise, which are, immediately before the appointed day, the rights, liabilities and obligations of the autonomous State of Meghalaya, including the rights, liabilities and obligations apportioned or to be apportioned to the share of the autonomous State of Meghalaya by virtue of section 58, of the Assam Reorganisation (Meghalaya) Act, 1969 (55 of 1969) shall, on and from the appointed day, be the rights, liabilities and obligations of the State of Meghalaya.

(2) All property and assets held by the autonomous State of Meghalaya immediately before the appointed day, including the property and assets apportioned or to be apportioned to the share of the autonomous State of Meghalaya by virtue of section 53 of the Assam Reorganisation (Meghalaya) Act, 1969 (55 of 1969), shall, on and from that day, pass to the State of Meghalaya.

(3) Subject to the provisions of sub-sections (1) and (2) of this section and section 52, all rights, liabilities and obligations whether arising out of any contract or otherwise, which are, immediately before the appointed day, the rights, liabilities and obligations of the existing State of Assam and all property and assets held by the existing State of Assam immediately before the appointed day shall be apportioned between the State of Assam and the State of Meghalaya in accordance with the provisions contained in the Sixth Schedule.

52. *Assets and liabilities (including public debt) relating to the Mizo District* : (1) All property and assets within the Mizo District which are, immediately before the appointed day, vested in the existing State of Assam shall, as from that day, rest in the Union.

(2) Unless the Central Government otherwise direct any stores, articles and other goods belonging to the existing State of Assam and situated outside the Mizo District immediately before the apointed day shall, as from that day, pass to the Union if such stores, articles or other goods are held for, or are relatable to, the administration of that District.

(3) All rights, liabilities and obligations of the existing State of Assam in relation to the Mizo District shall, as from the appointed day, be the rights, liabilities and obligations of the Union.

(4) The liability of the existing State of Assam to the Union in respect of the loans taken by that State from the Central Government shall be reduced by an amount which bears such proportion to the total public debt of that State immediately before the appointed day as the total expenditure on all capital works and other capital outlays incurred or deemed to have been incurred up to that day by the existing State of Assam in

the Mizo District bears to the total expenditure on all capital works and other capital outlays incurred or deemed to have been incurred by the existing State of Assam up to the appointed day:

Provided that for the purposes of this sub-section the total public debt of the existing State of Assam shall exclude the public debt apportioned or apportionable to the autonomous State of Meghalaya under section 58 of the Assam Reorganisation (Meghalaya) Act, 1969, (55 of 1969) and the total expenditure on all capital works and other capital outlays incurred or deemed to have been incurred by the existing State of Assam shall exclude such outlays incurred or deemed to have been incurred for the purposes of the autonomous State under the said section.

(5) Nothing in this section shall apply to any amount which may be payable by the Union to the existing State of Assam in respect of the expenditure incurred by the State in connection with internal disturbances in the Mizo District.

PART VII

Provisions as to certain Corporations

53. *Provisions as to certain Corporations* : (1) The following bodies corporate constituted for the existing State of Assam, namely:

(a) the State Electricity Board constituted under the Electricity (Supply) Act, 1948, (54 of 1948); and

(b) the State Warehousing Corporation established under the Warehousing Corporations Act, 1962, (58 of 1962),

shall, on and from the appointed day, continue to function in those areas in respect of which they were functioning immediately before that day, subject to the provisions of this section and to such direction as may, from time to time, be issued by the Central Government.

(2) Any directions issued by the Central Government under sub-section (1) in respect of the Board or the Corporation may include a direction that the Act under which the Board or the Corporation was constituted shall, in its application to that Board or Corporation, have effect subject to such exceptions and modifications as the Central Government thinks fit.

(3) The Board or the Corporation referred to in sub-section (1) shall cease to function as from, and shall be deemed to be dissolved on, the expiry of a period of two years from the appoined day or such earlier date as the Central Government may, by order, appoint; and upon such dissolution, its assets, rights and liabilities shall be apportioned between the successor States in such manner as may be agreed upon among them within one year of the dissolution of the Board or the Corporation, as the case may be, or if no agreement is reached, in such manner as the Central Government may, by order, determine.

(4) Nothing in the preceding provisions of this section shall be construed as preventing the Government of any of the successor States from constituting at any time on or after the appointed day, a State Electricity Board or a State Warehousing Corporation for that State under the provisions of the Act relating to such Board or Corporation; and if such a Board or a Corporation is so constituted in any of the successor States before the dissolution of the Board or the Corporation referred to in sub-section (1),—

(a) provision may be made by order of the Central Government enabling the new Board or the new Corporation to take over from the existing Board or Corporation all or any of its undertakings, assets, rights and liabilities in that State, and

(b) upon the dissolution of the existing Board or Corporation,

(i) any assets, rights and liabilities which would otherwise have passed to that State by or under the provisions of sub-section (3) shall pass to the new Board or the Corporation instead of to that State;

(ii) any employees who would otherwise have been transferred to or re-employed by that State under sub-section (3), read with clause (i) of sub-section (5), shall be transferred to or re-employed by the new Board or the Corporation instead of to or by that State.

(5) An agreement entered into between the successor States under sub-section (3) and an order made by the Central

Government under that sub-section or under clause (a) of sub-section (4) may provide for the transfer or re-employment of any employees of the Board or the Corporation referred to in sub-section (1),—

(i) to or by the successor States, in the case of an agreement under sub-section (3) or an order made under that sub-section;

(ii) to or by the new Board or the new Corporation constituted under sub-section (4), in the case of an order made under clause (a) of that sub-section;

and, subject to the provisions of section 58, also for the terms and conditions of service applicable to such employees after such transfer or re-employment.

54. *Continuance of arrangements in regard to generation and supply of electric power and supply of water* : If it appears to the Central Government that the arrangement in regard to the generation or supply of electric power or the supply of water for any area or in regard to the execution of any project for such generation or supply has been or is likely to be modified to the disadvantage of that area by reason of the fact that it is, by virtue of the provisions of Part II, outside the State in which the power stations and other installations for the generation and supply of such power or the catchment area reservoirs and other works for the supply of water, as the case may be are located, the Central Government may give such directions as it deems fit, to the State Government or other authority concerned for the maintenance, so far as practicable, of the previous arrangement.

55. *Provisions as to Assam State Financial Corporation*: (1) The Assam State Financial Corporation established under the State Financial Corporations Act, 1951 (63 of 1951), shall on and from the appointed day, continue to function in those areas in respect of which it was functioning immediately before that day, subject to the provisions of this section and to such directions as may, from time to time, be issued by the Central Government.

(2) Any direction issued by the Central Government under sub-section ( ) in respect of the Corporation may include a direction that the said Act, in its application to the Corporation,

shall have effect subject to such exceptions and modifications as may be specified in the direction.

(3) Notwithstanding anything contained in sub-section (1) or sub-section (2), the Board of Directors of the Corporation may, with the previous approval of the Central Government and shall, if so required by the Central Government, convene at any time after the appointed day a meeting for the consideration of a scheme for the reconstitution or re-organisation or dissolution as the case may be of the Corporation including proposals regarding the formation of new Corporations and the transfer thereto of the assets, rights and liabilities of the existing Corporation, and if such a scheme is approved at a general meeting by a resolution passed by a majority of the shareholders present and voting the scheme shall be submitted to the Central Government for its sanction.

(4) If the scheme is sanctioned by the Central Government either without modifications or with modifications which are approved at a general meeting, the Central Government shall certify the scheme, and upon such certification the scheme shall notwithstanding anything to the contrary contained in any law for the time being in force, be binding on the Corporations affected by the scheme as well as the shareholders and creditors thereof.

(5) If the scheme is not so approved or sanctioned the Central Government may refer the scheme to such Judge of the common High Court as may be nominated in this behalf by the Chief Justice thereof, and the decision of the Judge in regard to the scheme shall be final and shall be binding on the Corporations affected by the scheme as well as the shareholders and creditors thereof.

(6) Nothing in the preceding provisions of this section shall be construed as preventing the Government of the State of Meghalaya from constituting, at any time after the appointed day and with the approval of the Central Government, a State Financial Corporation for that State under the State Financial Corporations Act, 1951 (63 of 1951).

56. *General provisions as to statutory corporations* : (1) Save as otherwise expressly provided by the foregoing provisions of this Part, where any body corporate constituted under a Central Act, State Act, or Provincial Act for the existing State of Assam or any

part thereof has, by virtue of the provisions of Part II, become another State body corporate, then, the body corporate shall, on and from the appointed day continue to function and operate in those areas in respect of which it was functioning and operating immediately before that day, subject to such directions as may from time to time be issued by the Central Government, until other provision is made by laws in respect of the said body corporate.

(2) Any directions issued by the Central Government under sub-section (1) in respect of any such body corporate may include a direction that any law by which the said body corporate is governed shall, in its application to that body corporate, have effect, subject to such exceptions and modifications as may be specified in the direction.

57. *Temporary provisions as to continuance of certain existing road transport permits*: (1) Notwithstanding anything contained in section 63 of the Motor Vehicles Act, 1939, (4 of 1939), a permit granted by the State or a Regional Transport Authority in the existing State of Assam shall, if such permit was, immediately before the appointed day, valid and effective in any area therein, be deemed to continue to be valid and effective in that area after that day subject to the provisions of that Act, as for the time being in force in that area and it shall not be necessary for any such permit to be countersigned by any State or Regional Transport Authority for the purpose of validating it for use in such area:

Provided that the Central Government may, after consultation with the State Government or Governments concerned, add to amend or vary the conditions attached to the permit by the authority by which the permit was granted.

(2) No tolls, entrance fees or other charges of a like nature shall be levied after the appointed day in respect of any transport vehicle for its operations in any of the successor States under any such permit, if such vehicle was immediately before that day exempt from the payment of any such tolls, entrance fees or other charges for its operation within the existing State of Assam:

Provided that the Central Government may after consultation with the State Government or Governments concerned, authorises the levy of any such tolls, entrance fees or other charges as the case may be.

58. *Special provision relating to retrenchment compensation in certain cases*: Where, on account of the reorganisation of the existing State of Assam under this Act any body corporate constituted under a Central Act, State Act or Provincial Act, any cooperative society registered under any law relating to co-operative societies or any commercial or industrial undertaking of that State is reconstituted or reorganised in any manner whatsoever or is amalgamated with any other body corporate, co-operative society or undertaking, or is dissolved and in consequence of such reconstitution, reorganisation, amalgamation or dissolution, any workman employed by such body corporate of any such co-operative society or undertaking, is transferred to, or re-employed by any other body corporate, or in any other co-operative society or undertaking then notwithstanding anything contained in section 25F, 25FF or 25FFF of the Industrial Disputes Act, 1947, (14 of 1947) such transfer or re-employment shall not entitle him to any compensation under that section :

Provided that—

(a) the terms and conditions of service applicable to the workman after such transfer or re-employment are not less favourable to the workman than those applicable to him immediately before the transfer or re-employment; and

(b) the employer in relation to the body corporate, the co-operative society or the undertaking where the workman transferred or re-employed is, by agreement or otherwise, legally liable to pay to the workman, in the event of his retrenchment, compensation under section 25F, 25FF or 25FFF of the Industrial Disputes Act, 1947 (14 of 1947), on the basis that his service has been continuous and has not been interrupted by the transfer or re-employment.

59. *Special provisions as to income-tax* : Where the assets, rights and liabilities of any body corporate carrying on business are, under the provisions of this Part, transferred to any other bodies corporate which after the transfer carry on the same business, the losses or profits or gains sustained by the body corporate first mentioned which, but for such transfer, would have been allowed to be carried forward and set-off in accordance with the provisions of Chapter VI of the Income-Tax Act 1961 (43 of 1961), shall be apportioned amongst the transferee bodies corporate in accordance with the rules to be made by the Central Government in this behalf and, upon such apportionment, the share of loss allotted to each transferee body corporate shall be dealt with in accordance with the provisions of Chapter VI of the said Act, as if the transferee body corporate has itself sustained such loss in a business carried on by it in the years in which these losses were sustained.

60. *Continuance of facilities in certain State institutions*: (1) The Government of the State of Assam or Meghalaya or, as the case may be, the Central Government in relation to the Union territory of Mizoram shall, in respect of the institutions specified in the Seventh Schedule located in that State or Union territory, continue to provide facilities to any other Government aforesaid and the people of the States and Union territory aforesaid which shall not, in any respect, be less favourable to such Government and people than what were being provided to them before the appointed day, for such period and upon such terms and conditions (including those relating to any contributions to be made for the provision of such facilities) as may be agreed upon between the said Governments before the expiry of a period of one year from the appointed day or, if no agreement is reached before such expiry, as may be fixed by order of the Central Government.

(2) The Central Government may at any time before the expiry of a period of one year from the appointed day, by notification in the official Gazette, specify in the Seventh Schedule any other institution existing on the appointed day in the said States and Union territory and on the issue of such notification, the said Schedule shall be deemed to be amended by the inclusion of the said institution therein.

PART VIII

Provisions as to Services

61. *Provisions relating to All-India Services*: (1) In this section, the expression "joint cadre",—

(a) in relation to the Indian Administrative Service, has the meaning assigned to it in the Indian Administrative Service (Cadre) Rules, 1954;

(b) in relation to the Indian Police Service, has the meaning assigned to it in the Indian Police Service (Cadre) Rules, 1954; and

(c) in relation to the Indian Forest Service, has the meaning assigned to it in the Indian Forest Service (Cadre) Rules, 1966.

(2) On and from the appointed day, there shall be constituted for the States of Assam and Meghalaya a joint cadre of the Indian Administrative Service, a joint cadre of the Indian Police Service and a joint cadre of the Indian Forest Service.

(3) On and from the appointed day, there shall be constituted for the States of Manipur and Tripura a joint cadre of the Indian Administrative Service, a joint cadre of the Indian Police Service and a joint cadre of the Indian Forest Service.

(4) The initial strength and composition of the joint cadre referred to in sub-section (2) and (3) shall be such as the Central Government may, by order, determine before the appointed day.

(5) The members of each of the said Services borne on the Assam cadre thereof immediately before the appointed day shall be allocated to the joint cadre of the same Service constituted under sub-section (2) and to the Union Territroies cadre of that Service in such manner and with effect from such date or dates as the Central Government may, by order, specify.

(6) Such members of each of the said Services borne on the Union Territories cadre thereof immediately before the appointed day, as the Central Government may, by order, specify shall be allocated to the joint cadre of the same Service constituted under sub-section (3) with effect from such date or dates as may be specified in the order.

(7) Every person who, being a member of a State Civil

Service of the existing State of Assam, is borne on a Select List for promotion to the Assam Cadre of an All-India Service immediately before the appointed day shall, unless he is deemed to have been allocated to the Union under section 64, be deemed to have been included in the same order as in that List, in the Select List for promotion to the joint cadre of the same Service constituted under sub-section (2).

(8) Every person who, being a person deemed to have been allocated under section 62 for service in connection with the affairs of the State of Manipur or the State of Tripura, is borne on a Select List for promotion to the Union Territories cadre of an All-India Service immediately before the appointed day, shall be deemed to have been included in the same order as in the List, in the Select List for promotion to the joint cadre of the same Service constituted under sub-section (3).

(9) Every person who, being a person deemed to have been allocated to the Union under section 64, is borne on a Select List for promotion to the Assam cadre of an All-India Service immediately before the appointed day, shall be deemed to have been included in the Select List for promotion to the Union Territories cadre of the same Service and his position in the said Select List shall be determined by the Central Government in consultation with the Union Public Service Commission.

(10) Nothing in this section shall be deemed to affect the operation after the appointed day of the All-India Services Act, 1951 (61 of 1951), or the rules or regulations made thereunder.

62. *Provisions relating to Services in Manipur and Tripura*: Every person who immediately before the appointed day is serving in connection with the affairs of the Union under the administrative control of the Administrator of the Union territory of Manipur, or the Administrator of the Union territory of Tripura (including a person who has been placed on deputation by the Administrator concerned with any other authority), shall, unless otherwise directed by an order of the Central Government, be deemed to have been allocated for service as from that day in connection with the affairs of the State of Manipur or, as the case may be, of the State of Tripura :

Provided that no direction shall be issued under this section after the expiry of a period of one year from the appointed day.

63. *Special provisions relating to members of Central Health Service* : Notwithstanding the provisions of section 62, every member of the Central Health Service who immediately before the appointed day is holding any post in the Union territory of Manipur or the Union territory of Tripura, being a post included to the authorised strength of that Service, shall unless otherwise directed by the Central Government, be deemed to be on deputation on and from the appointed day, to the Government of the State of Manipur or, as the case may be, of the State of Tripura on the same terms and conditions of service as are applicable to him under the Central Health Service Rules, 1963, but without any deputation allowance :

Provided that the period of such deputation shall in no case extend beyond a period of three years from the appointed day.

Explanation : In this section, "Central Health Service" means the Central Health Service constituted under the Central Health Service Rules, 1963.

64. *Provisions relating to Services in the existing State of Assam* : (1) Such persons serving in connection with the affairs of the existing State of Assam (including persons borne on any cadre of that State and serving under the Government of the autonomous State of Meghalaya or on deputation to any other Government or authority) as may be determined at any time before or after the appointed day,—

(a) by agreement between the Government of the existing State of Assam and the Government of the autonomous State of Meghalaya or between the Government of the State of Assam and the Government of the State of Meghalaya, as the case may be, or

(b) in default of any such agreement, by the Central Government may, notwithstanding anything in their terms of appointment or their conditions of service:

(i) in a case referred to in clause (a), by one or more orders made by the Government of the existing State of Assam or the Government of the State of Assam, as the case may be, or

(ii) in a case referred to in clause (b), by one or more orders made by the Central Government, be required to serve in connection with the affairs of the State of Meghalaya and every such person shall accordingly be deemed to have been allocated to that State with effect from such date as may be specified in the order.

(2) Such persons serving in connection with the affairs of the existing State of Assam (including persons borne on any cadre of the existing State of Assam and serving under the Government of the autonomous State of Meghalaya or on deputation to any other Government or authority), as the Central Government may, at any time before or after the appointed day, determine in consultation with the Government of the existing State of Assam or the Government of the State of Assam, as the case may be, may, notwithstanding anything in the terms of their appointment or their conditions of service by one or more orders made by the Central Government, be required to serve in connection with the administration of the Union territory of Mizoram, and every such person shall accordingly, be deemed to have been allocated to the Union with effect from such date as may be specified in the order :

Provided that every person borne on any cadre of the existing State of Assam and serving in the Mizo District immediately before the appointed day shall unless otherwise directed by the Administrator of the Union territory of Mizoram, continue to serve on and from the appointed day, in connection with the administration of that Union territory until an order is made under this sub-section in respect of such person or the expiry of a period of three years from the appointed day, whichever is earlier.

65 *Provisions relating to Services in the autonomous State of Meghalaya*: Every person who immediately before the appointed day is serving in connection with the affairs of the autonomous State of Meghalaya (including a person on deputation from the Government of that autonomous State to any other Government or authority) not being a person to whom section 64 applies, shall be deemed to have been allocated to serve as from that day in connection with the affairs of the State of Meghalaya.

66. *Other provisions relating to Services*: (1) Nothing in this section or sections 62 to 65 (both inclusive) shall be deemed to affection or after the appointed day the operation of the provisions of Chapter I of Part XIV of the Constitution in relation to determination of conditions of service of persons serving in connection with the affairs of the State of Manipur, Meghalaya or Tripura or the Union territory of Mizoram:

Provided that the conditions of service applicable immediately before the appointed day in the case of any person deemed to have been allocated to the State of Manipur or the State of Tripura under section 62 or to the State of Meghalaya under sub-section (1) of section 64 or section 65 or to the Union under sub-section (2), of section 64 shall not be varied to his disadvantage except with the previous approval of the Central Government.

(2) All services prior to the appointed day rendered by a person—

(a) if he is deemed to have been allocated to any State under section 62 or section 64 or section 65, shall be deemed to have been rendered in connection with the affairs of the State,

(b) if he is deemed to have been allocated to the Union in connection with the administration of the Union territory of Mizoram, shall be deemed to have been rendered in connection with the affairs of the Union,

for the purposes of the rules regulating his conditions of service.

(3) The provisions of sections 62, 64 and 65 shall not apply in relation to members of any All-India Service.

67. *Provisions as to continuance of officers in same posts*: (1) Every person who, immediately before the appointed day is holding or discharging the duties of any post or office in connection with the administration of the Union territory of Manipur or Union territory of Tripura, shall continue to hold the same post or office in the State of Manipur, or, as the case may be, in the State of Tripura and shall be deemed, on and from that day, to have been duly appointed to the post or office by the Government of, or other appropriate authority in the State concerned.

(2) Where a person who immediately before the appointed day is holding or discharging the duties of any post or office in connection with the affairs of the existing State of Assam and as from the appointed day, such duties become duties in

connection with affairs of the State of Meghalaya or administration of the Union territory of Mizoram, then, he shall continue to hold the same post or office in that State or Union territory and shall be deemed on and from that day, to have been duly appointed to the post or office by the Government or Administrator of, or other appropriate authority in that State or Union territory, as the case may be.

(3) Where a person who immediately before the appointed day is holding or discharging the duties or any post or office in connection with the affairs of the autonomous State of Meghalaya and, as from the appointed day, such duties become dutics in connection with the affairs of the State of Meghalaya, then, he shall continue to hold the same post or office in the State of Meghalaya and shall be deemed on and from that day, to have been duly appointed to the post or office by the Government of, or other appropriate authority in the State of Meghalaya.

(4) Nothing in sub-section (1) or sub-section (2) or sub-section (3) shall be deemed to prevent a competent authority, on and from the appointed day, from passing in relation to any person referred to in that sub-section, any order affecting his continuance in such post or office.

68. *Advisory Committees*: The Central Government may, by order, establish one or more Advisory Committees for the purpose of assisting it in regard to—

(a) the discharge of any of its functions under this Part; and

(b) the ensuring of fair and equitable treatment to all persons affected by the provisions of this Part and the proper consideration of any representation made by such persons.

69. *Power of Central Government to give directions* : The Central Government may give such directions to the State Governments of Assam, Manipur, Meghalaya and Tripura and to the Administrator of the Union territory of Mizoram as may appear to it to be necessary for the purpose of giving effect to the foregoing provisions of this Part and the State Governments and the Administrator shall comply with such directions.

70. *Provisions as to State Public Service Commission* : (1) The Public Service Commission for the existing State of Assam shall, on and from the appointed day, be deemed to be the Public Service Commission for the State of Assam.

(2) Every person holding office immediately before the appointed day as Chairman or other member of the Public Service Commission for the existing State of Assam shall, as from the appointed day, be the Chairman or, as the case may be, the other member of the Public Service Commission for the State of Assam.

(3) Every person who becomes Chairman or other member of the Public Service Commission for the State of Assam on the appointed day under sub-section (2) shall—

(a) be entitled to receive from the Government of the State of Assam conditions of service not less favourable than those to which he was entitled under the provisions applicable to him immediately before the appointed day, and

(b) subject to the provision to clause (2) of article 316, hold office or continue to hold office until the expiration of his term of office as determined under the provisions applicable to him immediately before the appointed day.

PART IX

Legal and Miscellaneous Provisions

71. *Amendment of articles 210, 239A, 244A, 275, 332, 371B and Fifth and Sixth Schedules to the Constitution*: On and from the appointed day—

(a) in article 210, in the proviso to clause (2) for the words "Legislature of the State of Himachal Pradesh", the words "Legislatures of the States of Himachal Pradesh, Manipur and Meghalaya and Tripura" shall be substituted;

(b) in article 239A, in clause (1) the words "Manipur, Tripura", shall be omitted;

(c) in article 244,—

(i) in clause (1), for the words "the State of Assam" the worsds "the States of Assam and Meghalaya" shall be substituted;

(ii) in clause (2), for the words "the State of Assam" the words "the States of Assam and Meghalaya and the Union territory of Mizoram" shall be substituted;

(d) in article 244A, in clause (1), for the word and letter "Part A", the word and figure "Part 1" shall be substituted;

(e) in article 275, in clause (a) of the second proviso to clause (1), for the word and letter "Part A" the word and figure "Part 1" shall be substituted;

(f) in article 332,—

(i) in clause (5), the words "except in the case of the constituency comprising the cantonment and municipality of Shillong" shall be omitted;

(ii) in clause (6), the words "except from the constituency comprising the cantonment and municipality of Shillong" shall be omitted;

(g) in article 371B, for the word and letter "Part A" the word and figure "Part 1" shall be substituted;

(h) in the Fifth Schedule to the Constitution, in paragraph 1, for the words "State of Assam" the words "States of Assam and Meghalaya" shall be substituted;

(i) the Sixth Schedule to the Constitution shall stand amended as directed in the Eighth Schedule.

72. *Amendment of Act 2 of 1934*: On and from the appointed day, in section 21A, of the Reserve Bank of India Act, 1934, in sub-section (1), the brackets and words "(including the autonomous State of Meghalaya)" shall be omitted.

73. *Amendment of Act 64 of 1950*: On and from the appointed day, in section 47A of the Road Transport Corporations Act, 1950, in the Explanation to sub-section (1), after clause (ii), the following clause shall be inserted, namely:

"(iii) in relation to the Assam State Road Transport Corporation, shall mean the Government of the State of Assam or of Meghalaya as formed under the North-Eastern Areas (Reorganisation) Act, 1971."

74. *Amendment of Act 37 of 1956*: On and from the appointed day, in the States Re-organisation Act, 1956,—

(a) for clause (c) of section 15, the following clause shall be substituted, namely:

"(c) the Eastern Zone, comprising the States of Bihar, West Bengal and Orissa;";

(b) in sub-section (1) of section 16, clause (d) shall be omitted.

75. *Amendment of Act 20 of 1963*: On and from the appointed day, in the Government of Union Territories Act, 1963,—

(a) in clause (h) of sub-section (1) of section 2, the words "Manipur, Tripura," shall be omitted;

(b) in section 44, sub-section (2) shall be omitted;

(c) section 52 shall be omitted.

76. *Amendment of Act 56 of 1955 and the Tripura (Courts) Order, 1950* : On and from the appointed day,—

(a) the Manipur (Courts) Act, 1955, shall stand amended as directed in the Ninth Schedule;

(b) The Tripura (Courts) Order, 1950, shall stand amended as directed in the Tenth Schedule;

77. *Territorial extent of laws* : The provisions of Part II shall not be deemed to have effected any change in the territories to which any law in force immediately before the appointed day extends or applies, and the territorial references in any such law to the existing State of Assam or the autonomous State of Meghalaya or the Union territory of Manipur or the Union territory of Tripura or the North-East Frontier Agency shall, until otherwise provided by a competent Legislature or other competent authority, be construed as meaning the territories within that State or autonomous State or Union territory or Agency immediately before the appointed day.

78. *Continuance of existing District Councils and Regional Council and members thereof* : For the removal of doubt, it is hereby declared that all District Councils and the Regional Council constituted under the provisions of the Sixth Schedule to the Constitution and functioning immediately before the appointed day in the respective autonomous districts and in the autonomous region shall, as from that day, be deemed to have been constituted under the said Schedule as amended by

clause (i) of section 71, with the Eighth Schedule and accordingly,—

(a) every such District Council and the Regional Council shall, unless sooner dissolved, continue to function in the respective autonomous districts and in the autonomous region notwithstanding that any such district or region ceases to be comprised in the territories of the State of Assam, by virtue of the provisions of Part II; and

(b) every member of such District Council or Regional Council shall continue to be a member thereof for the unexpired term of his office as such.

79. *Power to adapt laws*: For the purpose of facilitating the application of any law in relation to any of the States or Union territories formed or established by the provisions of Part II, the appropriate Government may before the expiration of two years from the appointed day by order, make such adaptations and modifications of the law, whether by way of repeal or amendment, as may be necessary or expedient, and thereupon every such law shall have effect subject to the adaptations and modifications so made until altered, repealed or amended by a competent Legislature or other competent authority.

Explanation: In this section, the expression "the appropriate Government" means:—

(a) as respects any law relating to a matter enumerated in the Union List in the Seventh Schedule to the Constitution, the Central Government; and

(b) as respects any other law,—

(i) in its application to a State, the State Government, and

(ii) in its application to a Union territory, the Central Government.

80. *Power to construe laws*: (1) Notwithstanding that no provision or insufficient provision has been made under section 79 for the adaptation of a law made before the appointed day, any court, tribunal or authority required or empowered to enforce such law may for the purpose of facilitating its application in relation to the State of Assam, Manipur, Meghalaya or Tripura or to the Union territory of Mizoram or Arunachal Pradesh construe the law in such manner without affecting the substance, as may be necessary or proper in regard to the matter before the court, tribunal or authority.

(2) Any reference to the High Court of Assam or the High Court of Assam and Nagaland or to the Court of the Judicial Commissioner for Manipur or the Court of the Judicial Commissioner for Tripura in any law shall, unless the context otherwise requires, be construed, on and from the appointed day, as a reference to the common High Court.

81. *Power to name authorities, etc., for exercising statutory functions*: The Central Government, as respects the Union territory of Mizoram or Arunachal Pradesh and the State Government as respects any new State established or formed by the provisions of Part II may, by notification in the Official Gazette, specify the authority, officer or person who, as from the appointed day, shall be competent to exercise such functions exercisable under any law in force on that day as may be mentioned in that notification and such law shall have effect accordingly.

82. *Legal proceedings*: (1) Where immediately before the appointed day the Union is a party to any legal proceedings with respect to any property, right or liability and such property, right or liability devolves on the State of Manipur or the State of Tripura under this Act, then, the State of Manipur or, as the case may be, the State of Tripura shall be deemed to be substituted for the Union as a party to these proceedings and the proceedings may continue accordingly.

(2) Where immediately before the appointed day the autonomous State of Meghalaya is a party to any legal proceedings with respect to any property, right or liability of that State, and such property, right or liability devolves on the State of Meghalaya under this Act, then, the State of Meghalaya shall be deemed to be substituted for the autonomous State of Meghalaya as a party to those proceedings and the proceeedings may continue accordingly.

(3) Where immediately before the appointed day the existing State of Assam is a party to any legal proceeding with respect to any property, rights or liabilities subject to appointment under this Act, the successor State, which succeeds to, or

acquires a share in that property or those rights or liabilities by virtue of any provision of this Act, shall be deemed to be substituted for the existing State of Assam as a party to those proceeding or added as a party thereto, as the case may be, and the proceeding may continue accordingly.

83. *Rights of pleaders to practise in certain cases* : Any person who, immediately before the appointed day, is enrolled as a pleader entitled to practise in any subordinate courts in the existing State of Assam shall, for a period of one year from that day, continue to be entitled to practise in those courts, notwithstanding that the whole or any part of the territories within jurisdiction of those courts has been transferred to the State of Meghalaya or to a Union territory.

84. *Transfer of pending proceedings* : (1) Every proceeding pending immediately before the appointed day before a court (other than a High Court), tribunal, authority or officer in any area which on that day falls within a State or Union territory shall, if it is a proceeding relating exclusively to the territories which as from that day are the territories of another State or Union territory, stand transferred to the corresponding court, trribunal, authority or officer in that other State or Union territory, as the case may be.

(2) If any question arises as to whether any proceedings should stand transferred under sub-section (1), it shall be referred to the common High Court and the decision of that High Court shall be final.

(3) In this section,—

(a) "proceeding" includes any suit, case or appeal; and

(b) "corresponding court, tribunal, authority or officer" in a State or a Union territory means—

(i) the court, tribunal, authority or officer in that State or Union territory to which or before whom the proceeding would have lain if it had been instituted after the appointed day; or

(ii) in case of doubt, such court, tribunal, authority or officer in that State or Union territory as may be determined after the appointed day by the Government of that State or the Central Government, as the case may be, or before the appointed day by the

Government of the existing State of Assam or the Government of the autonomous State of Meghalaya or the Central Government, as the case may be, to be the corresponding court, tribunal, authority or officer.

85. *Provisions as to continuance of courts, etc.* : All courts and tribunals and all authorities discharging lawful functions throughout the existing State of Assam or the Union territory of Manipur or the Union territory of Tripura or any part of such State or Union territory immediately before the appointed day shall, unless their continuance is inconsistent with the provisions of this Act or until other provision is made by a competent Legislature or other competent authority, conitnue to exercise the respective functions.

86. *Effect of provisions of the Act inconsistent with other laws* : The provisions of this Act shall have effect notwithstanding anything inconsistent therewith contained in any other law.

87. *Power to remove difficulties* : (1) If any difficulty arises in giving effect to the provisions of this Act, the President may, by order, do anything not inconsistent with such provisions which appears to him to be necessary or expedient for the purpose of removing the difficulty.

(2) Every order made under this section shall be laid before each House of Parliament.

88. *Power to make rules* : (1) The Central Government may, by notification in the Official Gazette, make rules to give effect to the provisions of this Act.

(2) Every rule made under this section shall be laid, as soon as may be after it is made, before each House of Parliament while it is in session for a total period of thirty days which may be comprised in one session or in two successive sessions and if, before the expiry of the session in which it is so laid or the session immediately following, both Houses agree in making any modification in the rule or both Houses agree that the rule should not be made, the rule shall thereafter have effect only in such modified form or be of no effect, as the case may be, so, however, that any such modification or annulment shall be without prejudice to the validity of anything previously done under that rule.

THE FIRST SCHEDULE

[See Sections 14(2) and 20(5)]

Amendments to the Delimitation of Parliamentary and Assembly Constituencies Order, 1966

In Schedule II to the Delimitation of Parliamentary and Assembly Consituenies Order, 1966,—

(1) In Part A: PARLIAMENTARY CONSTITUENCIES,—

(a) for serial No. 1 and the entries relating thereto, the following shall be substituted, namely:

"1. Cachar.—(11) Silchar, (12) Sonai, (13) Dholai, (14) Lakhipur, (15) Udharbond, (16) Borkhola.";

(b) for serial No. 3 and the entries relating thereto, the following shall be substituted, namely:

"3. Diphu (S.T.).—(18) Haflong, (19) Bokajan, (20) Howraghat, (21) Baithalangso.";

(c) for serial No. 4 and the entries relating thereto, the following shall be substituted, namelv:

"4. Dhubri.—(31) Mankachar, (32) South Salmara, (33) Dhubri, (34) Gauripur, (35) Golakganj, (36) Biiasipara.";

(2) In Part B.—ASSEMBLY CONSTITUENCIES, serial Nos: 1, 2, 3 and 22 to 30 (both inclusive) and the entries relating thereto shall be omitted.

THE SECOND SCHEDULE

[See Section 25 (1)]

Amendments to the Constitution (Scheduled Castes) Order, 1950

In the Constitution (Scheduled Castes) Order, 1950.—

(1) in paragraph 2, for the figures "XIV" the figures "XVII" shall be substituted.

(2) in paragraph 4,—

(a) for the words and figures "and any reference in Part XIV", the words and figures "any reference in Part XIV" shall be substituted;

(b) the following shall be added at the end, namely:

"and any reference in Parts XV, XVI and XVII to a State shall be construed as a reference to the State constituted as from the day appointed under clause (b) of section 2 of the North-Eastern Areas (Reorganisation) Act, 1971";

(3) in the Schedule, after Part XIV, the following Parts shall be inserted, namely :

"Part XV—Manipur

Throughout the State :

1. Dhupi or Dhobi
2. Lois
3. Muchi or Ravidas
4. Namasudra
5. Patni
6. Sutradhar
7. Yaithibi

Part XVI—Meghalaya

Throughout the State :

1. Bansphor
2. Bhuinmali or Mali
3. Brittial-Bania or Bania
4. Dhupi or Dhobi
5. Dugla or Dholi
6. Hira
7. Jalkeot
8. Jhalo, Malo or Jhalo-Malo
9. Kaibartta or Jaliya
10. Lalbegi
11. Mahara
12. Mehtar or Bhangi
13. Muchi or Rishi
14. Namasudra
15. Patni
16. Sutradhar.

Part XVII—Tripura

Throughout the State :

1. Bagdi
2. Baiti
3. Bhuimali
4. Bhunar
5. Chamar or Muchi
6. Dandasi
7. Dhenuar
8. Dhoba
9. Duai
10. Dum
11. Ghasi
12. Gour
13. Gunar
14. Gur
15. Gorang
16. Jalia Kaibarta
17. Kahar
18. Kalindi
19. Kan
20. Kanda
21. Kanugh
22. Keot
23. Khadit
24. Kharia
25. Khemcha
26. Koch
27. Koir
28. Kol
29. Kora
30. Kotal
31. Mahisyadas
32. Mali
33. Mehtor
34. Musahar
35. Namasudra
36. Patni
37. Sabar."

THE THIRD SCHEDULE

[See Section 25(2)]

Amendments to the Constitution (Scheduled Castes) (Union Territories) Order, 1951

In the Constitution (Scheduled Castes) (Union Territories) Order, 1951,—

(1) for paragraph 4, the following paragraph shall be substituted, namely :

"4. Any reference in this Order to a Union territory in Part 1 of the Schedule shall be construed as a reference to the territory constituted as a Union territory as from the 1st day of November, 1956, any reference to a Union territory in Part II of the Schedule shall be construed as a reference to the territory constituted as a Union territory as from the 1st day of November, 1966 and any reference to a Union territory in Parts III and IV of the Schedule shall be construed as a reference to the territory constituted as a Union territory as from the day appointed under clause (b) of section 2 of the North-Eastern Areas (Reorganisation) Act, 1971.";

(2) in the Schedule,—

(a) Parts III and IV shall be omitted;

(b) Part V shall be renumbered as Part II and after that Part as so renumbered, the following Parts shall be inserted, namely :

"Part III—Mizoram

Throughout the Union Territory :

1. Bansphor
2. Bhuinmali or Mali
3. Brittial-Bania or Bania
4. Dhupi or Dhobi
5. Dugla or Dholi
6. Hira
7. Jalkeot
8. Jhalo, Malo or Jhalo-Malo
9. Kaibartta or Jaliya
10. Lalbegi
11. Mahara
12. Mehtar or Bhangi
13. Muchi or Rishi
14. Namasudra
15. Patni
16. Sutradhar.

Part IV—Arunachal Pradesh

Throughout the Union Territory :

1. Bansphor
2. Bhuinmali or Mali
3. Brittial-Bania or Bania
4. Dhupi or Dhobi
5. Dugla or Dholi
6. Hira
7. Jalkeot
8. Jhalo, Malo or Jhalo-Malo
9. Kaibartta or Jaliya
10. Lalbegi
11. Mahara
12. Mehtar or Bhangi
13. Muchi or Rishi
14. Namasudra
15. Patni
16. Sutradhar."

THE FOURTH SCHEDULE

[See Section 26(1)]

Amendments to the Constitution (Scheduled Tribes) Order, 1950

In the Constitution (Scheduled Tribes) Order, 1950,—

(1) in paragraph 2, for the figures "XIII", the figures "XVI" shall be substituted;

(2) in paragraph 3,—

(a) for the words and figures "and any reference in Part XIII", the words and figures "any reference in Part XIII" shall be substituted;

(b) the following shall be added at the end, namely :

"and any reference in Parts XIV to XVI to a State shall be construed as a reference to the State constituted as from the day appointed under clause (b) of section 2 of the North-Eastern Areas (Reorganisation) Act, 1971";

(3) in the Schedule :

(a) in Part II—Assam, paragraph 2 shall be omitted and in paragraph 3, for the words "excluding the Tribal areas"; the words "excluding the autonomous districts" shall be substituted;

(b) after Part XIII, the following Parts shall be inserted, namely :

"Part XIV—Manipur

Throughout the State :

1. Aimol
2. Anal
3. Angami
4. Chiru
5. Chothe
6. Gangte
7. Hmar
8. Kabui
9. Kacha Naga
10. Khoirao
11. Koireng
12. Kom
13. Lamgang
14. Any Mizo (Lushai) tribes
15. Maram
16. Maring
17. Mao
18. Monsang
19. Moyon
20. Paite
21. Purum
22. Ralte
23. Sema
24. Simte
25. Suhte
26. Tangkhul
27. Thadou
28. Vaiphui
29. Zou.

Part XV—Meghalaya

Throughout the State :

1. Chakma
2. Dimasa (Kachari)
3. Garo
4. Hajong
5. Hmar
6. Khasi and Jaintia (including Khasi, Synteng or Pnar, War, Bhoi or Lyngngam)
7. Any Kuki tribes including
   - (i) Biate or Biete
   - (ii) Changsan
   - (iii) Chongloi
   - (iv) Doungel
   - (v) Gamalhou
   - (vi) Gangte
   - (vii) Guite
   - (viii) Hanneng
   - (ix) Haokip or Haupit
   - (x) Haolai
   - (xi) Hengna
   - (xii) Hongsungh
   - (xiii) Hrangkhwal or Rangkhol
   - (xiv) Jongbe
   - (xv) Khawchung
   - (xvi) Khawathlang or Khothalong
   - (xvii) Khelma
   - (xviii) Kholhou
   - (xix) Kipgen
   - (xx) Kuki
   - (xxi) Lengthang
   - (xxii) Lhangum
   - (xxiii) Lhoujem
   - (xxiv) Lhouvun
   - (xxv) Lupheng
   - (xxvi) Mangjel

(xxvii) Misao
(xxviii) Riang
(xxix) Sairhem
(xxx) Selnam
(xxxi) Singson
(xxxii) Sitlhou
(xxxiii) Sukte
(xxxiv) Thado
(xxxv) Thangngeu
(xxxvi) Uibuh
(xxxvii) Vaiphei
8. Lakher
9. Man (Tai-Speaking)
10. Any Mizo (Lushai) tribes
11. Mikir
12. Any Naga tribes
13. Pawi
14. Synteng.

Part XVI—Tripura

Throughout the State :

1. Lushai
2. Mag
3. Kuki, including the following sub tribes :
   (i) Balte
   (ii) Belahut
   (iii) Chhalya
   (iv) Fun
   (v) Hajango
   (vi) Jangtoi
   (vii) Khareng
   (viii) Khephong
   (ix) Kuntei
   (x) Laifang
   (xi) Lantei
   (xii) Mizel
   (xiii) Namte
   (xiv) Paitu Paite
   (xv) Rangchan
   (xvi) Rangkhole
   (xvii) Thangluya
4. Chakma
5. Garoo
6. Chaimal
7. Halam
8. Khasia
9. Bhutia
10. Munda including Kaur
11. Orang
12. Lepcha
13. Santal
14. Bhil
15. Tripura or Tripuri, Tippera
16. Jamatia
17. Noatia
18. Riang
19. Uchai."

THE FIFTH SCHEDULE

[See section 26(2)]

Amendments to the Constitution (Scheduled Tribes) (Union Territories) Order, 1951

In the Constitution (Scheduled Tribes) (Union Territories) Order, 1951,—

(1) in paragraph 2, for the words and figures "Parts I to IV", the words and figures "Parts I to III" shall be substituted;

(2) for paragraph 3, the following paragraph shall be substituted namely :

"(3) Any reference in this Order to a Union territory in Part I of the Schedule shall be construed as a reference to that territory constituted as a Union territory as from the 1st day of November, 1956 and any reference to a Union territory in Parts II and III of the Schedule shall be construed as a reference to the territory constituted as a Union territory as from the day appointed under clause (b) of section 2 of the North-Eastern Areas (Reorganisation) Act, 1971".

(4) in the Schedule,—

(a) Parts II and III shall be omitted;

(b) Part IV shall be renumbered as Part I and after that Part as so renumbered, the following Parts shall be inserted, namely :

"Part II—Mizoram

Throughout the Union territory :

1. Chakma
2. Dimasa (Kachari)
3. Garo
4. Hajong
5. Hmar
6. Khasi and Jaintia (including Khasi, Synteng or Pnar, War, Bhoi or Lyngngam)
7. Any Kuki tribes including:
   (i) Baite or Biete
   (ii) Changsan
   (iii) Chongloi
   (iv) Doungel
   (v) Gamalhou
   (vi) Gangte
   (vii) Guite
   (viii) Hanneng
   (ix) Haokip or Haupit
   (x) Haolai
   (xi) Hengna
   (xii) Hongsungh
   (xiii) Hrangkhwal or Rangkhol
   (xiv) Jongbe
   (xv) Khawchung
   (xvi) Khawathlang or Khothalong
   (xvii) Khelma
   (xviii) Kholhou
   (xix) Kipgen
   (xx) Kuki
   (xxi) Lengthang
   (xxii) Lhangum
   (xxiii) Lhoujem
   (xxiv) Lhouvun

(xxv) Lupheng
(xxvi) Mangjel
(xxvii) Missao
(xxviii) Riang
(xxix) Sairhem
(xxx) Salnam
(xxxi) Singson
(xxxii) Sitlhou
(xxxiii) Sukte
(xxxiv) Thado
(xxxv) Thangngeu
(xxxvi) Uibuh
(xxxvii) Vaiphei

8. Lakher
9. Man (Tai-Speaking)
10. Any Mizo (Lushai) tribes
11. Mikir
12. Any Naga tribes
13. Pawi
14. Synteng."

"Part III—Arunachal Pradesh

Throughout the Union territory :—

All tribes of the Union territory including :

1. Abor
2. Aka
3. Apatani
4. Dafla
5. Galong
6. Khampti
7. Khowa
8. Mishmi
9. Momba
10. Any Naga tribes
11. Sherdukpen
12. Singpho."

THE SIXTH SCHEDULE

[See section 51 (3)]

Apportionment of Assets and Liabilities

1. *Definitions* : In this Schedule :

(a) "population ratio", in relation to the States of Assam and Meghalaya, means the ratio of 93.58 to 6.42; and

(b) "transferred territories" means the territories which, as from the appointed day, become the territories of the State of Meghalaya under section 5.

2. *Provisions of the Schedule to be applied to the apportionment of certain assets and liabilities* : Where any asset or liability is required to be apportioned to the autonomous State of Meghalaya by virtue of section 58, of the Assam Reorganization (Meghalaya) Act, 1969 (55 of 1969) but has not been so apportioned before the appointed day, the provisions of this Schedule shall be applied after apportionment under the said section has been effected.

3. *Apportionment of land, stores, etc* : (1) Subject to the other provisions contained in this Schedule, all land and all stores, articles and other goods belonging to the existing State of Assam shall, on and from the appointed day,—

(a) in a case where such land, stores, articles and other goods are situated within the transferred territories, pass to the State of Meghalaya; and

(b) in any other case, pass to the State of Assam :

Provided that where the Central Government is of the opinion that any goods or class of goods should be distributed among the States of Assam and Meghalaya otherwise than according to the situation of the goods, the Central Government may issue such directions, as it thinks fit, for a just and equitable distribution of the goods and the goods shall pass to the States of Assam and Meghalaya accordingly.

(2) (a) Such of those lands and buildings as are held by the existing State of Assam within the limits of the cantonment and municipality of Shillong immediately before the appointed day as may be agreed upon between the States of Assam and Meghalaya shall be available for the use of the State of Assam on the appointed day and thereafter for such period as may be agreed upon between the said States.

(b) Where no agreement is reached between the States of Assam and Meghalaya on any of the matters referred to in clause (a), the Central Government shall decide such matter and the decision of the Central Government thereon shall be binding on the said States.

(c) Different periods may be agreed upon under clause (a) or decided under clause (b) for different lands and buildings.

(d) Where any land or building is made available to the State of Assam under this sub-paragraph on or after the appointed day, then, notwithstanding anything contained in this Schedule, the debt or other liabilities in respect of such land or building shall pass to the State of Meghalaya only from the date from which possession of the land or building is given to the State of Meghalaya and the amount of such debt or other liability shall be determined by agreement between the States of Assam and Meghalaya or, in default of any such agreement by the Central Government.

(e) For so long as any land or building referred to in clause (a) is held by the State of Assam for its use, it shall be the responsibility of that State to properly maintain such land or building from its own funds.

(3) Stores relating to the Secretariat and the offices of Heads of departments having jurisdiction over the areas comprised partly in the transferred territories and partly in the State of Assam and unissued stores shall be divided between the State of Assam and Meghalaya in accordance with such directions as the Central Government may think fit to issue for a just and equitable distribution thereof.

Explanation : In this paragraph, the expression "land" includes immovable property of every description and any rights in or over such property, and the expression "goods" does not include coins, bank notes, and currency notes.

4. *Arrears of taxes* : The State of Meghalaya shall have the right to recover the arrears of tax or any duty, including the arrears of land revenue, on property situated in the transferred territories, and shall also have the right to recover the arrears of any other tax or duty if the place of assessment of that tax or duty is located in the transferred territories.

5. *Right to recover loans and advances* : (1) Save as provided in sub-paragraph (2) of paragraph 6, the right to recover any loans or advances made before the appointed day by the existing State of Assam to any local body, society, agriculturist or other person in the transferred territories shall belong to the State of Meghalaya.

(2) The right to recover loans and advances of pay and travelling allowances to a Government servant made before the appointed day by the existing State of Assam shall pass to the State of Meghalaya if, after the appointed day, that Government servant is required to serve in connection with the affairs of Meghalaya.

6. *Investments* : (1) The investments of the existing State of Assam immediately before the appointed day in any company or private commercial or industrial undertaking, in so far as such investments have not been made or deemed not to have

been made from the Cash Balance Investment Account, shall pass to the State of Meghalaya, if the principal seat of business of the company or undertaking is located in the transferred territories and where on that day the principal seat of business of the company or undertaking is located in the transferred territories and where on that day the principal seat of business of the company or undertaking is located outside the territories of the existing State of Assam, such investments shall be divided between the States of Assam and Meghalaya in the population ratio :

Provided that such investments in any Government company shall be divided between the States of Assam and Meghalaya in such proportion as may be agreed upon between those States or—

(a) in default of such agreement; or

(b) at the expiry of a period of one year from the appointed day, whichever is earlier, in such proportion as the Central Government may, by order, determine :

Provided further that nothing in this paragraph shall apply to any investment made by the existing State of Assam on or after the 2nd day of April, 1970 in any company or private commercial or industrial undertaking located outside the territories of the existing State of Assam.

(2) Where any body corporate constituted under a Central Act, State Act or Provincial Act or the existing State of Assam or any part thereof has, by virtue of the provisions of Part II, become an inter-State body corporate, the investments in, or loans or advances to, any such body corporate by the existing State of Assam made before the appointed day shall, save as otherwise expressly provided by or under this Act, be divided between the States of Assam and Meghalaya in the same proportion in which the assets of the body corporate are divided under the provisions of Part VII.

7. *Assets and liabilities of State Undertakings* : (1) The assets and liabilities relating to any commercial or industrial undertaking of the existing State of Assam shall pass to the State of Meghalaya if the undertaking is located in the transferred territories.

(2) Where a depreciation reserve fund is maintained by the existing State of Assam for any commercial or industrial undertaking the securities held in respect of investments made from

that fund shall pass to the State of Meghalaya if the undertaking is located in the transferred territories.

(3) Where any such undertaking is located partly in the State of Assam and partly in the State of Meghalaya, the assets and liabilities and the securities referred to in sub-paragraphs (1) and (2) respectively shall be divided in such manner as may be agreed upon between the Governments of the two States within one year from the appointed day, or in default of such agreement, as the Central Government may, by order, direct.

8. *Public debt* : (1) The public debt of the existing State of Assam attributable to loans raised by the issue of Government securities and outstanding with the public immediately before the appointed day shall continue to be the public debt of the State of Assam, and the State of Meghalaya shall be liable to pay to the State of Assam a share of the sums due from time to time for the servicing and repayment of the debt and for the purpose of determining the said share, the debt shall be deemed to be divided between the States of Assam and Meghalaya as if it were a debt referred to in sub-paragraph (5).

Explanation : In this sub-paragraph, the "public debt of the existing State of Assam", excludes the portion of such public debt the liability for servicing and repayment of which has been apportioned to the autonomous State of Meghalaya by virtue of section 58 of the Assam Reorganisation (Meghalaya) Act, 1969, (55 of 1969).

(2) Where a sinking fund or depreciation fund is maintained by the existing State of Assam for repayment of any loan raised by it, the securities held in respect of investment made from that fund shall be divided between the States of Assam and Meghalaya in the same proportion in which the total public debt is divided between the two States under this paragraph.

(3) The public debt of the existing State of Assam attributable to loans taken from the Central Government, the National Co-operative Development Co-operation or the Central Warehousing Co-operation or the Khadi and Village Industries Commission or from any other source for the express purpose of re-lending the same to a specific institution and outstanding immediately before the appointed day shall,—

(a) if re-lent to the Assam State Electricity Board, or any other institution which becomes an inter-State body corporate on the appointed day, be divided between the States of Assam and Meghalaya in the same proportion in which the assets of such body corporate are divided under the provisions of Part VII.

(b) if re-lent to any local body, body corporate or other institution in any local area, be the debt of the State in which the local area is included on the appointed day.

(4) Out of so much of the public debt of the existing State of Assam, other than the public debt referred to in sub-paragraphs (1) and (3), as is equal to loans and advances made by that State and outstanding on the appointed day, the share of the liability of the State of Meghalaya shall be for an amount equal to the loans and advances (not being re-lent amounts referred to in sub-paragraph (3) and outstanding immediately before the appointed day) recoverable by the State of Meghalaya under paragraph 5.

(5) The remaining public debt of the existing State of Assam attributable to loans taken from the Central Government, the Reserve Bank of India or any other body or bank outstanding immediately before the appointed day, shall be divided between the State of Assam and Meghalaya in proportion to the total expenditure on all capital works and other capital outlays incurred or deemed to have been incurred by the existing State of Assam up to the appointed day in the territories remaining in the State of Assam and the total expenditure on all capital works and other capital outlays incurred or deemed to have been incurred by the existing State of Assam up to the appointed day in the transferred territories, other than such outlays incurred or deemed to have been incurred before the 2nd day of April, 1970 in the autonomous State of Meghalaya for the purposes of the autonomous State as defined in paragraph 1 of the Third Schedule to the Assam Reorganisation (Meghalaya) Act, 1969 (55 of 1969).

(6) For the purpose of this paragraph "Government security" means a security created and issued by the existing State of Assam for the purpose of raising a public loan and having any of the forms specified in, or prescribed under, clause (2) of Section 2 of the Public Debt Act, 1944 (18 of 1944).

(7) For the purpose of this paragraph, "the public debt of

the existing State of Assam attributable to the loans taken from the Central Government" means the public debt of the State as reduced in accordance with the provisions of sub-section (4) of section 52.

9. *Refund of taxes collected in excess* : After the appointed day it shall be the liability of the State of Meghalaya to refund any tax or duty on property, including land revenue, collected in excess or any property situate in the transferred territories or any other tax or duty collected in excess, if the place of assessment of that tax or duty is situate in the transferred territories.

10. *Deposits etc.* : (1) The liability of the existing State of Assam in respect of any civil deposit or local fund deposit, made before the appointed day in any place situate in the transferred territories shall become the liability of the State of Meghalaya.

(2) The liability of the existing State of Assam in respect of any charitable or other endowment shall, as from the appointed day, be the liability of the State of Meghalaya, if the institution entitled to the benefit of the endowment is located in the transferred territories, or if the objects of the endowment, under the terms thereof, are confined to the transferred territories.

11. *Arrears of pay and allowances* : The liability of the existing State of Assam in respect of any arrears of pay or allowances due to any Government servant for the period prior to the appointed day shall, if the Government servant is required to serve in connection with the affairs of the State of Meghalaya, be the liability of the State of Meghalaya.

12. *Provident Fund etc.* : The liability of the existing State of Assam in respect of the Provident Fund and Special Deposit Fund accounts of a Government servant required to serve in connection with the affairs of the State of Meghalaya shall, on and from the appointed day, be the liability of the State of Meghalaya.

13. *Pensions* : The liability of the State of Assam or the State of Meghalaya in respect of pensions shall be apportioned between the two States in such manner as may be agreed upon between them or in default of such agreement, in such manner as the Central Government may, by order, specify.

14. *Contracts* : (1) Where, before the appointed day, the

existing State of Assam has made any contract in exercise of its executive power for any purposes of that State, that contract shall be deemed to have been made in the exercise of the executive power,—

(a) if such puropses are, as from the appointed day, exclusively purposes of either the State of Assam or the State of Meghalaya, of the State of Assam or, as the case may be, of the State of Meghalaya; and

(b) in any other case, of the State of Assam,

and all rights and liabilities which have accrued or may accrue under any such contract shall, to the extent to which they would have been rights or liabilities of the existing State of Assam, be rights or liabilities of the State of Assam, or, as the case may be, of the State of Meghalaya:

Provided that in any such case as is referred to in clause (b), the initial allocation of rights and liabilities made under this sub-paragraph shall be subject to such financial adjustment as may be agreed upon between the States of Assam and Meghalaya, or, in default of such agreement, as the Central Government may, by order, direct.

(2) For the purposes of this paragraph, there shall be deemed to be included in the liabilities which have accrued or may accrue under any contract,—

(a) any liability to satisfy an order or award made by any court or tribunal in proceedings relating to the contract; and

(b) any liability in respect of expenses incurred in, or in connection with, any such proceedings.

(3) This paragraph shall have effect subject to the other provisions of this Schedule relating to the apportionment of liabilities in respect of loans, guarantees and other financial obligations; and bank balances and securities shall, notwithstanding that they partake of the nature of contractual rights, be dealt with under those provisions.

15. *Liability in respect of actionable wrong* : Where, immediately before the appointed day, the existing State of Assam is subject to any liability in respect of any actionable wrong, other than breach of contract, that liability shall,—

(a) if the cause of action arose wholly within the territories, which as from that day, are the territories of the State of Assam or the State of Meghalaya, be the liability of the State of Assam or, as the case may be, of the State of Meghalaya; and

(b) in any other case, be initially the liability of the State of Assam, but subject to such financial adjustment as may be agreed upon between the States of Assam and Meghalaya or, in default of any such agreement, as the Central Government may, by order, direct.

16. *Liability as guarantor* : Where, immediately before the appointed day, the existing State of Assam is liable as guarantor in respect of any liability of a registered co-operative society or other person, that liability shall,—

(a) if the area of operation of such society or person is limited to the territories which, as from that day, are the territories of the State of Assam or of the State of Meghalaya, be the liability of the State of Assam or, as the case may be, of the State of Meghalaya; and

(b) in any other case, be initially the liability of the State of Assam, subject to such financial adjustment as may be agreed upon between the State of Assam and Meghalaya or, in default of such agreement, as the Central Government may, by order, direct.

17. *Items in suspense* : If any item in suspense is ultimately found to affect an asset or liability of the nature referred to in any of the foregoing provisions of this Schedule, it shall be dealt with in accordance with that provision.

18. *Residuary provisions* : The benefit or burden of any asset or liability of the existing State of Assam not dealt with in the foregoing paragraphs of this Schedule shall pass to the State of Assam in the first instance, subject to such financial adjustment as may be agreed upon between the States of Assam and Meghalaya within one year from the appointed day or, in default of such agreement, as the Central Government may, by order, direct.

19. *Apportionment of assets and liabilities by agreement*: Where the States of Assam and Meghalaya agree that the benefit or burden of any particular asset or liability should be apportioned between them in a manner other than that as provided for in the foregoing paragraphs of this Schedule, then, notwithstanding anything contained therein, the benefit or burden of that asset or liability shall be apportioned in the manner so agreed upon.

20. *Power of Central Government to order allocation or adjustment in certain cases* : Where, by virtue of any of the provisions of this Schedule, the State of Assam or the State of Meghalaya is entitled to any property, or obtains any benefits or becomes subject to any liability, and the Central Government is of opinion on a reference made to it within a period of three years from the appointed day by the State of Assam or the State of Meghalaya, as the case may be, that it is just and equitable, that property or those benefits should be transferred to one of the two States or shared between them, or that a contribution towards that liability should be made by either of the States, the said property or benefits shall be allocated in such manner, or the State of Meghalya or the State of Assam shall make to the other State primarily subject to the liability such contribution in respect thereof, as the Central Government may, after consultation with the Government of Assam and the Government of Meghalaya, by order, determine.

THE SEVENTH SCHEDULE

[See Section 60(1)]

List of Institutions where existing facilities shall be continued

1. Assam Forest Training School, Jhalukbari.
2. Survey School for Mandals, Gauhati.
3. Assam Survey Training School, Gauhati.
4. Assam Co-operative Training Centre, Joysagar.
5. Gram Sevikas Training Centre, Jorhat.
6. Police Training College, Dergaon.
7. Forensic Science Laboratory, Gauhati.
8. Finger Print Bureau, Shillong.
9. Public Health Laboratory, Shillong.
10. Administrative Training School, Gauhati.
11. Reid Chest T.B. Hospital, Shillong.
12. Gauhati Medical College, Gauhati.
13. Assam Medical College, Dibrugarh.

14. Medical College, Silchar.
15. Pasteur Institute, Shillong.
16. State Malaria Institute, Shillong.
17. Ayurvedic College, Gauhati.
18. Mental Hospital, Tezpur.
19. Primary Health Centre, Chabua.
20. Assam Engineering College, Jhalukbari.
21. Jorhat Engineering College, Jorhat.
22. Assam Government Press, Shillong.
23. Assam Agriculture College. } Under the Agricultural University, Jorhat.
24. Assam Veterinary College. }

THE EIGHTH SCHEDULE

[See Section 71 (i)]

Amendments to the Sixth Schedule to the Constitution

1. In the Sixth Schedule to the Constitution (hereafter in this Schedule referred to as the Sixth Schedule), in the heading, for the word "Assam", the words "the States of Assam and Meghalaya and in the Union territory of Mizoram" shall be substituted.

2. In paragraph 1 of the Sixth Schedule,—

(i) in sub-paragraph (1), for the word and letter "Part A," the words and figures "Parts I and II and in Part III" shall be substituted;

(ii) in sub-paragraph (3),—

(i) in clauses (a) and (b), for the word and letter "Part A" the words "any of the Parts" shall be substituted;

(ii) after the existing proviso, the following proviso shall be inserted, namely :

"Provided further that any order made by the Governor under this sub-paragraph may contain such incidental and consequential provisions (including any amendment of paragraph 20 and of any item in any of the Parts of the said table) as appear to the Governor to be necessary for giving effect to the provisions of the order."

3. In paragraph 3 of the Sixth Schedule, in the proviso to clause (a) of sub-paragraph (1) for the words "by the Government of Assam or the Government of Meghalaya", the words "by the Government of the State concerned" shall be substituted.

4. In paragraph 4 of the Sixth Schedule,—

(i) in sub-paragraph (3), the words "of Assam" shall be omitted.

(ii) in sub-paragraph (5), for the words "after consulting the Government of Assam or, as the case may be, the Government of Meghalaya", the words "after consulting the Government of the State concerned" shall be substituted.

5. In paragraph 6 of the Sixth Schedule, in sub-paragraph (2), the words "of Assam or Meghalaya, as the case may be", shall be omitted.

6. In paragraph 8 of the Sixth Schedule, in sub-paragraph (1), for the words "by the Government of Assam in assessing lands for the purpose of land revenue in the State of Assam generally", the words "by the Government of the State in assessing lands for the purpose of land revenue in the State generally" shall be substituted.

7. In paragraph 9 of the Sixth Schedule, in sub-paragraph (1), for the words "the Government of Assam", in both the places where they occur, the words "the Government of the State" shall be substituted.

8. In paragraph 12 of the Sixth Schedule,—

(i) for the heading, the following heading shall be substituted, namely :

"Application of Acts of Parliament and of the Legislature of the State of Assam to autonomous districts and autonomous regions in the State of Assam";

(ii) in sub-paragraph (1) :

(a) in clause (a), for the words "Legislature of the State" in both the places where they occur, the words "Legislature of the State of Assam" shall be substituted and after the words "any autonomous district or autonomous region" the words "in that State" shall be inserted;

(b) in clause (b), for the words "Legislature of the State", the words "Legislature of the State of Assam", shall be substituted and after the words "an autonomous district or an autonomous region", the words "in that State" shall be inserted.

9. For paragraph 12A of the Sixth Schedule, the following paragraphs shall be substituted, namely :

"12-A. *Application of Acts of Parliament and of the Legislature of the State of Meghalaya to autonomous districts and autonomous regions in the State of Meghalaya*:—Notwithstanding anything in this Constitution :

(a) if any provision of a law made by a District or Regional Council in the State of Meghalaya with respect to any matter specified in sub-paragraph (1) of paragraph 3 of this Schedule or if any provision of any regulation made by a District Council or a Regional Council in that State under paragraph 8 or paragraph 10 of this Schedule, is repugnant to any provision of a law made by the Legislature of the State of Meghalaya with respect to that matter, then, the law or regulation made by the District Council or, as the case may be, the Regional Council whether made before or after the law made by the Legislature of the State of Meghalaya, shall, to the extent of repugnancy, be void and the law made by the Legislature of the State of Meghalaya shall prevail;

(b) the President may, with respect to any act of Parliament, by notification, direct that it shall not apply to an autonomous district or an autonomous region in the State of Meghalaya, or shall apply to such district or region or any part thereof subject to such exceptions or modifications as he may specify in the notification and any such direction may be given so as to have retrospective effect.

12B. *Application of Acts of Parliament and other Acts to autonomous districts and autonomous regions in the Union territory of Mizoram* : Notwithstanding anything in this Constitution, the President may with respect to any Act of Parliament and the Administrator may with respect to any other Act, by notification, direct that it shall not apply to an autonomous district or an autonomous region in the Union territory of Mizoram or shall apply to such district or region or any part thereof subject to such exceptions or modifications as he may specify in the notification and any such direction may be given so as to have retrospective effect."

10. In paragraph 13 of the Sixth Schedule, the words "of Assam" shall be omitted.

11. In paragraph 14 of the Sixth Schedule, in sub-paragraph (2), for the words "the Government of Assam", the words "the Government of the State" shall be substituted.

12. In paragraph 17 of the Sixth Schedule, for the words "the Legislative Assembly of Assam", the words "the Legislative Assembly of Assam or Meghalaya" shall be substituted and after the words "autonomous district", the words "in the State of Assam or Meghalaya, as the case may be", shall be inserted.

13. Paragraph 18 of the Sixth Schedule, shall be omitted.

14. For paragraphs 20 and 20A of the Sixth Schedule, the following paragraphs shall be substituted, namely,—

"20. *Tribal areas*: (1) The areas specified in Parts I, II and III of the table below shall respectively be the tribal areas within the State of Assam, the State of Meghalaya and the Union territory of Mizoram.

(2) Any reference in the table below to any district shall be construed as a reference to the territories comprised within the autonomous district of that name existing immediately before the appointed day under clause (b) of section 2 of the North-Eastern Areas (Reorganisation) Act, 1971:

Provided that for the purposes of clauses (e) and (f) of sub-paragraph (1) of paragraph 3, paragraph 4, paragraph 5, paragraph 6, sub-paragraph (2), clauses (a), (b) and (d) of sub-paragraph (3) and sub-paragraph (4) of paragraph 8 and clause (d) of sub-paragraph (2) of paragraph 10 of this Schedule, no part of the area comprised within the municipality of Shillong shall be deemed to be within the United Khasi-Jaintia Hills District."

TABLE

Part I

1. The North Cachar Hills District.
2. The Mikir Hills District.

Part II

1. The United Khasi-Jaintia Hills District.
2. The Jowai District.
3. The Garo Hills District.

Part III

The Mizo District.

20A. *Interpretation* : Subject to any express provision made in this behalf, the provisions of this Schedule shall, in their application to the Union territory of Mizoram, have effect—

(1) as if references to the Governor and Government of the State were references to the Administrator of the Union territory appointed under article 239 and references to State (except in the expression "Government of the State") were references to the Union territory of Mizoram;

(2) as if—

(a) in sub-paragraph (3) of paragraph 1,—

(i) after clause (g), the following clause had been inserted, namely :

"(h) divide any autonomous region into two or more autonomous regions and define the boundaries thereof";

(ii) the first proviso had been omitted;

(b) in sub-paragraph (5) of paragraph 4 the provision for consultation with the Government of the State concerned had been omitted;

(c) in sub paragraph (2) of paragraph 9, the words "in his discretion" had been omitted;

(d) paragraph 13 had been omitted;

(e) sub-paragraphs (2) and (3) of paragraph 14 had been omitted;

(f) sub-paragraph (2) (including the proviso thereto) of paragraph 15 had been omitted;

(g) in paragraph 16,—

(i) in sub-paragraph (I), in clause (b), the words "subject to the previous approval of the Legislature of the State" and the second proviso to that sub-paragraph had been omitted;

(ii) sub-paragraph (3) had been omitted."

THE NINTH SCHEDULE

[See section 76(a)]

Amendments to the Manipur (Courts) Act, 1955

In the Manipur (Courts) Act, 1955 (56 of 1955) :

(i) through the Act save as otherwise expressly provided,—

(a) for the words "Chief Commissioner", the words "State Government" shall be substituted, and for the words "Judicial Commissioner" or "Court of the Judicial Commissioner", the words "High Court" shall be substituted, and such consequential amendments, as the rules of grammar may require, shall be made;

(b) for the words "Union Territory of Manipur", the words "State of Manipur" shall be substituted;

(ii) in the long title, the words "a Judicial Commissioner's Court and other" shall be omitted.

(iii) in section 2,—

(a) clause (i) shall be omitted;

(b) after clause (iii), the following clause shall be inserted, namely :

(iiia) "High Court", means the Gauhati High Court (the High Court of Assam, Nagaland, Meghalaya, Manipur and Tripura);

(iv) Chapter II shall be omitted;

(v) in section 16, the words "the Court of the Judicial Commissioner and" shall be omitted;

(vi) in section 17,—

(a) the brackets and figure "(1)" shall be omitted;

(b) sub-section (2) shall be omitted;

(vii) in section 18, for sub-section (1), the following sub-section shall be substituted, namely :

"(1) When the business pending before the court of a district judge requires the aid of an additional district judge for its speedy disposal, one or more additional district judges may be appointed";

(viii) section 19 shall be omitted;

(ix) for section 23, the following section shall be substituted, namely :

"23. *Local limits of the jurisdiction of courts of subordinate judges and munsiffs* : (1) The local limits of the jurisdiction of the court of a subordinate judge or a munsiff shall be such as the State Government may, after consultation with the High Court, by notification in the Official Gazette define.

(2) When a subordinate judge is posted to a district, the local limits of the district shall, in the absence of any direction to the contrary, be the local limits of his jurisdiction.";

(x) in section 25, sub-section (4) shall be omitted;

(xi) section 33, 34, 35 and 40 shall be omitted;

(xii) in sub-section (1) of section 43, the words "the Court of the Judicial Commissioner and" shall be omitted;

(xiii) section 46 shall be omitted.

THE TENTH SCHEDULE

[See section 76 (b)]

Amendments to the Tripura (Courts) Order, 1950

In the Tripura (Courts) Order, 1950—

(i) throughout the Order, save as otherwise expressly provided, for the words "Chief Commissioner", the words "State Government" shall be substituted, and for the words "Judicial Commissioner" or "Court of the Judicial Commissioner", the words "High Court", shall be substituted, and such consequential amendments, as the rules of grammar may require, shall be made;

(ii) in paragraph 2,—

(a) clause (i) shall be omitted;

(b) for clause (iii), the following clauses shall be substituted, namely:

'(iii) "High Court" means the Gauhati High Court (the High Court of Assam, Nagaland, Meghalaya, Manipur and Tripura);

(iiia) "Tripura" means the State of Tripura';

(iii) Chapter II shall be omitted;

(iv) in paragraph 15, the words "the Court of the Judicial Commissioner and" shall be omitted;

(v) in paragraph 16,—

(a) the brackets and figure "(1)" shall be omitted;

(b) sub-paragraph (2) shall be omitted.

(vi) in paragraph 17 for sub-paragraph (1), the following sub-paragraph shall be substituted, namely:—

"(1) When the business pending before the Court of District Judge requires the aid of an Additional Judge or Judges for its speedy disposal, one or more Additional District Judges may be appointed.";

(vii) paragraph 18 shall be omitted;

(viii) for paragraph 22, the following paragraph shall be substituted, namely:—

22. *Local limits of jurisdiction of Courts of Subordinate Judges and Munsiffs:* (1) The local limits of the jurisdiction of the Court of a Subordinate Judge or Munsiff shall be such as the State Government may, after consultation with the High Court, by notification in the Official Gazette, define.

(2) When a Subordinate Judge is posted to a district, the local limits of the district shall, in the absence of any directions to the contrary, be the local limits of his jurisdiction.";

(ix) paragraph 31 shall be omitted;

(x) for paragraph 32, the following paragraph shall be substituted, namely:—

"32. *Finality of appellate decrees of District Court*: Subject to the provisions of section 100 of the Code of Civil Procedure, 1908 (5 of 1908), an appellate decree of a District Court shall be final";

(xi) paragraphs 33, 34, 35 and 41 shall be omitted;

(xii) in sub-paragraph (1) of paragraph 42, the words "the Court of Judicial Commissioner and" shall be omitted.

5. THE CONSTITUTION (TWENTY-SEVENTH AMENDMENT) ACT, 1971

An Act

Further to amend the Constitution of India.

Be it enacted by Parliament in the Twenty-second Year of the Republic of India as follows:

1. *Short title and commencement* : (1) This Act may be called the Constitution (Twenty-seventh Amendment) Act, 1971.

(2) This section and section 3 shall come into force at once and the remaining provisions of this Act shall come into force on such date, being a date not earlier than the day appointed under clause (b) of section 2 of the North Eastern Areas (Reorganisation) Act, 1971, as the Central Government may, by notification in the Official Gazette, appoint.

2. *Amendment of article 239A* : In article 239A of the Constitution, in clause (i) for the words "Goa, Daman and Diu, and Pondicherry" the words "Goa, Daman and Diu, Pondicherry and Mizoram" shall be substituted.

3. *Insertion of new article 239B* : After article 239A of the Constitution, the following article shall be inserted, namely :—

"239B. *Power of administrator to promulgate Ordinances during recess of Legislature* : (1) If at any time, except when the Legislature of a Union territory referred to in clause (1) of article 239A is in session, the administrator thereof is satisfied that circumstances exist which render it necessary for him to take immediate action, he may promulgate such Ordinances as the circumstances appear to him to require :

Provided that no such Ordinance shall be promulgated by the administrator except after obtaining instructions from the President in that behalf :

Provided further that whenever the said Legislature is dissolved, or its functioning remains suspended on account of any action taken under any such law as is referred to in clause (1) of article 239A, the administrator shall not promulgate any Ordinance during the period of such dissolution or suspension.

(2) An Ordinance promulgated under this article in pursuance of instructions from the President shall be deemed to be an Act of the Legislature of the Union territory which has been duly enacted after complying with the provisions in that behalf contained in any such law as is referred to in clause (1) of article 239A, but every such Ordinance,—

(a) shall be laid before the Legislature of the Union territory and shall cease to operate at the expiration of six weeks from the re-assembly of the Legislature or if, before the expiration of that period, a resolution disapproving it is passed by the Legislature, upon the passing of the resolution; and

(b) may be withdrawn at any time by the administrator after obtaining instructions from the President in that behalf.

(3) If and so far as an Ordinance under this article makes any provision which would not be valid if enacted in an Act of the Legislature of the Union territory made after complying with the provisions in that behalf contained in any such law as is referred to in clause (1) of article 239A, it shall be void."

4. *Amendment of article 240* : In article 240 of the Constitution,—

(a) in clause (1),—

(i) after entry (e), the following entries shall be inserted, namely :—

"(f) Mizoram;

(g) Arunachal Pradesh";

(ii) in the proviso, for the words "Union territory of Goa, Daman and Diu or Pondicherry", the words "Union territory of Goa, Daman and Diu, Pondicherry or Mizoram" shall be substituted;

(iii) after the proviso as so amended, the following further proviso shall be inserted, namely :—

Provided further that whenever the body functioning as a Legislature for the Union territory of Goa, Daman and Diu, Pondicherry or Mizoram is dissolved, or the functioning of that body as such Legislature remains suspended on account of any action taken under any such law as is referred to in clause (1) of article 239A, the President may, during the period of such dissolution or suspension, make regulations for the peace, progress and good government of that Union territory.";

(b) in clause (2), for the words "any existing law", the words "any other law" shall be substituted.

5. *Insertion of new article 371C*: After article 371B of the Constitution, the following article shall be inserted, namely :—

'371C. *Special provision with respect to the State of Manipur*: (1) Notwithstanding anything in this Constitution, the President may, by order made with respect to the State of Manipur, provide for the constitution and functions of a committee of the Legislative Assembly of the State consisting of members of that Assembly elected from the Hill Areas of that State, for the modifications to be made in the rules of business of the Government and in the rules of procedure of the Legislative Assembly of the State and for any special responsibility of the Governor in order to secure the proper functioning of such committee.

(2) The Governor shall annually, or whenever so required by the President, make a report to the President regarding the administration of the Hill Areas in the State of Manipur and the executive power of the Union shall extend to the giving of directions to the State as to the administration of the said areas.

Explanation: In this article, the expression "Hill Areas" means such areas as the President may, by order, declare to be Hill Areas'.

6. THE GOVERNMENT OF UNION TERRITORIES (AMENDMENT) ACT, 1971

An Act

Further to amend the Government of Union Territories Act, 1963 and also further to amend the Sixth Schedule to the Constitution and the Representation of the People Act, 1950.

Be it enacted by Parliament in the Twenty-second Year of the Republic of India as follows :—

1. *Short title and commencement*: (1) This Act may be called the Government of Union Territories (Amendment) Act, 1971.

(2) It shall come into force on such date, being a date not earlier than the day appointed under clause (b) of section 2 of

the North-Eastern Areas (Reorganisation) Act, 1971, as the Central Government may, by notification in the Official Gazette, appoint.

2. *Amendment of section 1*: In section 1 of the Government of Union Territories Act, 1963, (20 of 1963) hereinafter referred to as the principal Act, in sub-section (2),—

(i) before the existing proviso, the following proviso shall be inserted, namely:—
"Provided that it shall come into force in the Union territory of Mizoram on such date, being a date not earlier than the date of commencement of the Government of Union Territories (Amendment) Act, 1971, as the Central Government may, by notification in the Official Gazette, appoint";

(ii) in the existing proviso, for the words "Provided that" the words "Provided further that" shall be substituted.

3. *Amendment of section 2* : In section 2 of the principal Act, in sub-section (1), in clause (h), for the words "Goa, Daman and Diu, and Pondicherry", the words "Goa, Daman and Diu, Pondicherry and Mizoram" shall be substituted.

4. *Amendment of section 3* : In section 3 of the principal Act:

(i) in sub-section (4), for the words "in the Legislative Assembly of every Union territory other than the Union Territory of Goa, Daman and Diu", the words "in the Legislative Assembly of the Union territory of Pondicherry" shall be substituted;

(ii) in sub-section (5), for the words "of any Union territory", the words "of the Union territory of Pondicherry" shall be substituted;

(iii) in sub-section (6), for the words "in the Legislative Assemblies of the Union territories", the words "in the Legislative Assembly of the Union territory of Pondicherry" shall be substituted.

5. *Amendment of section 20* : Section 20 of the principal Act shall be re-numbered as sub-section (2) thereof and after sub-section (1) as so re-numbered, the following sub-section shall be inserted, namely:

"(2) The provisions of article 304 shall, with the necessary modifications, apply in relation to any law passed by the Legislative Assembly of a Union territory with respect to any of the matters referred to in that article as they apply in relation to any law passed by the Legislature of a State with respect to those matters."

6. *Substitution of new section for section 21* : For section 21 of the principal Act, the following section shall be substituted namely,—

"21. *Inconsistency between laws made by Parliament and laws made by Legislative Assembly* : (1) If any provision of a law made by the Legislative Assembly of a Union territory is repugnant to any provision of a law made by Parliament, then, subject to the provisions of sub-section (2), the law made by Parliament, whether passed before or after the law made by the Legislative Assembly of the Union territory, shall prevail and the law made by the Legislative Assembly of the Union territory shall, to the extent of the repugnancy, be void.

(2) Where a law made by the Legislative Assembly of a Union territory with respect to any of the matters enumerated in the Concurrent List or the State List in the Seventh Schedule to the Constitution contains any provision repugnant to the provisions of an earlier law made by Parliament with respect to that matter, or where a law made by the Legislative Assembly of a Union territory with respect to any matter enumerated in the Concurrent List aforesaid is repugnant to the provisions of any earlier law, other than a law made by Parliament, with respect to that matter, then, in either case, the law so made by the Legislative Assembly of the Union territory shall, if it has been reserved for the consideration of the President and has received his assent, prevail in that Union territory :

Provided that nothing in this sub-section shall prevent Parliament from enacting at any time any law with respect to the same matter including a law adding to, amending, varying or replacing the law so made by the Legislative Assembly of the Union territory."

7. *Substitution of new section for section 25* : For section 25 of the principal Act, the following sections shall be substituted namely :

"25 *Assent to Bills* :—When a Bill has been passed by the Legislative Assembly of a Union territory, it shall be presented to the Administrator and the Administrator shall declare either that he assents to the Bill or that he withholds assent therefrom or that he reserves the Bill for the consideration of the President:

Provided that the Administrator may, as soon as possible after the presentation of the Bill to him for assent, return the Bill if it is not a Money Bill together with a message requesting that the Assembly will reconsider the Bill or any specified provisions thereof, and, in particular, will consider the desirability of introducing any such amendments as he may recommend in his message and, when a Bill is so returned, the Assembly will reconsider the Bill accordingly, and if the Bill is passed again with or without amendment and presented to the Administrator for assent, the Administrator shall declare either that he assents to the Bill or that he reserves the Bill for the consideration of the President :

Provided further that the Administrator shall not assent to, but shall reserve for the consideration of the President, any Bill which,—

(a) in the opinion of the Administrator would, if it became law, so derogate from the powers of the High Court as to endanger the position which that Court is, by the Constitution, designed to fill; or

(b) relates to any of the matters specified in clause (1) of article 31A; or

(c) the President may, by order, direct to be reserved for his consideration; or

(d) relates to matters referred to in sub-section (5) of section 7 or section 17 or section 34 or sub-section (6) of section 45 or in entry 1 or entry 2 of the State List in the Seventh Schedule to the Constitution :

Provided also that without prejudice to the provisions of the second proviso, the Administrator shall not assent to, but shall reserve for the consideration of the President, any Bill which has been passed by the Legislative Assembly of the Union territory of Mizoram and which relates to any area comprised in any autonomous district in that Union territory under the Sixth Schedule to the Constitution.

Explanation : For the purposes of this section and section 25A a Bill shall be deemed to be a Money Bill if it contains only provisions dealing with all or any of the matters specified in sub-section (1) of section 23 or any matter incidental to any of those matters and, in either case, there is endorsed thereon the certificate of the Speaker of the Legislative Assembly signed by him that it is a Money Bill.

25A. *Bills reserved for consideration* : When a Bill is reserved by an Administrator for the consideration of the President, the President shall declare either that he assents to the Bill or that he withholds assent therefrom :

Provided that where the Bill is not a Money Bill, the President may direct the Administrator to return the Bill to the Legislative Assembly together with such a message as is mentioned in the first proviso to section 25 and, when a Bill is so returned, the Assembly shall reconsider it accordingly within a period of six months from the date of receipt of such message and, if it is again passed by the Assembly with or without amendment, it shall be presented again to the President for his consideration."

8. *Amendment of section 33* : To sub-section (2) of section 33 of the principal Act, the following proviso shall be added, namely :—

"Provided that the provisions of this sub-section shall apply in relation to the Legislative Assembly of the Union territory of Mizoram as if for the words "the State of Uttar Pradesh", the words "the State of Assam" had been substituted".

9. *Amendment of section 38* : In section 38 of the Principal Act,—

(i) in clause (a) the words, figures, and letter "or with the Election Commission under section 43A" shall be added at the end;

(ii) after clause (b), the following clause shall be inserted, namely :

(bb) "Election Commission" means the Election Commission appointed by the President under article 324".

10. *Insertion of new section 43A* : After section 43 of the principal Act, the following section shall be inserted, namely :

"43A. *Special provision for delimitation of constituencies of Mizoram Legislative Assembly* : (1) The provisions of sections

39 to 43 (both inclusive) shall not apply to the delimitation of constituencies for the purpose of elections to the Legislative Assembly of the Union territory of Mizoram.

(2) The Election Commission shall, in the manner herein provided, distribute the seats assigned to the Legislative Assembly of the Union territory of Mizoram under sub-section 2 of section 3 to single member assembly constituencies and delimit them on the basis of the latest census figures having regard to the provisions of the Constitution and the following provisions,—

(a) all constituencies shall, as far as practicable be geographically compact areas;

(b) in delimiting the constituencies, regard shall be had to physical features, existing boundaries of administrative units, facilities of communication and public convenience.

(3) For the purpose of assisting in the performance of its functions under sub-section (2), the Election Commission shall associate with itself as associate members,—

(a) all the persons who, having been elected to the Legislative Assembly of the State of Assam from the Lungleh, Aijal East and Aijal West territorial constituencies are members of that Assembly immediately before the day appointed under clause (b) of section 2 of the North-Eastern Areas (Reorganisation) Act, 1971; and

(b) such three elected members of the District Council of the Mizo District as the Chairman thereof may nominate :

Provided that none of the associate members shall have a right to vote or sign any decision of the Election Commission.

(4) If, owing to death or resignation, the office of an associate member falls vacant, it shall be filled, if practicable, in accordance with the provisions of sub-section (3).

(5) The Election Commission shall—

(a) publish its proposals for the delimitation of constituencies, together with the dissenting proposals, if any, of any associate member who desires publication thereof in the Official Gazette and in such other manner as the Commission may consider fit, together with a notice inviting objections and suggestions in relation to the proposals and specifying a date on or after which the proposals will be further considered by it;

(b) consider all objections and suggestions which may have been received by it before the date so specified;

(c) after consideration of objections and suggestions which may have been received by it before the date so specified, determine by one or more orders the delimitation of constituencies and cause such order or orders to be published in the Official Gazette; and upon such publication the order or orders shall have the full force of law and shall not be called in question in any court.

(6) The Election Commission may, from time to time, by notification in the Official Gazette,—

(a) correct any printing mistake in any order made under sub-section (5) or any error arising therein from inadvertent slip or omission;

(b) where the boundaries or name of any territorial division mentioned in any such order or orders are or is altered, make such amendments as appear to it to be necessary or expedient for bringing such order up-to-date.

(7) Every order made under sub-section (5) and every notification issued under sub-section (6) shall be laid as soon as may be after it is made or issued before the Legislative Assembly of the Union territory of Mizoram.

(8) All things done, and all steps taken, before the commencement of this Act in the Union territory of Mizoram with a view to delimiting territorial constituencies of that Union territory for purposes of elections to the Legislative Assembly of that Union territory shall, in so far as they are in conformity with the foregoing provisions of this section, be deemed to have been done or taken under those provisions as if those provisions were in force at the time such things were done or such steps were taken."

11. *Amendment of section 44* : In section 44 of the principal Act,—

(a) to sub-section (1), the following further proviso shall be added, namely:

"Provided further that in the Union territory of Mizoram

every decision taken by a Minister or by the Council of Ministers in relation to any matter concerning any area comprised in any autonomous district in that Union territory under the Sixth Schedule to the Constitution shall be subject to the concurrence of the Administrator and nothing in this sub-section shall be construed as preventing the Administrator in case of any difference of opinion between him and his Ministers from taking such action in respect of the administration of such area as he, in his discretion, considers necessary.";

(b) after sub-section (1) as so amended the following sub-section shall be inserted, namely:—

"(2) In the exercise of his functions, the Administrator of the Union territory of Mizoram shall have special responsibility for the security of the border and for that purpose he may issue such directions and take such measures as he may think necessary."

12. *Substitution of new sections for section 54*: For section 54 of the principal Act, the following section shall be substituted, namely :—

"54. *Transitional provisions for administration of justice in certain areas in the Union territory of Mizoram* : On and from the commencement of this Act in the Union territory of Mizoram and until other provisions in this behalf are made by a competent Legislature or other competent authority, the administration of justice in those areas of that Union territory which are not comprised in any autonomous district under the Sixth Schedule to the Constitution shall be carried on, so far as may be, in accordance with the provisions of paragraphs 4 and 5 of that Schedule, as if those areas were comprised in an autonomous district under that Schedule and the provisions of the said paragraphs were in force in those areas and for this purpose,—

(i) all powers and functions of a District Council under the provisions of the said paragraph 4 shall be exercised and discharged by the Administrator or any officer appointed by him in this behalf;

(ii) the said paragraph 5 shall have effect as if references to the District Council, the Regional Council and the

Courts constituted by the District Council, by whatever form of words, had been omitted therefrom; and

(iii) references to Governor in the said paragraphs 4 and 5 shall be construed as references to the Administrator."

13. *Amendment of Sixth Schedule to the Constitution*: On and from the day on which the Legislative Assembly of the Union territory of Mizoram has been duly constituted under and in accordance with the provisions of the principal Act, in the Sixth Schedule to the Constitution:

(i) for paragraph 12B, the following paragraph shall be substituted, namely :—

"12B. *Application of Acts of Parliament and of the Legislature of the Union territory of Mizoram to autonomous districts and autonomous regions in the Union territory of Mizoram*: Notwithstanding anything to this Constitution,—

(a) if any provision of a law made by a District Council or a Regional Council in the Union territory of Mizoram with respect to any matter specified in sub-paragraph (1) of paragraph 3 of this Schedule or if any provision of any regulation made by a District Council or a Regional Council in that Union territory under paragraph 8 or paragraph 10 of this Schedule, is repugnant to any provision of a law made by the Legislature of the Union territory of Mizoram with respect to that matter, then, the law or regulation made by the District Council or, as the case may be, the regional Council, whether made before or after the law made by the Legislature of the Union territory of Mizoram, shall, to the extent of repugnancy, be void and the law made by the Legislature of the Union territory of Mizoram shall prevail;

(b) the President may with respect to any Act of Parliament, by notification, direct that it shall not apply to an autonomous district or an autonomous region in the Union territory of Mizoram, or shall apply to such district or region or any part thereof subject to such exceptions or modifications as he may specify in the notification and any such direction may be given so as to have retrospective effect.";

(ii) in paragraph 20, in Part III of the table, the words, "The Mizo District" shall be omitted;

(iii) for paragraph 20A, the following paragraphs shall be substituted, namely :—

"20A. *Dissolution of the Mizo District Council* : (1) Notwithstanding anything in this Schedule, the District Council of the Mizo District existing immediately before the prescribed date (hereinafter referred to as the Mizo District Council) shall stand dissolved and cease to exist.

(2) The Administrator of the Union territory of Mizoram may, by one or more orders, provide for all or any of the following matters, namely :—

(a) the transfer, in whole or in part, of the assets, rights and liabilities of the Mizo District Council (including the rights and liabilities under any contract made by it) to the Union or to any other authority;

(b) the substitution of the Union or any other authority for the Mizo District Council or the addition of the Union or any other authority as a party to any legal proceedings to which the Mizo District Council is a party;

(c) the transfer or re-employment of any employees of the Mizo District Council to or by the Union or any other authority, the terms and conditions of service applicable to such employees after such transfer or re-employment;

(d) the continuance of any laws, made by the Mizo District Council and in force immediately before its dissolution, subject to such adaptations and modifications, where by way of repeal or amendment, as the Administrator may make in this behalf, until such laws are altered, repealed or amended by a competent Legislature or other competent authority;

(e) such incidental, consequential and supplementary matters as the Administrator considers necessary.

Explanation : In this paragraph and in paragraph 20B of this Schedule, the expression "prescribed date" means the date on which the Legislative Assembly of the Union territory of Mizoram is duly constituted under and in accordance with the provisions of the Government of Union Territories Act, 1963 (20 of 1963).

20B. *Autonomous regions in the Union territory of Mizoram to be autonomous districts and transitory provisions consequent thereto* : (1) Notwithstanding anything in this Schedule,—

(a) every autonomous region existing immediately before the prescribed date in the Union territory of Mizoram shall, on and from that date, be an autonomous district to that Union territory (hereafter referred to as the corresponding new district) and the Administrator thereof may, by one or more orders, direct that such consequential amendments as are necessary to give effect to the provisions of this clause shall be made in paragraph 20 of this Schedule (including Part III of the table appended to that paragraph) and thereupon the said paragraph and the said Part shall be deemed to have been amended accordingly;

(b) every Regional Council of an autonomous region in the Union territory of Mizoram existing immediately before the prescribed date, (hereinafter referred to as the existing Regional Council) shall, on and from that date and until a District Council is duly constituted for the corresponding new district, be deemed to be the District Council of that district (hereafter referred to as the corresponding new District Council).

(2) Every member whether elected or nominated of an existing Regional Council shall be deemed to have been elected or, as the case may be, nominated to the corresponding new District Council and shall hold office until a District Council is duly constituted for the corresponding new district under this Schedule.

(3) Until rules are made under sub-paragraph (7) of paragraph 2 and sub-paragraph (4) of paragraph 4 of this Schedule by the corresponding new District Council, the rules made under the said provisions by the existing Regional Council and in force immediately before the prescribed date shall have effect in relation to the corresponding new District Council subject to such

adaptations and modifications as may be made therein by the Administrator of the Union territory of Mizoram.

(4) The Administrator of the Union territory of Mizoram may, by one or more orders, provide for all or any of the following matters, namely,—

(a) the transfer in the whole or in part of the assets, rights and liabilities of the existing Regional Council (including the rights and liabilities under any contract made by it) to the corresponding new District Council;

(b) the substitution of the corresponding new District Council for the existing Regional Council as a party to the legal proceedings to which the existing Regional Council is a party;

(c) the transfer or re-employment of any employees of the existing Regional Council to or by the corresponding new District Council, the terms and conditions of service applicable to such employees after such transfer or re-employment;

(d) the continuance of any laws made by the existing Regional Council and in force immediately before the prescribed date, subject to such adaptations and modifications, whether by way of repeal or amendment, as the Administrator may make in this behalf until such laws are altered, repealed or amended by a competent Legislature or other competent authority;

(e) such incidental consequential and supplementary matters as the Administrator considers necessary.

20C. *Interpretation* : Subject to any provision made in this behalf, the provisions of this Schedule shall, in their application to the Union territory of Mizoram, have effect,—

(1) as if references to the Governor and Government of the State were references to the Administrator of the Union territory appointed under article 239, references to State (except in the expression "Government of the State") were references to the Union territory of Mizoram and references to the State Legislature were references to the Legislative Assembly of the Union territory of Mizoram;

(2) as if—

(a) in sub-paragraph (5) of paragraph 4, the provision for consultation with the Government of the State concerned had been omitted;

(b) in sub-paragraph (2) of paragraph 6, for the words "to which the executive power of the State extends", the words "with respect to which the Legislative Assembly of the Union territory of Mizoram has power to make laws" had been substituted;

(c) in paragraph 13, the words and figures "under article 202" had been omitted."

14. *Amendment of Act 43 of 1950* : On and from the day on which the Legislative Assembly of the Union territory of Mizoram has been duly constituted and in accordance with the provisions of the principal Act, in section 27A of the Representation of the People Act, 1950,—

(i) in sub-section (4), for the words "The electoral college for the Union territory of Pondicherry", the words "The electoral college for each of the Union territories of Pondicherry and Mizoram" shall be subsituted;

(ii) in sub-section (5), for the words "to each of the Union territories of Mizoram and Arunachal Pradesh" the words "to the Union territory of Arunachal Pradesh" shall be substituted.

15. *Elections to the Legislative Assembly of Mizoram* : As soon as may be after the commencement of this Act, elections shall be held in the Union territory of Mizoram in accordance with the provisions of the principal Act as amended by this Act for constituting a Legislative Assembly for that Union territory and every endeavour shall be made to hold such elections within a period of four months of such commencement.

7. THE NORTH-EASTERN COUNCIL ACT, 1971

An Act

to provide for the setting up of a Council for the north-eastern areas of India to be called the North-Eastern Council and for matters connected therewith.

Be it enacted by Parliament in the Twenty-second Year of the Republic of India as follows :

1. *Short title and commencement* : (1) This Act may be called the North-Eastern Council Act, 1971.

(2) It shall come into force on such date, being a date not earlier than the day appointed under clause (b) of section 2 of the North-Eastern Areas (Reorganisation) Act, 1971, as the Central Government may, by notification in the Official Gazette, appoint.

2. *Definitions* : In this Act unless the context otherwise requires,—

(a) "Council" means the North-Eastern Council set up under section 3;

(b) "north-eastern area" means the area comprising the States of Assam, Manipur, Meghalaya, Nagaland and Tripura and the Union territories of Arunachal Pradesh and Mizoram; and

(c) "State" include the Union territories of Arunachal Pradesh and Mizoram.

3. *Setting up and composition of the North-Eastern Council* : (1) There shall be a Council to be called the North-Eastern Council which shall consist of the following members, namely,—

(a) the person or persons for the time being holding the office of the Governor of the States or the office of Administrator of the Union territories in the north-eastern area;

(b) the Chief Ministers of the States of Assam, Manipur, Meghalaya, Nagaland and Tripura and of the Union territory of Mizoram; and

(c) one of the Counsellors to the Administrators of the Union territory of Arunachal Pradesh appointed under section 18 of the North-East Frontier Agency (Administration) Supplementary Regulation, 1971, to be nominated by the Administration:

Provided that if there is no Council of Ministers in any State referred to in clause (b) or in the Union territory referred to in that clause, the President may nominate not more than one person to represent such State or Union territory in the Council for so long as there is no Council of Ministers in such State or Union territory.

(2) Notwithstanding anything contained in sub-section (1), the President may, if he deems it necessary so to do, nominate a Union Minister to be a member of the Council.

(3) One of the members of the Council to be nominated by the President shall be the Chairman of the Council.

(4) The President may, if he deems it necessary so to do, nominate another member of the Council to act as Vice Chairman of the Council.

4. *Functions of the Council*: (1) The Council shall be an advisory body and may discuss any matter in which some or all of the States represented in that Council, or the Union and one or more of the States repersented in that Council, have a common interest and advise the Central Government and the Government of each State concerned as to the action to be taken on any such matter, and, in particular, may discuss and make recommendations with regard to,—

(i) any matter of common interest in the field of economic and social planning;

(ii) any matter concerning inter-State transport and communications;

(iii) any matter relating to power or flood control projects of common interest.

(2) For securing the balanced development of the north-eastern area, the Council shall forward proposals,—

(a) formulating for the States represented in the Council a united and co-ordinated regional plan (which will be in addition to the State Plan) in regard to matters of common importance to that area;

(b) regarding the priorities of the projects and schemes included in the regional plan and the stages in which the regional plan may be implemented; and

(c) regarding the location of the projects and schemes included in the regional plan,

to the Central Government for its consideration.

(3) The Council shall,—

(a) review, from time to time, the implementation of the projects and schemes included in the regional plan and recommend measures for effecting co-ordination among the Governments of the States concerned in the matter of implementation of such projects and schemes;

(b) where a project or scheme is intended to benefit two or more States, recommend the manner in which,—

(i) such project or scheme may be executed or implemented and managed or maintained; or

(ii) the benefits therefrom may be shared; or

(iii) the expenditure thereon may be incurred;

(c) on a review of progress of the expenditure, recommend to the Central Government the quantum of financial assistance to be given, from time to time, to the State or States entrusted with the execution or implementation of any project or scheme included in the regional plan;

(d) recommend to the Government of the State concerned or to the Central Government the undertaking of necessary surveys and investigation of projects in any State represented in the Council to facilitate consideration of the feasibility of including new projects in the regional plan.

(4) The Council shall review from time to time the measures taken by the States represented in the Council for the maintenance of security and public order therein and recommend to the Governments of the States concerned further measures necessary in this regard.

5. *Meetings of the Council* : (1) The Council shall meet at such times as the Chairman of the Council may appoint in this behalf and shall, subject to the other provisions of this section, observe such rules of procedure in regard to transaction of business at its meetings as it may lay down from time to time.

(2) The Chairman or in his absence the Vice-Chairman, if any, or in the absence of both the Chairman and the Vice-Chairman, any other member chosen by the members present from amongst themselves, shall preside at a meeting of the Council.

(3) The proceedings of every meeting of the Council shall be forwarded to the Central Government and also to the Government of each State represented on the Council.

6. *Nomination of certain Officers to attend the meeting of the Council* : In order to assist the Council in the discharge of its

functions, each of the Ministries of the Central Government dealing with matters relating to Defence, Finance, Home Affairs and Planning shall nominate an officer to attend the meetings of the Council.

7. *Officers and Staff of the Council*: (1) The Council shall have a Secretarial Staff consisting of a Secretary, a Planning Adviser, a Financial Adviser and a Security Adviser and such other officers and employees as the Central Government may, by order, determine.

(2) The Secretarial Staff of the Council shall function under the direction, supervision and control of the Chairman of the Council.

(3) The office of the Council shall be located at such place as may be determined by the Council.

(4) The Administrative expenses of the said office, including the salaries and allowances payable to, or in respect of, members of the Secretarial Staff of the Council, shall be borne by the Central Government out of the moneys provided by Parliament for the purpose.

8. *Repeal*: The North-Eastern Council Act, 1970 (26 of 1970) is hereby repealed.

8. THE MANIPUR (HILL AREAS) DISTRICT COUNCILS ACT, 1971

An Act

to provide for the establishment of District Councils in the Hill Areas in the Union territory of Manipur.

Be it enacted by Parliament in the Twenty-second Year of the Republic of India as follows:

CHAPTER I

Preliminary

1. *Short title and extent*: (1) This Act may be called the Manipur (Hill Areas) District Councils Act, 1971.

(2) It extends to the whole of the Union territory of Manipur.

2. *Definitions*: In this Act, unless the context otherwise requires,—

(a) "Administrator" means the administrator of the Union

territory of Manipur appointed under article 239 of the Constitution;

(b) "autonomous district" means an autonomous district referred to in sub-section (1) of section 3;

(c) "building" includes a house, out-house, stable, latrine, urinal, shed, hut, wall (other than boundary wall) and any other structure (whether of masonry, bricks, wood, mud or other material) but does not include any portable or temporary shelter;

(d) "constituency" means a District Council constituency provided by order made under section 5 for the purpose of elections to the District Council;

(e) "Deputy Commissioner", in relation to any District Council, means the officer appointed as such by the Administrator, by notification in the Official Gazette, to perform the functions of the Deputy Commissioner under this Act in the autonomous district for which such District Council has been constituted;

(f) "Hill Areas" means the Hill Areas determined by the President by any notification issued under sub-section (2) of section 52 of the Government of Union Territories Act, 1963 (20 of 1963) and in force immediately before the commencement of this Act;

(g) "Hill Areas Committee" means the Standing Committee referred to in section 52 of the Government of Union Territories Act, 1963 (20 of 1963);

(h) "market" includes any place where persons assemble for the sale of, or for the purpose of exposing for sale of meat, fish, fruit, vegetables, animals intended for human food or any other articles of human food whatsoever with or without the consent of the owner of such place notwithstanding that there may be no common regulation for the concourse of buyers and sellers and whether or not any control is exercised over the business of, or the persons frequenting, the market by the owner of the place or by any other persons;

(i) "member" means a member of a District Council constituted under this Act;

(j) "Official Gazette" means the Gazette of the Union territory of Manipur;

(k) "person" does not include a body of persons;

(l) "prescribed" means prescribed by rules made under this Act;

(m) "Scheduled Tribes" has the same meaning assigned to it in clause (25) of article 366 of the Constitution;

(n) "vehicle" includes a carriage, cart, hand-cart, bicycle, tricycle and every wheeled conveyance which is used or is capable of being used on a street but does not include a mechanically propelled vehicle.

CHAPTER II

Constitution of District Councils

3. *Division of Hill Areas into autonomous districts:* (1) As soon as may be after the commencement of this Act, the Administrator shall cause all the Hill Areas to be divided into not more than six autonomous districts.

(2) The Administrator may, by order notified in the Official Gazette,—

(a) declare that any area in any autonomous district which is, or is intended to be, included within the limits of any municipality, cantonment or town committee shall cease to be a part of such autonomous district;

(b) increase the area of any autonomous district;

(c) diminish the area of any autonomous district;

(d) unite two or more autonomous districts or parts thereof so as to form one autonomous district;

(e) define the boundaries of any autonomous district;

(f) alter the name of any autonomous district.

(3) No order under sub-section (2) shall be made by the Administrator except after consultation with the Hill Areas Committee.

(4) Any order made by the Administrator under sub-section (2) may contain such incidental and consequential provisions as appear to the Administrator to be necessary for giving effect to the provisions of the order.

4. *Constitution of District Councils and their composition* : (1) For each autonomous district there shall be a District Council as from such date as the Administrator may, by notification in the Official Gazette, appoint in this behalf.

(2) The total number of seats in the District Council to be filled by persons chosen by direct election on the basis of adult suffrage from territorial constituencies shall be not more than eighteen.

(3) The Administrator may nominate not more than two persons, not being persons in the service of Government, to be members of any District Council.

5. *Delimitation of constituencies* : The Administrator shall, by order, determine:

(a) the constituencies (which shall be single member constituencies) into which an autonomous district shall be divided for the purpose of election of members to the District Council of that district; and

(b) the extent of each constituency.

6. *Power to alter or amend delimitation orders* : The Administrator may, from time to time, by order, alter or amend any order made under section 5.

7. *Qualifications for membership* : A person shall not be qualified to be chosen as a member of a District Council of any autonomous district unless he is an elector for any District Council constituency in that autonomous district.

8. *Disqualifications for membership* : (1) A person shall be disqualified for being chosen as a member of a District Council if he is for the time being disqualified for being chosen as a member of either House of Parliament or holds any office of profit under any District Council.

(2) For the purposes of this section, a person shall not be deemed to hold an office of profit under a District Council by reason only that he is a member thereof.

9. *Electors on electoral rolls* : (1) The persons entitled to vote at elections of members of a District Council shall be the persons entitled, by virtue of the provisions of the Constitution and the Representation of the People Act, 1950 (43 of 1950), to be registered as voters at elections to the House of the People.

(2) So much of the electoral roll for any parliamentary constituency for the time being in force as relates to the areas comprised within a constituency formed under section 5 shall

be deemed to be the electoral roll for that constituency for the purposes of this Act.

10. *Right to vote* : (1) Every person whose name is, for the time being, entered in the electoral roll of a constituency shall be entitled to vote at the election of a member of the District Council from that constituency.

(2) Every person shall give one vote and no more to any one candidate at an election.

11. *Election of members* : Election of members of a District Council shall be held in accordance with the rules made under section 21 on such date or dates as the Administrator may, by notification in the Official Gazette direct :

Provided that a casual vacancy shall be filled as soon as may be after the occurrence of the vacancy :

Provided further that no election shall be held to fill up a casual vacancy occurring within four months prior to the holding of a general election under this section.

12. *Notification of results of elections* : The names of all persons elected or nominated to be members of a District Council shall be published by the Administrator in the Official Gazette.

13. *Term of office of members* : (1) Save as otherwise provided in this section, the term of office of a member shall be five years and shall commence from the date of the notification of his election or nomination under section 12 or from the date on which the vacancy in which he is elected or nominated has occurred, whichever date is later :

Provided that the Administrator may, when satisfied that it is necessary in order to avoid administrative difficulty, extend the term of office of all the members by such period not exceeding one year as he thinks fit.

(2) The term of office of a member elected to fill a casual vacancy shall commence from the date of the notification of his election and shall continue so long only as the member in whose place he is elected would have been entitled to hold office if the vacancy had not occurred.

14. *Disputes as to elections* : (1) No election of a member shall be called in question except by an election petition presented to the court of the District Judge having jurisdiction in the area in which the constituency concerned is situated, within thirty days from the date of the notification of the result of the election under section 12.

(2) An election petition calling in question any such election may be presented on one or more of the grounds specified in section 16 by any candidate at such election or by any elector of the constituency.

(3) A petitioner shall join as respondents to his petition all the candidates at the election.

(4) An election petition—

(a) shall contain a concise statement of the material facts on which the petitioner relies;

(b) shall, with sufficient particulars, set forth the ground or grounds on which the election is called in question; and

(c) shall be signed by the petitioner and verified in the manner laid down in the Code of Civil Procedure, 1908 (5 of 1908), for the verification of pleadings.

15. *Relief that may be claimed by petitioner* : A petitioner may, in addition to claiming a declaration that the election of all or any of the returned candidates is void, claim a further declaration that he himself or any other candidate has been duly elected.

16. *Grounds on which an election may be called in question* : The election of a returned candidate may be called in question on any one or more of the following grounds, namely :

(a) that on the date of his election the returned candidate, was not qualified to be elected, or he was disqualified for being elected, as a member under this Act; or

(b) that the nomination paper of any candidate at the election has been improperly rejected; or

(c) that the result of the election has been materially affected by the improper acceptance of a nomination paper or by the improper acceptance or refusal of a vote or by any other cause.

17. *Procedure to be followed by the District Judge* : The procedure provided in the Code of Civil Procedure, 1908 (5 of 1908) in regard to suits shall be followed by the court of the District Judge, as far as it can be made applicable in the trial and disposal of an election petition under this Act.

18. *Decision of the District Judge* : (1) At the conclusion of the trial of an election petition, the court of the District Judge shall make an order—

(a) dismissing the election petition; or

(b) declaring the election of all or any of the returned candidates to be void; or

(c) declaring the election of all or any of the returned candidates to be void and the petitioner or any other candidate to have been duly elected.

(2) If any person who has filed an election petition has, in addition to calling in question the election of the returned candidate, claimed a declaration that he himself or any other candidate has been duly elected and the court of the District Judge is of opinion—

(a) that in fact the petitioner or such other candidate received a majority of the valid votes; or

(b) that but for the votes obtained by the returned candidate, the petitioner or such other candidate would have obtained a majority of the valid votes,

the court of the District Judge shall, after declaring the election of the returned candidate to be void, declare the petitioner or such other candidate, as the case may be, to have been duly elected.

19. *Procedure in case of equality of votes* : If during the trial of an election petition it appears that there is equality of votes between any candidates at the election and that the addition of a vote would entitle any of those candidates to be declared elected, then, the court of the District Judge shall decide between them by lot and proceed as if the one on whom the lot falls had received an additional vote.

20. *Finality of decisions* : (1) An order of the court of the District Judge on an election petition shall be final and conclusive.

(2) An election of a member not called in question in accordance with the foregoing provisions shall be deemed to be a good and valid election.

21. *Power to make rules regulating the election of members* : The Administrator may make rules to regulate all or any of the following matters for the purpose of the holding of elections of members under the Act, namely :

(a) the manner of the splitting up of electoral rolls for parliamentary constituencies into parts for the purpose of constituting one or more of such parts into electoral roll for a constituency; and the officer or authority by whom such splitting up is to be carried out;

(b) the drawing up of the programme of election;

(c) the appointment of returning officers, presiding and polling officers for election;

(d) the nomination of candidates and the scrutiny of such nomination;

(e) the deposits to be made by candidates and the time and manner of making such deposits;

(f) the withdrawal of candidatures;

(g) the appointment of agents of candidates;

(h) the time and manner of holding elections;

(i) the general procedure at the elections including the time, place and hours of poll and the method by which votes shall be cast;

(j) the fee to be paid on an election petition;

(k) any other matter relating to elections or election disputes in respect of which the Administrator deems it necessary to make rules under this section or in respect of which this Act makes no provision or makes insufficient provision and provision is, in the opinion of the Administrator, necessary.

22. *Incorporation of District Councils* : Each District Council shall be a body corporate by the name respectively of "the District Council of (name of autonomous district)" and shall have perpetual succession and a common seal with power to acquire, hold and dispose of property and to contract and may be the said name sue and be sued.

23. *Chairman and Vice-Chairman* : (1) A District Council shall, as soon as may be, choose two members to be respectively Chairman and Vice-Chairman thereof and, so often as the office of Chairman or Vice-Chairman becomes vacant, the Council shall choose another member to be Chairman or Vice-Chairman, as the case may be :

Provided that the Administrator may nominate the first Chairman who shall hold office for a period not exceeding one year.

(2) If a resolution for the removal of an elected Chairman is passed by not less than two-thirds of the total membership of the Council at a meeting convened in accordance with the provisions of sub-section (3), such resolution shall have the effect of removing the Chairman from his office as from the date on which the resolution is so passed and if such resolution is passed by less than two-thirds but not less than one-half of the total membership of the Council, the Administrator may, by order in writing, remove, for reasons to be recorded, the Chairman from his office as from such date as may be specified in the order :

Provided that no such resolution shall be brought within one year from the date of election of the Chairman:

Provided further that if the resolution is not passed by not less than two-thirds of the total membership of the Council, no other resolution for the removal of the Chairman shall be allowed to be considered within one year from the date on which such resolution was considered.

(3) A notice in writing of the intention to move a resolution referred to in sub-section (2) signed by not less than one-third of the total membership of the Council together with a copy of the proposed resolution shall be delivered to the Deputy Commissioner in accordance with the rules made by the Deputy Commissioner in this behalf and the Deputy Commissioner shall, after giving not less than fifteen days' notice thereon, convene for consideration of the resolution a meeting of the Council to be held in the office of the Council on a date not later than thirty days from the date on which the notice was delivered to him and he shall preside over the meeting.

(4) The Chairman of the Council shall be a whole-time functionary and shall be entitled to such salary or allowances as may be fixed by the Administrator.

24. *Oath or affirmation by members* : Every member shall, before taking his seat, make and subscribe at a meeting of the District Council, an oath or affirmation in the prescribed form.

25. *Vacation of seats* : (1) No person shall be a member both of the Legislative Assembly of the Union territory of Manipur and of a District Council and if a person is chosen a member both of the Legislative Assembly and of a District Council, then at the expiration of fourteen days from the date of publication in the Official Gazette that he has been so chosen, that person's seat in the District Council shall become vacant unless he has previously resigned his seat in the Legislative Assembly.

(2) If a member—

(a) becomes subject to any of the disqualifications mentioned in section 8; or

(b) resigns his seat by writing under his hand addressed to the Chairman of the District Council,

his seat shall thereupon become vacant.

(3) If during the six successive months a member is, without the permission of the District Council, absent from all meetings thereof, the Council may declare his seat vacant.

(4) If any question arises as to whether a member has become subject to any of the disqualifications mentioned in section 8, it shall be referred to the District Judge having jurisdiction in the area in which the constituency concerned is situated and his decision shall be final.

26. *Allowances of members* : Subject to the provisions of sub-section (4) of section 23, every member shall be entitled to receive such allowances as may be determined by the Administrator.

27. *Liability of members* : Every person shall be liable for the loss, waste or misappropriation of any money or other property belonging to a District Council, if such loss, waste or misappropriation is a direct consequence of his neglect or misconduct while a member of the District Council and a suit for compensation may be instituted against him by the Council with the previous sanction of the Deputy Commissioner or by the Deputy Commissioner with the previous sanction of the Administrator.

28. *Members to be deemed to be public servants* : Every member shall be deemed to be a public servant within the meaning of section 21 of the Indian Penal Code (45 of 1860).

CHAPTER III

Functions of District Councils

29. *Functions of District Councils* : (1) Subject to such exceptions and conditions as the Administrator may make and impose, the following matters shall be under the control and administration of a District Council, namely:—

(i) the maintenance and management of such property, movable and immovable, and institutions as may be transferred to that Council by the Administrator;

(ii) the construction, repair and maintenance of such of the roads, bridges, channels and buildings as may be transferred to that Council by the Administrator;

(iii) the establishment, maintenance and management of primary schools and the construction and repair of all buildings connected with these institutions and institution of scholarships;

(iv) the establishment, maintenance and management of dispensaries;

(v) the establishment and maintenance of cattle pounds including such functions under the Cattle Trespass Act, 1871 (1 of 1871) as may be transferred to that Council by the Administrator;

(vi) the establishment, maintenance and management of markets and fairs and the construction, repair and maintenance of all buildings connected therewith;

(vii) the supply, storage and prevention from pollution of water for drinking, cooking and bathing purposes;

(viii) the construction, repair and maintenance of embankments and the supply, storage and control of water for agricultural purposes;

(ix) the preservation and reclamation of soil;

(x) the preservation, protection and improvement of live-stock and prevention of animal diseases;

(xi) public health and sanitation;

(xii) the management of such ferries as may be entrusted to the charge of that Council by the Administrator;

(xiii) the initiation, inspection and control of relief works;

(xiv) the allotment, occupation or use, or the setting apart of land, other than land acquired for any public purpose or land which is a reserved forest, for the purpose of agriculture or grazing or for residential or other non-agricultural purposes or for any other purposes likely to promote the interests of the inhabitants of any village or town situated within the autonomous district for which that council is constituted;

(xv) the management of any forest not being a reserved forest;

(xvi) the regulation of the practice of *Jhum* or other form of shifting cultivation; and

(xvii) any other matter which the Administrator may, in consultation with the Hill Areas Committee, entrust to the District Council in the field of agriculture, animal husbandry, community development, social and tribal welfare, village planning or any other matter referred to in section 52 of the Government of Union Territories Act, 1963 (20 of 1963).

(2) It shall be competent for a District Council to recommend to the Government of the Union territory of Manipur legislation relating to the following matters in so far as they concern members of the Scheduled Tribes, namely :

(a) appointment or succession of Chiefs ;

(b) inheritance of property;

(c) marriage and divorce; and

(d) social customs.

CHAPTER IV

Procedure and Staff of District Councils

30. *Conduct of business* : A District Council shall conduct its business in such manner and in accordance with such procedure as may be prescribed.

31. *Committees* : A District Council may, from time to time, appoint out of its own body such and so many committees for the efficient discharge of its duties as may be necessary.

32. *Officers and staff* : (1) For every District Council there shall be a Chief Executive Officer, who shall be appointed by the Administrator.

(2) If a resolution for removal of the Chief Executive Officer is passed at a meeting of the District Council by a majority of

not less than two-thirds of the total membership of the Council, the Administrator shall remove him forthwith.

(3) The District Council shall appoint such officers and staff as may be necessary for the proper and efficient execution of its duties and make regulations for their conditions of service.

(4) The power of appointing officers and staff (whether temporary or permanent) shall be exercised in accordance with the rules framed for the purpose by the Administrator.

(5) The conditions of service applicable to a person immediately before his appointment to a post under a District Council shall not be varied to his disadvantage except with the previous approval of the Administrator.

(6) Every officer or member of staff of a District Council shall be deemed to be a public servant within the meaning of section 21 of the Indian Penal Code (45 of 1860).

CHAPTER V

Finance of District Councils and Vesting of Property

33. *Powers of taxation* : Notwithstanding anything to the contrary contained in any other law for the time being in force, a District Council shall have the power to levy all or any of the following taxes within the autonomous district for which the Council is constituted, that is to say—

(a) taxes on professions, trades, ceilings and employments;
(b) taxes on animals, vehicles (other than mechanically propelled vehicles) and boats;
(c) taxes on entry of goods into a market for sale therein and tolls on passengers and goods carried in ferries;
(d) taxes for the maintenance of schools, dispensaries or roads; and
(e) any other tax falling under List II of the Seventh Schedule to the Constitution which the Legislature of the Union territory of Manipur may, by law, empower the District Council to levy.

34. *Levy of fees* : A District Council may fix and levy—

(a) school fees; and
(b) fees for the use of, or benefits derived from any of the works done or services rendered under section 29.

35. *Procedure for imposing taxes* : (1) A District Council may resolve at a meeting specially convened for the purpose to propose the imposition of any of the taxes mentioned in section 33.

(2) When a resolution has been passed, the Council shall publish a notice in the Official Gazette and also in the prescribed manner, defining the class of persons or description of property proposed to be taxed, the amount or rate of tax to be imposed and the system of assessment to be adopted.

(3) Any person, directly or indirectly affected by the proposed tax and objecting to it, may, within thirty days from the publication of the notice, send his objections in writing to the Council and the Council shall, at a specially convened meeting, take all such objections into consideration.

(4) If no objection is sent within the said period of thirty days or if the objections received are deemed insufficient, the Council may submit its proposals to the Administrator with the objections, if any, and its decision thereon.

(5) The Administrator may then sanction the proposals or refuse to sanction them or return them to the Council for further consideration.

(6) When the proposal in respect of a tax has been sanctioned, the Administrator shall notify its imposition in the Official Gazette and specify a date not later than three months from the date of notification on which the tax shall come into force.

36. *Abolition or reduction of taxes* : The Administrator may, by notification in the Official Gazette, and a District Council may with the previous approval of the Administrator by a resolution passed at a meeting specially convened for the purpose abolish or reduce any tax imposed under section 33.

37. *Recovery of taxes and fees* : All arrears of taxes and fees levied under this Act may be recovered under the law for the time being in force for the recovery of public dues as if such arrears were public dues.

38. *Assessment and collection of taxes and fees* : A District Council may, by notification in the Official Gazette, determine the person by whom any tax or fee shall be assessed and collected and make rules for the assessment and collection of such tax or fee and direct in what manner persons employed in the assessment or collection shall be remunerated.

39. *Appeals* : (1) In matters connected with the assessment and collection of any tax or fee levied under this Act, an appeal shall lie from the order of any person authorised to make assessment or collections to such person as the Administrator may appoint or designate for the purpose.

(2) An appeal under sub-section (1) shall be presented within thirty days from the date of the order.

(3) The order passed on the appeal shall be final.

40. *Instalments of taxes and fees* : A District Council may, by notification in the Official Gazette and with the previous approval of the Deputy Commissioner, prescribed by what instalments and what times any tax or fee shall be payable.

41. *Power to exempt from taxation* : A District Council, may with the previous approval of the Administrator, by notification in the Official Gazette, remit or reduce any tax or fee or exempt any persons or class of persons or any description of property, wholly or in part, from liability as to any tax or fee and cancel any such remission, reduction or exemption.

42. *Recoveries of moneys claimable by the Council* : (1) Save as provided by section 37, all moneys claimable by a District Council may be recovered on an application to a Magistrate having jurisdiction in the area where the person from whom the money is claimable may, for the time being, be resident, by the distress and sale of any movable property or by the attachment and sale of any immovable property, within the limits of his jurisdiction belonging to such person and the cost of such proceedings shall be recoverable in the same manner as the said moneys.

(2) An application for recovery of money shall be in writing and shall be signed by an officer authorised in this behalf by order of the Chairman of the Council.

43. *Council Fund* : (1) All moneys received by or on behalf of a District Council under the provisions of this Act or any other law for the time being in force shall be credited to a fund which shall be called the "Council Fund" and it shall be held by the District Council in trust for the purposes of this Act.

(2) All expenditure of the Council shall be defrayed out of the Council Fund.

(3) The Administrator may make rules for the management of the Council Fund and for the procedure to be followed in

respect of payment of money into the said Fund, the withdrawal of moneys therefrom, the custody of moneys therein and any other matter connected with or ancillary to the matters aforesaid.

(4) The accounts of a District Council shall be kept in such form as may be prescribed.

44. *Property vested in District Council*: Subject to any order of the Administrator, all property of the nature specified below and situated in the autonomous district shall vest in and belong to the District Council for which it is constituted and shall, with all other property which may become vested in the Council, be under its direction, management and control and shall be held and applied for the purposes of this Act—

(a) all public buildings, constructed or maintained out of the Council Fund;

(b) all public roads which have been constructed or are maintained out of the Council Fund and the stones and other materials thereof and also all trees, erections, materials, implements and things provided for such roads;

(c) all land or other property transferred to the District Council by the Administrator or by gift, sale or otherwise for public purposes.

45. *Budget* : (1) A District Council shall, on or before a prescribed day in each year submit to the Administrator an estimate of the income and expenditure of the Council for the next financial year in such form as may be prescribed.

(2) The Administrator may, on or before a prescribed day, return the estimate of the Council with or without modification.

(3) When a budget is returned with modifications under sub-section (2), the Council shall consider the proposed modifications, take a decision thereon and report the same to the Administrator.

(4) The budget estimate finally adopted by the Council shall be the budget of the District Council.

(5) Any subsequent alteration in the budget or reappropriation or transfer of provision within the estimate shall be made with the approval of the Administrator.

CHAPTER VI

Control

46. *Control*: (1) It shall be the duty of the Chairman of a District Council to furnish to the Deputy Commissioner a copy of the proceedings of the meetings of the Council and such other information as the Deputy Commissioner may require.

(2) The Deputy Commissioner shall have the power to give to any District Council all such directions as he may consider necessary in respect of subjects, curricula, text books and standards of teaching in schools vested wholly or partly in the Council and in schools wholly or partly maintained by grants payable from the Council Fund and the Council shall comply with such directions.

(3) The Deputy Commissioner may, by order, and for reasons to be recorded, suspend the execution of any resolution or order of any District Council or prohibit the doing of any act which is about to be done, or is being done, in pursuance of or under cover of any provision of the law relating to the constitution or functions of the District Council, if, in his opinion, the resolution, order or act is in excess of the powers conferred by law or the execution of the resolution or order or the doing of the act is likely to lead to a breach of the peace, or to cause annoyance or injury to the public or to any class or body of persons:

Provided that the Council may, within fifteen days of the date of the order of the Deputy Commissioner offer such explanation as it deems fit in relation to the execution of the resolution or order which has been suspended or the doing of the act has been prohibited.

(4) When the Deputy Commissioner makes any order as aforesaid he shall forthwith send a copy of it to the Administrator with a statement of the reasons for making it and forward in due course to the Administrator the explanation, if any, offered by the Council and the Administrator may, thereupon, confirm, modify or rescind the order of the Deputy Commissioner.

47. *Supersession of the District Council*: (1) If, on receipt of a report from the Deputy Commissioner or otherwise, the Administrator is of opinion that—

(a) any District Council is not competent to perform, or persistently makes default in the performance of, the duties imposed on it by or under this Act or any other law; or

(b) any District Council exceeds or abuses its powers; or

(c) the financial position and credit position of any District Council is seriously threatened; or

(d) a situation has arisen in which the administration of any District Council cannot be carried on in accordance with the provisions of this Act,

the Administrator may, by an order published, together with a statement of reasons therefor, in the Official Gazette, supersede such Council for such period, not exceeding one year, as may be specified in the order:

Provided that before making an order of supersession as aforesaid under clause (a) or clause (b) or clause (c), reasonable opportunity shall be given to such Council to show cause why such order of supersession should not be made:

Provided further that the period of supersession may be extended for any further period or periods not exceeding six months at a time in consultation with the Hill Areas Committee.

(2) When any District Council is superseded by an order under sub-section (1),—

(a) all the members of the Council (including the Chairman and Vice-Chairman thereof) shall, on such date as may be specified in the order, vacate their offices as such members without prejudice to their eligibility for election or nomination under clause (d);

(b) during the period of supersession of the Council, all powers and duties conferred and imposed upon the Council by or under this Act or any other law shall be exercised and performed by such officer or authority as the Administrator may appoint in this behalf;

(c) all property vested in the Council shall, until it is reconstituted, vest in the Central Government;

(d) before the expiry of the period of supersession, election or nomination, as the case may be, of members to the

Council shall be held or made for the purpose of reconstituting the Council.

48. *Effect of certain provisions during the period when the Hill Areas Committee is not functioning* : Where at any time, consequent on the dissolution of the Legislative Assembly of the Union territory of Manipur, the Hill Areas Committee is not functioning, then, during the period when such Committee is not functioning,—

(i) section 3 shall have effect as if sub-section (3) thereof had been omitted;

(ii) clause (xvii) of section 29 and the second proviso to sub-section (1) of section 47 have effect as if the words "in consultation with the Hill Areas Committee" had been omitted therefrom.

CHAPTER VII

Offences and Penalties

49. *Penalty for obstruction*: If any person wilfully obstructs a District Council or any officer or servant of a District Council or any person authorised by the District Council in the exercise of its powers, he shall be punishable with fine which may extend to fifty rupees.

50. *Penalty for entering into any contract with the Council*: If any member, officer or other employee of a District Council enters into any contract with the Council, he shall be deemed to have committed an offence under section 168 of the Indian Penal Code (45 of 1860).

CHAPTER VIII

Rules and Bye-Laws

51. *Power of Administrator to make rules*: (1) Without prejudice to the power to make rules under any other provision of this Act, the Administrator may, after previous publication, make, by notification in the Official Gazette, rules for the purpose of carrying out the provisions of this Act.

(2) In particular and without prejudice to the generality of the foregoing power, such rules may—

(i) regulate the conduct of business of a District Council;

(ii) prescribe the forms in which the budget estimate is to

be prepared and the dates for the various stages of its completion;

(iii) determine the language in which the business of a District Council will be transacted;

(iv) regulate the powers of a District Council to transfer property;

(v) regulate the powers of a District Council to contract and do other things necessary for the purposes of its constitution and the mode of executing contracts;

(vi) regulate the employment, payment, suspension and removal of officers and staff of a District Council;

(vii) protect the terms and conditions of service of Government servants transferred to a District Council;

(viii) prescribe the forms for statements, registers, estimates and accounts of a District Council and regulate the keeping, checking and publication of such accounts;

(ix) prescribe the authority by whom and the manner in which the accounts of a District Council shall be audited; and

(x) provide for any other matter for which rules have to be made under this Act.

52. *Power to make bye-laws*: (1) Subject to the provisions of this Act and of the rules made thereunder, a District Council may make bye-laws to provide for all or any of the following matters in the autonomous district for which it is constituted or in any part thereof, namely—

(a) the maintenance and management of schools and grants of stipends and scholarships;

(b) control and administration of dispensaries, their construction and repairs, the supply of medicines and the measures to be taken during the prevalence of diseases;

(c) the protection from pollution of such tanks, springs, wells or parts of rivers, streams, channels or water courses as are set apart for drinking or culinary purposes;

(d) any other matter which is necessary for carrying out all or any of the provisions of this Act and the rules made thereunder.

(2) A bye-law made under sub-section (1) shall not have effect until it has been confirmed by the Administrator and published in such manner as he may direct.

(3) The Administrator, in confirming a bye-law, may make any change therein which appears to him to be necessary.

53. *Penalty for infringement of rules or bye-laws* : (1) In making any rule, the Administrator, and in making any bye-law, a District Council, may direct that the breach of the same shall be punishable with fine which may extend to one hundred rupees and in the case of a continuing breach with a further fine which may extend to ten rupees of every day during which the breach is continued after the offender has been convicted of such breach.

(2) In default of payment of any fine, the defaulter shall be punishable with imprisonment for a term which may extend to fifteen days.

INDEX